Hog Meat and Hoecake

Food Supply in the Old South,

1840–1860

SAM BOWERS HILLIARD

Southern Illinois University Press   Feffer & Simons, Inc.

Carbondale and Edwardsville   *London and Amsterdam*

HD 9007 . A13 HS4
1972

Contents

Figures

Tables

Acknowledgments

To acknowledge one's debts for a work such as this is not easy. So many persons from all parts of the globe and from a variety of professions have contributed in one manner or another to the final product.

A special word of gratitude must be extended to Dr. Andrew H. Clark of the University of Wisconsin for it was he who nurtured me through the formative stages of the work and prodded me into persevering. Others on the Wisconsin campus whose influence and encouragement are appreciated are Drs. Clarence W. Olmstead and Morton Rothstein. Encouragement to continue probing into the geography of self-sufficiency has come from all quarters and none has been more helpful than Dr. Merle C. Prunty, Jr. of the University of Georgia.

I also owe special thanks to the Cartographic Laboratory of Southern Illinois University, and to the Geography secretarial staff for cartographic and stenographic aid.

I also owe a debt, deeper than one can imagine, to my wife, Joyce, for simply being there.

S. B. H.

Hog Meat and Hoecake

1 Self-sufficiency
The developing American farm

On Christmas day in 1827 Mrs. Frances Trollope, an English-woman, arrived at the mouth of the Mississippi River to begin a three and one-half year stay in America. Her observations on life in the new country, published five years later, proved to be a scathing commentary on the manner and customs of Americans. Food and cooking were especially repugnant yet, despite this, she recognized the general availability of food and observed that the "ordinary mode of living is abundant." She was impressed by the food market in Cincinnati "which, for excellence, abundance, and cheapness can hardly, I should think, be surpassed in any part of the world." [1] Three quarters of a century earlier, Peter Kalm described a similar abundance in the Delaware River Valley area:

> The annual harvest, I am told, always affords plenty of bread for the inhabitants. . . . A venerable Septuagenarian Swede . . . assured me that in his lifetime there had been no failure of crops but that the people had always had plenty. . . . Nor is it likely that any great famine can happen in the country unless it please God to afflict it with extraordinary punishments. [2]

These impressions of foodstuff "abundance" were not unique since most European travelers in America reacted similarly. After having seen and heard of food shortages in both Europe and Asia, many saw America as a "land of plenty" whose resources were abundant and production virtually unlimited.

On the whole, such impressions were well founded. Few areas have served the food needs of their people so unstintingly and few have responded so bountifully to a minimum of effort expended on agriculture. Blessed by an extraordinary combination of factors which made it highly productive, American agriculture has seen over production rather than shortage become the rule. The constant expansion of agricultural land in America over a period of more than three centuries has managed to keep the reserve of producing land well above the demands of an increasing population. This, together with a rapidly expanding farm technology, has maintained agricultural productivity in America at an extremely high level. In fact, during the eighteenth and early nineteenth centuries, when American agriculture was being maligned by European visitors as shamefully wasteful and inefficient, the American farmer was producing an abundance for home consumption as well as a substantial surplus for export.

While the overall supply of foodstuffs in the United States generally has been adequate, individual farm units rarely were diversified enough for each farmer to produce all the agricultural products he needed. As far back as the colonial period most farmers concentrated on a few crops while either doing without or depending upon other producers for items they could not or would not produce themselves. Limitations of soil, climate, plant or animal diseases, lack of skills—any number of inhibiting factors —made it difficult or impossible for farmers to produce all the commodities needed for subsistence. Moreover, the desire for exotic goods such as sugar, coffee, salt or other condiments as well as for manufactured goods required a cash outlay and encouraged agriculturists to produce in commercial quantities those goods they were best able to market. Thus, while producing a variety of goods for domestic use, the American farmer also directed a portion of his resources toward the production of commercial goods.

Despite this tendency toward the growing of commercially marketable crops to be used in buying or trading, the typical farm of the eighteenth and much of the nineteenth centuries was a highly independent and self-supplying entity with a diversified production of plants and animals answering most of the farmer's own needs. On the whole, most farmers wanted to be as self-contained as possible. The degree to which this wish was realized depended upon a number of factors, varying from place to place within the country and changing with time. The location of the farm in relation to markets, the farmer's ability to produce foodstuffs and other items for his own use, the cost of producing such goods as compared with their market value, and the farmer's own personal predilections concerning the crops or livestock he produced, all affected the level of his subsistence and dependence upon extrafarm sources. For example, an agricultural unit located in a remote area such as the back country of the central Appalachians or in interior New England might be forced into a high degree of self-reliance, since marketing of its own farm produce and purchasing other needs was difficult. In contrast, a unit along the coast of South Carolina or Georgia might find that foodstuffs could not be produced as easily or cheaply as they could be purchased. For whatever reason, individual units varied greatly with respect to foodstuff self-sufficiency.

While this fact was true of American agriculture in general, the rapid expansion and subsequent regional specialization that occurred during the first half of the nineteenth century created a number of "regions" with each concentrating on certain products. Each of these agricultural regions developed both commercial and subsistence elements in their economies, and there were marked differences in the relative levels of each element. Just as some landholdings achieved a higher level of subsistence than others, some regions became virtually self-sufficient while others had vital trade links with other producing regions. Of course, this had always been true to some extent as sugar, spices, and other exotics are traditional "trade items" not normally produced on farms. However, a number of the agricultural systems that developed in parts of the United States (especially the South) became so highly specialized that they concentrated on only one or two products for sale and depended in varying degrees upon other areas for their subsistence needs. The classic example of this is the twentieth-century American commercial farm region, such as the wheat belt, but a few areas in the South began moving in that direction quite early. The sugar producing area of Louisiana is perhaps the best example, but others had similar tendencies.

This attempt toward agricultural specialization in parts of the South has not gone unnoticed; in fact, it has been one of the major themes in discussions of both the southern and national economies.[3] The implications of this argument are enormous. If, for example, we assume that the South (or parts of it) imported a large part of its food needs, then several vital questions are raised: 1] Where did the food come from and what effects did its sale have on the economy of the producing area? 2] What

role did interregional trade have in the development of transportation networks?   3] What effects did this trade have on the overall national economy?   4] How did it affect the southern economy, e.g., was it a drain of resources or a boon to agricultural
specialization?   5] How did it affect regional development and
regional loyalties?   6] What were the effects on southern agriculture?   7] How did it relate to the plantation-slave regime? Obviously, these are important questions and there are others, but
these serve to point up the importance of the subject.[4] This study
certainly makes no attempt to answer all these questions, but it
does address itself to the overall theme of southern foodstuff self-
sufficiency. It will examine the major southern food sources, the
regional production of a number of commodities, and their role
in the subsistence economy. It will also investigate food habits,
cultural attitudes, and food consumption among various groups.
Finally, it will look at the foodstuff trade and speculate on its importance.

However, before we get immersed in the details of the southern system, it seems appropriate to look at the development of
agriculture in the United States and present a summary of regional development. In this way, the southern system can be seen
as it emerged and the regional differences can be pointed out. The
emphasis, of course, will be on the relative importance of food
production to each region's total agricultural economy.

Eighteenth-century American agriculture

Before the end of the colonial period, American agriculture
had expanded inland from the original coastal settlements in a
rather broad band from New England to Georgia. Along this band
of some 1,200 miles in length were exhibited a variety of landholding sizes and patterns, systems of production, market orienta-
tions, and crop-livestock emphases. Taking advantage of favorable growing seasons and abundant precipitation, the southern
colonies concentrated on a few semitropical crops and, with a
growing demand for such crops in Europe, these areas were the
first to enter the European market effectively. Tobacco, indigo,
rice, and cotton were the products first exported in large quantities since they tended to complement rather than compete with
European farm output. On the other hand, colonies to the north

were forced to channel their energies in other directions since they produced temperate-zone food crops for which the demand in western Europe was not very great at the time. In attempting to participate in world markets, the New England and middle colonies resorted to several alternatives; they developed nonagricultural resources such as forests and fisheries, expanded shipping and commercial activities, and developed a rather extensive trading network with the West Indies, the fishing stations of British North America, and Mediterranean Europe. Unlike western Europe, these markets were quite receptive to livestock and temperate-zone crops such as cereals.[5]

Of the three major colonial divisions, New England probably devoted a smaller proportion of its economic efforts to agricultural production. The New England farm was never able to produce *export* goods comparable to those of the middle or southern colonies.[6] The notable trade in livestock and livestock products moving out of New England ports during the eighteenth century indicates that agricultural surpluses were produced, but the total quantities and regional importance of such items were not impressive. Despite this limited output of export goods, New England farmers did produce a variety of goods for their own consumption and they supplied most of the food needed in the increasingly important urban markets nearby. An exception was the production of wheat. New England farmers had difficulty raising wheat enough for local consumption, although they did satisfy the home demand for other small grains. They also grew corn, root crops, fruits, and vegetables in abundance. Corn was more common than wheat, especially in southern New England, and was the chief cereal item in the diet during the seventeenth and early eighteenth centuries. Later, New Englanders came to prefer wheat over corn, but this choice was based on western rather than locally produced wheat.

By colonial standards, the New England livestock industry was substantial, though the care given to animals was considered inexcusably inadequate by Europeans traveling in the country. Almost all New England farmers kept livestock and most had a wide variety. The cattle were quadruple-purpose, that is, they were used as draft animals as well as for hides, meat, and milk. The typical farmer probably kept a dozen or so to provide food for his own family and a small surplus of butter, cheese, or slaughter animals for the local market. Even urban dwellers often kept one or more cows for their needs. Part of the livestock and livestock products went into urban markets to fill local consumption needs while the remainder provisioned ships or moved to the West Indies or other market areas.

In addition to cattle, almost all New England farmers kept swine and slaughtered several each year. Since pork was relatively inexpensive to produce and easily preserved, it served as an important element in the diet and also was in demand for provisioning ships. Sheep, kept on about half the region's farms, served primarily to supply wool rather than meat. Other animals helped round out the barnyard menagerie, especially poultry which was undoubtedly quite common.

Farmers in the middle colonies were more successful than those of New England in producing crops in quantities ample for both subsistence and sale.[7] The variety of domestic plants and animals on farms in the middle colonies did not differ appreciably from that of New England. Corn was a major crop but wheat was of much greater commercial importance. Wheat yielded better than in New England, and many farms produced it commercially. The market was good with both wheat and flour moving into southern Europe, the West Indies, and other parts of continental America. Long before the end of the eighteenth century, an embryonic wheat belt had developed with its axis running southwest from the lower Hudson River valley into North Carolina. Pennsylvania farmers grew more wheat than corn since it did extremely well, especially on the limestone soils of many eastern Pennsylvania valleys, and the advantage in value and marketability of wheat over corn made it the preferred crop. Both wheat and corn were grown extensively and, along with rye and oats, made up the core crops for most farms.[8] In some areas, notably southeastern Pennsylvania, hemp and flax were fairly important and both were commercially marketed. Other food crops were barley, root crops, fruits, and garden vegetables which rounded out the farm's production to ensure an adequate array of food for subsistence and feed for livestock.

In the commercial economy of the middle colonies, livestock was perhaps less important than in New England, primarily because of the increased place of wheat and flour as export items. Nevertheless, most farmers depended heavily upon livestock for subsistence, and each farm possessed a variety. Along the flood plains of the Hudson, Delaware, and Susquehanna rivers, as well as some lesser streams, natural meadows were available for pasturing stock. These meadows were made up of native grasses, but increasingly European grasses were imported to replace the native species. In some cases these meadows were irrigated part of the year to ensure additional pasturage and hay. In the absence of such meadows, the stock was fed straw or allowed to forage in the forests. Corn served to fatten animals for slaughter and as a feed for work stock. Most farmers kept cattle, swine, and poultry with perhaps half also raising sheep.

The treatment of animals by farmers in the mid-Atlantic area was poor by European standards, and the general quality of the stock was little, if any, better than New England. In some areas, notably southeastern Pennsylvania, there was some improvement in both the treatment and quality of livestock, but the really significant advances in selective breeding did not come until the nineteenth century.[9]

Wheat and flour exports were important to these "bread colonies" but so was the foreign market for livestock and other provisions. Equally important to the commercial farmer, though, were the growing urban centers of New York, Philadelphia, and Baltimore. By the end of the eighteenth century these cities, along with other, smaller urban areas had become significant consumers in their own right and were absorbing sizeable quantities of foodstuffs from the surrounding farms. Ultimately, of course, this domestic market completely overshadowed the export market and provided a basis for much of the later agricultural development in Trans-Appalachia.

Early in the colonial period, the area south of the Susquehanna developed a number of characteristics that readily distinguished it from the other colonies.[10] Agriculture, in particular, was notably different since it concentrated on the production of semitropical nonfood crops for export on relatively large landholdings using indentured or slave labor.[11]

The Chesapeake Bay region was a major exporter, principally of tobacco, throughout the entire colonial period. Most agriculturists, whether small farmers or planters, cultivated as much tobacco as their labor would permit. During much of the seventeenth century, tobacco production was confined to the estuarine coasts on both sides of the Chesapeake Bay, but by the end of the eighteenth century, tobacco growers had penetrated deeply into the Piedmont of Virginia and the Carolinas. Scattered production extended into the valleys of the Appalachians, across into Tennessee and Kentucky and southward, with farmers along the tributaries of the Savannah River in South Carolina and Georgia shipping tobacco through Savannah and Charleston.

Coupled with this tobacco growing was an impressive output of food crops for subsistence and for market. In fact, such crops usually eclipsed tobacco as the primary crops on many farms, especially in the interior. Wheat growing extended southward into North Carolina, and a number of farmers depended upon wheat and flour as cash items.[12] Corn, as elsewhere in the country, was grown by virtually all agriculturists and was the most important cereal crop—often the first major crop for new settlers—throughout the southern area. Occasionally corn was exported but, for the most part, it was too cheap to bear the cost of transportation over long distances and too nearly ubiquitous to enter into local trade in large quantities.

While tobacco, wheat, and corn occupied the Chesapeake Bay coast and extended inland toward the south and west, the coastal strip south from about Cape Fear to Florida was utilized for the commercial production of indigo, rice, and sea island cotton with rice the dominant cash crop. Unlike the tobacco region where both small farms and plantations produced cash crops, the southern coast had a high proportion of plantation-sized landholdings.[13] Coastal plantations grew a more limited variety of crops than inland farms, since a number of food crops did not do well in the poorly drained coastal lowlands nor under the high temperatures prevalent in the extreme south.

Most farms and plantations produced a number of food crops with corn being the most outstanding. Wheat was grown in most of the inland areas but did not yield quite as well as in the middle colonies. Consequently, there was a greater dependence upon corn for food than in other parts of the country. Minor crops, such as peas, and beans, root crops, and fruits occupied a place in the food economy similar to that farther north, but with minor changes. For example, the white potato did not do well in the warmer southern climate and was replaced by the sweet potato and small grains such as rye and barley were less common than in the Northeast.

Livestock raising was relatively important in the total economy of the southern colonies during the eighteenth century and the area had natural conditions that favored livestock grazing. An important aspect of southern colonial settlement was the relatively haphazard system under which landholdings were granted, whereby the settlement of noncontiguous plots was encouraged, thus leaving much of the less desirable land unsettled and uncleared for a number of years. This expanse of uncleared land encouraged a grazing industry productive in numbers, if not quality, of livestock. Cattle grazing was practiced by the whole gamut of the farmer-planter continuum, but in especially favored areas, conditions were such that fulltime cattlemen operated. Herds often were quite large, especially in the pine forests and prairies near the coast. Markets for these stock were in the cities along the mid-Atlantic coast, Charleston, and the West Indies.[14]

Swine were as common as cattle and, compared with the colonies to the north, were more important in the subsistence economy. Being inexpensive to produce and easily preserved, pork was the preferred meat of whites and was the flesh most commonly issued to the slaves. During the nineteenth century, this preference for pork came to be a distinctive element of southern culture and as a food item, pork completely eclipsed all others.

Compared to the colonies to the north, the region placed a stronger emphasis on cash crops such as rice, indigo and tobacco than subsistence crops but most southern colonial farmers and planters produced provisions enough for home use. The Carolina coastal plantations probably were the exceptions, but inland settlers were so isolated they were quite independent. Consequently, they differed little from their counterparts in the mid-Atlantic and New England colonies.

Nineteenth-century agricultural expansion

Several events occurred in the two or three decades around 1800 which greatly altered the course of agricultural development in the United States. The most important was the rapid increase in the area available for settlement. Prior to the Revolution, British policy aimed at preventing settlement west of the Appalachians, as evidenced by the Proclamation Line of 1763. It was ineffective in restraining westward movement during the late eighteenth century and was abolished under the newly created

federal government. In its place, the United States government
substituted a system of land disposal which encouraged rather
than impeded westward settlement. In return for concessions
from the new federal government, the original thirteen states
gave up their claims to western land, thereby creating a public
domain under the control of the national government.[15] This land
soon became available for settlement and during the two or three
decades after 1800 much of it was transferred from public to
private hands. Spurred by a rapidly growing population and rising
land values in the East, settlers pushed into the Appalachian valleys and hill lands and, as these were filled, moved onto the vast
and fertile plains beyond. During the same period, a similar expansion occurred south of the Appalachians with the Gulf Plains
being settled almost as rapidly as the area farther north.

During the same general period, developments along the
eastern seaboard created economic conditions which stimulated
development in the West. Due to high birth rates and unlimited
immigration, population in the East rose to the point where the
older states supplied increasing numbers of settlers for the relatively sparsely populated West. Moreover, population in the north
eastern states was becoming urbanized and industrialized requiring substantial quantities of commercially marketed foodstuffs. The older agricultural areas east of the Appalachians were
finding it increasingly difficult to compete effectively with the
West in supplying this market. New England, an importer of
certain kinds of foods even during the colonial period, became increasingly important as a food deficit area throughout the nineteenth century. As manufacturing establishments began to flour-
ish and urban populations increased, other areas began to look
more to the West for food. Baltimore, Philadelphia, and New York
actively imported western foodstuffs as early as 1820, and this
trade increased rapidly after the Erie Canal was opened in 1825.
In addition to the burgeoning domestic market, the ambitious activities of American shipping carried goods into foreign markets,
thereby enhancing the role of eastern seaboard cities as market
places for agricultural goods.

Finally, while these developments worked toward a rapid
alteration of the agricultural patterns inherited from the colonial
period, another series of events added a new dimension to the
already complex American agricultural scene. These were the

revolutionary technological achievements that made possible an almost explosive increase in the world production and use of one commodity—cotton. This series of innovations included the perfection of power looms and spinning machines and culminated in the development of a simple, workable cotton gin by Whitney in the last decade of the eighteenth century. Coming as they did when the United States was in the proces of rapid agricultural, commercial, and industrial expansion, these developments served to unite the country into a giant complex of interrelated regions which were to exhibit remarkable economic progress in the next half century and, at the same time, provide the basis for the growth of powerful centrifugal forces which would eventually lead to national disunion.

The internal migration and resettlement that occurred during the three or four decades after 1800 were unprecedented in both volume and rapidity. Moreover, it involved an area almost completely devoid of prior European settlement and, as such, necessitated the development of agricultural practices and marketing techniques to fit the new environment. Indeed, even the fundamental techniques of survival itself were essential to the very early settlers. The process of settling an empty area was not a new experience to many Americans, but the vastness of the western land with the distances involved to and from markets together with the magnitude and rapidity of the movement of population westward created special problems. The nineteenth-century frontier differed from that of the eighteenth century in scale if in no other way.

In 1800, the bulk of the nation's population was scattered along the Atlantic seaboard from Maine to Georgia in a strip that extended westward to the Appalachian Mountains. Although there were a number of settlements in the mountains and along the river valleys of the West, the core of settlement was in the mid-Atlantic states with the major cities being New York, Philadelphia, and Baltimore. The western settlements were primarily riverine, located along the Mississippi River and its tributaries. As settlement spread westward it moved first down the Ridge and Valley region of Virginia, then westward into the creek and river valleys of the Allegheny-Cumberland Plateau, and later into the fertile Kentucky and Tennessee basins as well as stream valleys along the upper Ohio. For the most part, settlement was non-

contiguous with some outliers, such as the French villages on the
Mississippi, separated from the communities in Tennessee, Kentucky, and Ohio by hundreds of miles. Most settlers, however,
were in the states of Tennessee and Kentucky, parts of western
Pennsylvania and southern Ohio. For a number of years, migration to the south and north of this area was blocked rather effectively by well-organized Indian nations. In 1803, the purchase
of the Louisiana Territory added the settlements along the lower
Mississippi to the Union, but not until after the War of 1812 did
settlement proceed rapidly into the areas north of the Ohio River
and south of the Tennessee. One could describe, in a very general
way, the settled portions of the United States as a huge triangle
with its base along the Atlantic seaboard and its apex at the junc-
tion of the Ohio and Mississippi rivers.

With the removal of Indian claims to the land in the Lake
and Gulf Lowlands after the War of 1812, the rich farming land
became available for the millions of people who were to settle
there during the next few decades. In a series of waves lasting
until 1850, and only temporarily slowed by the economic depres-
sions of 1819 and 1837, the settlement of the area east of the
Mississippi was completed.

As people moved onto the western lands, they carried with
them the farming practices, crop preferences, and cultural institutions prevalent in the areas from which they came. These
cultural accoutrements were modified of course by varying environmental or economic conditions, but there was a strong tendency to re-create, as nearly as possible, the agricultural systems
prevalent in the parent states. Thus, the Old Northwest tended
to reflect patterns in the mid- and north-Atlantic states while the
Gulf Plains more closely paralleled the Georgia-Carolina-Virginia
systems. Due to the influx of settlers from Tennessee and Kentucky into the Old Northwest, there was a strong "southern" influence in the southern portions of Illinois, Indiana, and Ohio,
but the agricultural systems that developed in the Old Northwest
were more akin to those of the Northeast than the South. There
were, of course, a number of innovations and modifications in
these transplanted agricultural systems, yet many features of the
older states were retained. Both the Old Northwest and the Southwest generally offered similar obstacles to human settlement and,
at the same time, offered similar attractions to prospective agri-

culturists. There were basic differences, however, in the crops grown as well as differences in markets and (more important to the major themes in this work) the degrees of subsistence achieved by the two regions.

Farm making in the Trans-Appalachian region north of the Ohio River during the first decades after 1800 was at the same time both easy and difficult. It was easy in that land was both abundant and relatively cheap with an inherent fertility well above that of the eastern states. Once cleared and cultivated, western lands yielded well with a minimum of effort and specialized knowledge. The difficulties lay in clearing or breaking the land and bringing it into cultivation, constructing the farmstead buildings, hauling crops to distant markets, and the not inconsiderable task of surviving until the farm could provide sustenance for the farm family.

The nineteenth-century western pioneer was a relatively independent individual who obtained many of his needs directly from the farm or nearby forests and streams. Considering the relative abundance of game and the exceptional fertility of western land during the pioneer period, one would expect an abundance of food even if it lacked variety.[16] The heavy dependence upon game and gathered food during the early years declined rapidly as the amount of tilled land increased. Consequently, as farm food production increased, there was a shift from "natural food" to a dependence upon food grown on the farm. In either case, the reliance was chiefly upon local sources with virtually no importation of foods other than exotics such as sugar, coffee, and condiments. However, this high degree of subsistence made possible by the abundant and varied production of western farms did not preclude the production of goods for market. The common and uncritical use of terms such as "subsistence" and "self-sufficient" to describe early settlers of the period has led to a stereotyping of the pioneer as an independent, self-contained hero who, given bare sustenance for his growing family, sought nothing for himself save solitude and freedom from restriction. Indeed, the words "pioneer" and "frontier" have come to symbolize such attributes to the point where the often highly commercial nature of early western agriculture is obscured.[17] The pioneer, whether he was a slaveowner looking for cotton lands or a yeoman farmer seeking a new homestead, was more often than not an economically oriented entrepreneur. He was looking for opportunity in a land where he thought the potential was good. While this is a generally recognized trait of the expansion-minded southern planter, somehow the farmer who moved into the Old Northwest has been seen as less of an opportunist and more of an idealist. Actually, the early search for commercial crops in both the plateau-mountain area and the Lake Plains was just as intense (and often as rewarding) as in the cotton states of the Gulf South. The early attempts at livestock droving out of the upper Ohio Valley, the establishment of meat packing industries in Cincinnati and the surrounding area, and the very early rafting of agricultural goods down the Mississippi all point to an early genesis of commercial agriculture in the Old Northwest.

Unfortunately for the western pioneer, however, farm-to-market distances were almost prohibitive. The cost of transporting and marketing western agricultural goods discriminated strongly against heavy and bulky inanimate products and perishable goods. Livestock, primarily cattle and swine, became the most important early products since they traveled to market under their own power. The Ohio Valley became the source region for an early livestock trade between the Old Northwest and the eastern seaboard cities and, to a lesser extent, the southern cities and plantations.[18] Supplementing this "live" market after about 1820 was the pork packing industry centered on Cincinnati. Most of its output during the early years moved down the Mississippi for coastwise transfer to eastern cities, for consumption in the South, for provisioning ships, and for foreign markets.[19]

Although other cereals as well as minor food crops and grasses were grown, the major crops in the Old Northwest came to be corn and wheat. The first Trans-Allegheny wheat belt developed in the Mohawk and tributary valleys of New York. Later, as lands of the Old Northwest were brought under the plow, western production increased to the point where the wheat belt shifted permanently to the West. Like pork, wheat first was shipped down river to New Orleans in small quantities. But, with the opening of the Erie Canal in New York and the development of local canals in the West, and especially with the extension of railroads, it moved effectively into the eastern markets. With a good market and adequate transportation, wheat came to be the major cash cereal crop of the Old Northwest.[20] Often it was the only money crop, at times even serving as a medium of exchange. It was wheat that paid the mortgage, bought the luxuries, and (as they became available) paid for the reaper, plow, and thresher.

Corn also was a major cereal. It yielded well and was the favorite food and animal feed during the early years. Unlike wheat, corn could be grown under widely varying conditions and was so commonly grown that corn prices did not justify shipment over long distances. Toward the end of the antebellum period in the Old Northwest, it was used less for human consumption and more for livestock fattening. In the valleys of western Pennsylvania and along the droving routes in Ohio, corn was sold to drovers as nightly feed for their animals. After pork-packing became more widespread, it also was in demand for fattening hogs. Most farmers grew both corn and hogs and conducted their own feeding operations. Corn surpluses were used either by purchasing pigs and feeding them out or by selling the corn to the professionals who ran huge fattening operations. On the whole, the role of corn in the region's agricultural economy was not greatly unlike the one it enjoyed in the corn belt a century later. Other commercial crops produced by western farmers included hemp, flax, tobacco, along with dairy products and wool, but the bulk of the commercial agriculture of the Old Northwest rested upon wheat and animals fattened on corn.

While the Old Northwest developed into a relatively diversified agricultural region, the Old Southwest became a continuation of the cotton kingdom which originated in the Carolinas and Georgia. The differential economic development which had distinguished the southern colonies from those of the northeast during the late eighteenth century tended, in many respects, to be perpetuated as the Old Southwest was settled. The plantation and the slave, vital ingredients of the Atlantic Seaboard South, remained an integral part of the picture as settlement moved into Alabama, Mississippi and Louisiana; only the crop emphases were different. The primary difference was that the nineteenth-century Gulf South came to be a "Cotton South." The preeminence of cotton both in the regional and national economies after about 1810 made it the undisputed "king" of the southern crops. It is with this new cotton kingdom that the major part of this study deals; not necessarily with the production of cotton itself but with the "system" of cotton production within which the growing of food crops often was an ancillary business, but absolutely prerequisite to the proper functioning of the cotton-producing system.

Before 1800, cotton growing in the United States was limited to the Atlantic coastal area, primarily the Sea Islands of Georgia. The rather rigid environmental limits of the "sea island" variety inhibited production over a wide area, while upland cotton could not be produced and sold in large quantities because of the technical problem of separating the fiber from the seed. When this difficulty was overcome by the perfection of a workable cotton gin around the turn of the nineteenth century, an increasing world market for cotton and an increase in available western land encouraged the rapid expansion of agricultural settlement and cotton production.

Although cotton production began along the coasts of South Carolina and Georgia, each year saw it extending into the interior. At first the spread was in all directions, inland into upper Georgia and South Carolina, northward into North Carolina and southern Virginia, and westward into Georgia; later, the spread was westward into Alabama, Mississippi, Louisiana, and Texas. During the early 1800s production increased rapidly in the South Atlantic states, but they were quickly displaced as the leading cotton producers by the Gulf states in the second quarter of the century. Cotton growers began moving westward around 1800, but the process was relatively slow until after Indian removal. Parts of the Old Southwest, such as the Tennessee River Valley, the area around Mobile, and the Natchez District of Mississippi, were settled by a few farmers and planters who raised cotton on a small scale before 1812.[21] After about 1815, a host of ambitious planters and farmers dispersed from these small nuclei searching for new lands from which they hoped to wrest a living or perhaps a modest fortune. As soon as land became available for white settlement, there were usually those who were willing to gamble life, labor, and money (not necessarily their own) for the profits to be made in cotton planting.

This rapid influx of potential cotton growers began about 1815 and was spurred by the Treaty of Fort Jackson in 1816, which opened land for settlement. It reached a peak in 1817 and 1818 with settlers pouring out of Georgia and the Carolinas searching for new homes, farms, and plantations. The influx of settlers was so rapid that food supplies often were inadequate and had to be supplemented from elsewhere.[22] This boom was short-lived and the period of apparently unlimited credit and abundant money ended with the economic depression of 1819 which slowed expansion of the cotton belt considerably.

Although a great deal of Indian land was made available for settlement before 1820, large areas were held by Indians until well after that date. One by one the Indian groups were forced (or rather "persuaded") to abandon their lands, and piece by piece the area became open to aspiring planters and farmers. By the 1830s virtually all the former Indian lands had been released and new settlement again reached floodlike proportions. Alabama and Mississippi as well as the Cherokee lands of Georgia were inundated with land-seeking, cotton-growing settlers as well as speculators who were seeking their fortunes in real estate. Slowed only temporarily by the economic panic of 1837 and its accompanying decrease in available credit and money, settlers proceeded to fill in the remaining lands and by 1860 effectively occupied most of what is commonly regarded as the Deep South (fig. 1).

During the same general period, the Mississippi River acted as a transportation artery into Louisiana, Arkansas, and western Mississippi. Lower Louisiana, of course, had been settled since about 1700, and sugar plantations were common along the rivers and bayous of the delta. However, as cotton culture moved into the lower Mississippi Valley, it did not compete directly with sugarcane; the cotton producer found northern Louisiana better suited to his needs. Somewhat stymied by poorly drained soils and periodic flooding, cotton growers were slow to take advantage of the rich alluvial soils of the Mississippi floodplain. In fact, many bypassed the low-lying floodplain in their migration westward, some pushing on into Texas even before it became a state. In time, though, they penetrated western Mississippi and Tennessee, northern Louisiana, and eastern Arkansas. By 1840, the general outline of what was later called the cotton belt was established (fig. 2). Only the filling in of a few areas and the intensification of agriculture on lands already settled was yet to be accomplished. The extent to which the cotton belt expanded and intensified during the following two decades is shown by comparing figures 2 and 3. A few areas such as northern Mississippi and the upper Mississippi River floodplain were opened up during

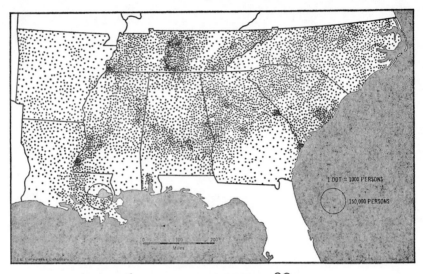

1. POPULATION, 1860.

the period 1840–60, but for the most part, all other areas within the South that produced cotton in 1860 were doing so on a lesser scale in 1840. Thus, the great increase in production during that period took place in the settled areas rather than through the opening of extensive new areas.

While cotton growing was the *raison d'être* of settlement in the interior South and the maker of fortunes for some of its inhabitants, the product was useless unless it could reach market. In this respect, most southern producers were in an advantageous position since they had a relatively close network of rivers extending inland into most producing areas, where their output could be floated to market in the coastal ports. Thus, from the outset, many of the services catering to cotton producers were concentrated in the port cities. In this respect, the cotton kingdom had a parallel in the tobacco region of the Chesapeake Bay, a factor which later worked to the detriment of inland urbanization and the development of local food marketing in the South.[23]

It would be difficult to overemphasize the importance of cotton to the southern economy or, for that matter, the economy of the entire nation. The South had a number of other exports, such as tobacco, rice, sugar, and forest products, yet during the antebellum period none approached the importance of cotton. Moreover, if attention is focused upon the major cotton-producing

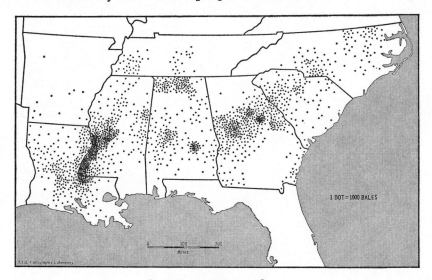

2. COTTON, 1840.

states its position was even more preeminent. One could point to the areas within the South not concentrating on cotton as providing contradictory evidence, yet when confronted with the *overwhelming* economic importance of cotton within the cotton belt, the slavish dependence of the coastal cities upon cotton for their very existence, the extravagant application of labor to the crop, the cotton-oriented landholding patterns and agricultural systems and, finally, the partial dependence upon other regions of the country for foodstuffs and other supplies, it is difficult to see the South as anything other than "cotton country." For South Carolina, Georgia, Alabama, Mississippi, and Louisiana, cotton kingdom, a term so often used in nineteenth-century literature, was appropriately descriptive. Not always linked directly to all human activity in the area, cotton was the main force behind its culture and economy. It enriched the planter, impoverished the soil, made big farmers out of little ones and planters out of farmers. It paid the taxes, bought the supplies, paid off the mortgages, and built the railroads. Finally, it sustained the institution of slavery, making it a central element of the regional society and economy. Like the major theme in a symphony, it wove its way through the entire area, on occasion light and subtle, but more often strong and distinct. And though it is not the major concern of this study, the development and functioning of the cotton

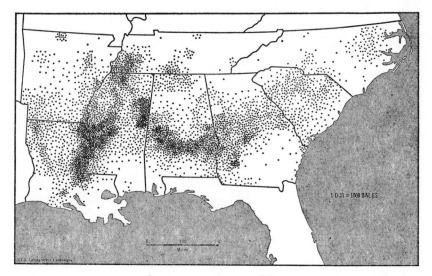

3.   COTTON, 1860.

system was so important that it must be considered. In many respects, the food producing industry was merely an adjunct of the cotton system and its character must be assessed in light of the demands of "King Cotton." Where cotton prevailed, food production became a secondary occupation finding itself closely intertwined (though, curiously, often in competition) with cotton production. Food was essential to the sustenance of the area's population, but in some areas the temptation to grow cotton resulted in periodic shortages and, consequently, a dependence upon other areas for food. Even so, cotton was not the only cash crop which affected food production. Both the sugar and rice producing areas depended upon imported food to a large extent, more, in fact, than the cotton areas since both had easy access to water-transported provisions and possessed poor natural conditions for the production of some foodstuffs, but this discussion must wait until later.

2 The problems of subsistence

In the preceding chapter, it was suggested that the South differed from the remainder of the nation in its attention to commercial nonfood crops. This fact should not be particularly surprising to students of American agriculture, since the South has traditionally been seen as a land of cotton, rice, tobacco, and sugarcane. Yet, few attempts have been made to assess the role of food production in the total southern agricultural system, establish the areas where food production was below the need, or to determine the reasons underlying specific conditions. In the following chapters we will address ourselves to these questions by looking at the production and consumption of a number of commodities. But, before a detailed analysis of the individual food products is begun, we must have a brief look at the southern agricultural system and its environmental conditions with an eye toward identifying specific characteristics that might have affected food production.

Southern agriculture and food production

That the South should have "problems" of food supply is in itself somewhat perplexing. Admittedly, it developed agricultural systems somewhat different from those in the remainder of the nation, but these differences often were minor and in much of the area appeared unrelated to the production of food crops. The South produced enormous quantities of food, and in some areas the commercial nonfood crops such as cotton were unimportant. In fact, there were many parts of the nation that placed just as high an emphasis on cash crops as did much of the South. However, we cannot ignore the abundant evidence that food shortages did occur on occasion and that agriculturists in some areas made no real effort to provide foodstuffs enough for their own use.

Therefore, it seems appropriate at the moment to examine some of the characteristics of southern agriculture that may have inhibited food production or encouraged its neglect.

One of the most distinctive features of southern agriculture, and indeed the southern landscape in general, was the plantation. It was introduced into the Atlantic seaboard during the late seventeenth and early eighteenth centuries and, when supplied with abundant, low-cost labor, proved itself to be an efficient and highly remunerative unit for producing a number of cash crops. Encouraged by the ready market for cotton, rice, and sugar; the availability of large tracts of land; and an apparently unlimited supply of slaves; the plantation became increasingly important during the antebellum period. It penetrated all parts of the South but reached its greatest development in the areas capable of specializing in such crops (figs. 4 and 5).[1]

The southern plantation had no inherent characteristics that necessarily inhibited food production. For centuries plantations all over the world have produced immense quantities of food for the commercial market; indeed, this has been one of their major contributions to world agricultural production. Yet, there were certain features about the organization and function of the plantation as it existed in the South that encouraged either a neglect of food production or a deliberate decision to buy rather than grow foodstuffs. Perhaps the most important of these factors was the competition from the cash crops themselves. Aside from the romantic notions that have developed about the planter, his love of the land and his paternalism toward his chattels, we must face the obvious fact that the plantation existed primarily to accumulate wealth. (There were plenty of "show plantations" in the South, *but* they became such only after the money had been made). The means whereby this was accomplished was growing and selling crops for cash. Obviously, foodstuffs not grown on the plantation cost money to buy, but since the plantation's *raison d'être* was making money, then cash crops received the highest priority. Cotton, rice, and sugarcane all required a great deal of labor during certain times of the year, a fact that forced many operators to make choices in the allocation of labor. When competition arose between food and cash crops, it was tempting to favor the cash crop, especially since cash crops often were so remunerative that the income realized from a given amount of

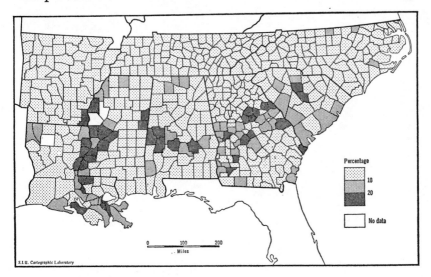

Percentage

10

20

No data

0   100   200
. . Miles

S.I.U. Cartographic Laboratory

4.   PROPORTION OF LANDHOLDINGS OVER 500
ACRES, 1860.

labor expended on them would buy more provisions than if the same labor had been devoted to food production. Of course, in the case of cotton, this comparative advantage may have been illusory since many food crops did not necessarily have to compete with it. This was especially true on well-managed plantations where labor allocation was planned judiciously. Yet, there is little doubt that the cash crops were so tyrannical in their demands for labor that other crops often suffered.[2]

For the planter to have had the opportunity to concentrate on cash crop production, he needed assurance of reliable sources from which he could purchase foodstuffs. In some cases, the concentration on cash crops was encouraged by the existence of very close ties with merchants (factors) located in port cities. A close economic relationship between the two could have tempted the planter to devote more of his resources to the production of cash crops, since he could purchase food directly from the factor who also carried his cash-crop account. A necessary link in this food-supply chain existed between the food surplus areas of Tennessee, Kentucky, and the Old Northwest and the southern port cities. Just as the planters depended upon the port city as a food source, so did the port merchant or factor look to the surplus food produc-

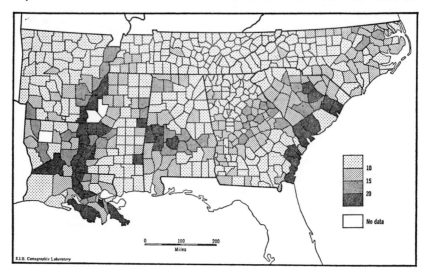

5. AVERAGE NUMBER OF SLAVES PER SLAVEHOLDER, 1860.

ing areas for his supply. Admittedly, the source areas were separated from the consumer by hundreds of miles, yet transportation
costs did not make such goods prohibitively expensive. Throughout most of the antebellum period, the food supply chain was
rather strictly confined to the existing waterways via the factors
in the southern port cities, thus limiting the number of areas that
could be served conveniently. A number of railroads were con-
structed before 1860 and some provisions moved over these roads,
but their importance as freight haulers was minimal. Moreover,
many planters disdained any dependence upon extraregional
sources for food and chose not to buy food from the factors. Nevertheless, the point is that such a food-supply chain did exist and
was available to many planters in certain areas of the South; it
offered them the choice to buy foodstuffs or not.

    Another feature of the cash crop system which made food
production somewhat of a problem was the dualistic nature of the
planter's output. The usual plantation output was a nonfood crop
which could not be consumed when food supplies were low. (Both
sugar and rice were foods but only rice could be considered a
staple of which large quantities could be consumed.) In order to
achieve self-sufficiency, the planter had to divert a portion of his
time and labor from the cash crop into the *separate and distinct*

food-crop effort. The typical farmer in the Old Northwest or the Hill South, on the other hand, did not face such a dichotomy of interest and effort since his cash products consisted of surpluses in cattle, hogs, wheat, pork, butter, cheese, and corn, all of which were food commodities. Only occasionally did he deal exclusively in nonfood items such as wool or hemp. This contrast may not seem significant and, under normal conditions, there was little difference. But, this functional distinction became important during lean years when the planter, who normally planned to produce only enough foodstuffs "to do," found himself in short supply while the farmer, who relied on surplus foodstuffs for sale, suffered only a reduction in that surplus. The farmer, unlike the planter, did not face a possible foodstuff deficit during the next year.

The planter's indifference to the production of foodstuffs was due principally to competition from cash crops but, in addition, he had little incentive to produce food surpluses in an area where local markets were so poorly developed. A surprising paradox existed in that market channels between many planters and the port city factors were well developed and fairly reliable, yet interior markets often were small and undependable, so that few planters counted on them as large-scale suppliers of foodstuffs or as markets for any surpluses the planter might produce.[3] One wonders, though, why small holders did not take advantage of this obvious market for foodstuffs, the plantation. The answer is that many did, and this trade will be discussed later, but a major factor that must be considered is that the small holder also was attracted to the cash crops. This was especially true in the production of cotton since the capital investment needed to grow cotton successfully was considerably less than that needed for either sugar or rice.

Another feature of the plantation that must be examined is absentee ownership. It was fairly common, especially in the newly settled parts of Alabama, Mississippi, and Louisiana and in both the sugar and rice producing areas where planters often owned more than one plantation. Since these units had to be managed, the system created a new professional person—the plantation overseer who resided on the plantation and was responsible for its function. The overseer often has been pictured as an uneducated, drunken lout who had to be watched closely to avoid his bankrupting the owner, and there were probably many who deserved this characterization, but for our purposes we are interested only in his ability as a food producer.[4] In some cases, he entered into a contract with the planter where his responsibilities and the plantation operation was spelled out in detail, but in others he was engaged on a very loose basis and left to run the plantation on his own. It seems logical to assume that a resident planter would be more sensitive to the food needs of his labor force than the presumably less responsible overseer whose greatest concern was making a good cash crop. There was, on occasion, some monetary incentive for the overseer to produce foodstuffs, since some absentee planters offered bonuses for the production of adequate provisions. On the other hand, the very necessity of offering such bonuses strongly suggests that overseers were not, under normal conditions, completely satisfactory as managers of foodstuff production. The fault, however, might not have lain with the overseer, since many planters wished a maximum return on their investment and felt it could be accomplished best by a strong emphasis upon cotton, often to the detriment of provisions. Consequently, many overseers were judged not by the provisions they grew but how many bales they hauled to the gin.[5]

In addition to the problems associated with the plantation, the slave often has been at the center of criticism for the South's failure to provide fully for its own food needs. Much of this has been directed toward his inability or unwillingness to function effectively under the slave system. There seems some justification in considering slavery partially responsible for the problems of the food-producing system, but the slave's ineffectiveness seems to be related to his position in the "system" rather than to any inherent personal qualities.

The slave neither owned land nor did he have any well-defined rights to its use such as "soil" or "tenancy" rights. He was, in every sense of the word, a slave and as such enjoyed only those privileges permitted by his master. There is good reason to believe that slavery, as it was practiced in the United States, was perhaps a more "complete" form of slavery than other slave systems existing in the New World at the same time. This does not necessarily mean that it was more cruel or that the slave was subjected to more physical abuse or deprivation, but that the slave had a lower legal status than was the case in parts of Latin

America. The prohibition against slaves' owning property, the attitude toward slave mobility and family ties, and the efforts to impede manumission, all point to the existence of a highly restrictive system which placed the slave in an extremely dependent position.[6] Often the slave was allowed a plot of land to work on his own and frequently was the possessor of some livestock, yet his status placed him in a disadvantageous position when it came to utilizing this food for himself. The plain and unadorned attire he was issued annually or semiannually and the dearth of amenities in his existence often led him to seek cash for purchasing a few coveted items such as cloth, choice foods, tobacco, and perhaps whiskey. Frequently, he obtained money for such "luxuries" by selling or trading the produce of his own agricultural plots. As a consequence, he restricted his own food supply and by so doing forced himself back into even more complete dependence upon his master.

There was nothing in the slave's innate ability which might have reduced his food producing potential. In fact, he did very well under the circumstances, often showing surprising ingenuity in providing for himself and his family under adverse conditions. Yet, his servile condition, his place in the agricultural community, and (again) his *dependent* position in the economy, led to his being completely left out of the decision-making and, consequently, without any significant voice in the food-producing effort. The slave was, in an economic sense, a domestic animal to be fed, housed, and worked at the pleasure of his owner.

The physical system and food production

In addition to the economic or cultural factors which might have affected food production, a number of natural conditions also were involved. For example, most of the South was particularly suited to the growing of tropical or semitropical crops and, during the colonial period, most colonies were expected to produce exotic goods for European needs. However, in time the hot, damp summers and poorly drained soils of the South came to be looked upon as unsuitable for some food crops. A few "southern" crops, such as corn, could be grown virtually anywhere in the nation, but some items have come to be identified specifically with the South and others have been virtually absent from its fields and gardens. Therefore, we must ask whether environmental conditions were important factors contributing to the "problem" of the southern subsistence economy.

The physical characteristics of the South varied considerably within the area and, depending upon the commodity produced, could be considered either beneficial or inhibitive to agricultural production. There are few "absolutes" in the relationship between the physical base of agriculture and the kinds of crops grown. Plants require optimum conditions to produce best, but they also have a tolerance range which allows them to be grown under less favorable conditions but usually with diminished returns. Obviously, this optimum varies considerably from one crop to another or even among varieties with a single crop species. Consequently, a grower must concentrate on the production of a few crops or expect yields disproportionate to the land and labor involved from plants less well suited to the existing conditions.

While the optimum conditions for each plant or animal vary, the range of tolerance for each also varies; some are severely limited while others do well under widely differing conditions. For example, sugarcane must have virtually frost-free conditions with an abundance of moisture and relatively rich soils; thus it is restricted to a few very limited parts of the South. At the other extreme on the scale of tolerance is corn or maize which thrives under widely varying temperature and moisture conditions. Of all the food crops of nineteenth-century America, it had the largest areal extent, being grown from Maine to Florida and west into the arid areas of Arizona and New Mexico. To be sure, corn had certain conditions under which it did best and many strains were developed for a number of different conditions, yet its wide tolerance and its extreme usefulness made it a favorite nearly everywhere.

The most obvious environmental element that distinguishes the South from the rest of the nation is its climate. With most of the South lying south of the 36th parallel (latitude of the Strait of Gibralter), it was expected to be a replacement for the Orient in the production of exotic crops such as silk and spices. Although such aspirations were never realized, it was to a very large extent the mild winters and long growing season which encouraged attempts to grow a host of tropical and semitropical crops and finally led to the dominance of cotton as the cash crop of the

South. Moreover, climate was influential in the choice of crops used for food, though perhaps less so than in the case of commercially marketed crops.

Since both temperature and precipitation are so important to plant growth, it seems appropriate to look at climate in the South and point out some of its influence of food production. Referred to by climatologists as a "humid subtropical" area, the southeastern United States is characterized by hot summers and mild winters. Subfreezing temperatures occur infrequently, thus, the growing season in much of the South is relatively long. Applying the criterion often used, namely the number of frost-free days per year, all of the area except eastern Tennessee, extreme northern Georgia, and western North Carolina has a growing season of 200 or more days. Near the coast, the season approaches 300 days (fig. 6). Average annual temperatures in the area vary from about 60°F along the Virginia–North Carolina border to about 70°F along the Gulf Coast. In July, the monthly average is about 80°F for most of the area while the January average varies from about 40°F in the North to 55°F or so in the South (figs. 7 and 8). Temperature, of course, varies considerably from these means with the difference between the coldest and warmest days of the year being between 70 and 90 degrees. Though commonly in the thirties and forties during January in the South, the thermometer sometimes plunges to nearly zero and in rare cases goes below. The average annual minimum temperature is about 15°F for places such as Augusta and Columbus, Georgia, Montgomery, Alabama, and Jackson, Mississippi.[7]

Most of the South receives more than 45 inches of rainfall annually; in fact, parts of the Gulf and Hill South average over 50 inches (fig. 9). Moreover, rainfall reliability is high, at least on an annual basis, with the annual precipitation seldom falling below 40 inches. An exception is the central and coastal areas of both Carolinas where 30–35 inches is received on occasion. However, averages tend to obscure one characteristic especially important for farming, namely a fairly frequent late summer drought. Near the Gulf and Atlantic coasts most summers record 12 to 14 inches of precipitation, but in the interior of the Gulf Plains (the core of the cotton belt) summers are sometimes dry enough to impair plant growth severely. Corn, in particular, is susceptible to these droughts since it has high moisture require-

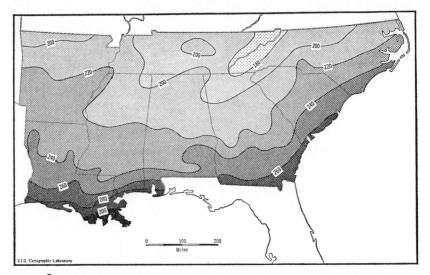

6. AVERAGE LENGTH OF GROWING SEASON.

ments while in the tasseling and fruiting stage. Although such
dry summer periods occur in the interior, Gulf and Atlantic coast
stations record a marked increase in rainfall in the late summer–
early fall period. This increase, related to tropical disturbances
in the Caribbean, is of particular significance, since it inhibits
maturation of some crops and delays the harvest of others.

Applying these general remarks to specific food crops we
find that only a few, such as citrus fruits and sugarcane, were
limited climatically to the South. A few others (sweet potatoes,
peanuts, melons, and sorghums) could be grown in other parts
of the country, yet they did best in the South. The climatic feature
that probably did more to affect southern food production was
the growing season. Not only did it permit the growth of long-
maturing plants, it allowed a much longer season in which many
food crops were available. Garden vegetables, for example, mature in 60 to 110 days thus, one could plant not one but several
gardens during the year. Judicious planting provided the table
with many vegetables from June until frost and a few vegetables,
such as turnip greens, the year round. On the other hand, the
long, hot summers proved disadvantageous to the growth of a
number of other vegetables. White potatoes, green peas, and cabbage do best in cool summers, though southerners ofter circumvented this climatic limitation by planting in the fall for winter

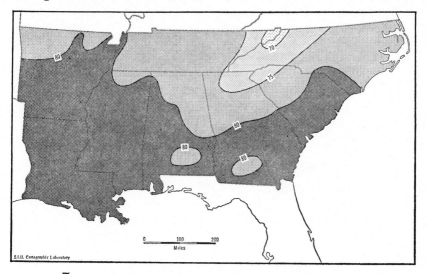

7. AVERAGE TEMPERATURE FOR JULY.

use or in January for early spring harvest. Southern orchards produced substantial quantities of apples and pears though the yields were highest where summers were not too hot (over 80°F). Peaches, plums, apricots, and vine fruits did quite well. Citrus fruits were planted along the coasts and often bore fruit but seldom were very successful over long periods since the occasional "severe" winter usually did lethal damage.

With abundant precipitation characteristic of most of the South, a wide variety of crops was grown and only occasionally was moisture deficiency a serious problem such as that of moisture availability for corn during "fruiting" period. In fact, the humid conditions found in most of the area were decidely unfavorable for small grain. Wheat rust becomes a problem where rainfall approaches 50 inches, a fact which did not prohibit wheat growing but did reduce yields. Furthermore, the rather erratic and showery nature of southern precipitation sometimes cut down yields by delaying crop harvesting.[8] Abrupt, intense rain showers, common during the summer months, often flattened small grain, making harvest difficult, and inhibited the curing of hay. While hay itself was not a food crop, there was an apparent relationship between the scarcity of good hay and the relatively underdeveloped livestock industry in the South.[9]

In addition to the more obvious effects of climate on food

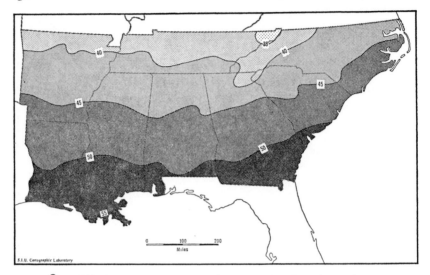

8. AVERAGE TEMPERATURE FOR JANUARY.

crop production, other elements in the physical milieu also affected the southern subsistence economy. Of these, the most important was the natural vegetation, which not only harbored a
fauna that could be harvested for food but also offered special
conditions that encouraged woods-grazing of farm animals.

The major part of the South was forested at the time of
initial settlement. The types of forests and the plant species varied, of course, from one area to another, and the plant associations often were complex in composition and varied in character,
but there were a number of large areas that exhibited considerable homogeneity with respect to species, size, and association.

The dominant trees unquestionably were the pines, with one
species or another being found over almost the entire area.
Roughly a third of the area was dominated by pines while in perhaps another fifth to a quarter of the area they were common. The
pine reached its most imposing proportions in the so-called "piney
woods" where it often reigned unchallenged as the upper story
plant cover. John Claiborne described the pine-forested area of
Mississippi as land

> thickly planted with an almost unvaried forest of yellow
> pine. Finer, straighter, loftier trees the world does not pro-
> duce. For twenty miles at the stretch in places you may ride
> through these ancient woods and see them as they have

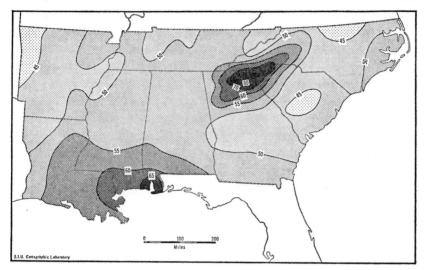

9. AVERAGE ANNUAL PRECIPITATION.

stood for countless years . . . this growth of giant pines is unbroken on the route we pursued for an hundred miles or more, save where rivers or large water courses intervene.[10]

One of the more striking aspects of the southern pine forests, especially to early travelers, was their open, parklike appearance with relatively little undergrowth. Charles Lyell, the noted British geologist described the condition, "we had many long rides together through those woods, there being no underwood to prevent a horse from galloping freely in every direction." [11] This parklike appearance was due to the custom of periodically burning the forests. Indians had burned the forests for centuries before Columbus, and white settlers were quick to adopt the custom.[12] In fact, it was recommended as a means of providing forage for cattle, since fire had the effect of eliminating brushy undergrowth and preventing the maturation of competing hardwoods. It also aided the fire-resistant pine since it was not a highly competitive species. This lack of undergrowth coupled with the fact that the pine tree canopy was relatively open led to a rich growth of grasses and herbs around and under the pines. Farmers, planters, herders, and Indians fired the forest every year or so to encourage the growth of this verdant carpet. Captain Basil Hall, while traveling through the area, witnessed one of these fires and recorded his impressions.

> It was an exceedingly pretty sight. A bright flaming ring, about a foot in height, and three or four hundred yards in diameter, kept spreading itself in all directions, meeting and enclosing trees, burning up shrubs with great avidity.[13]

The burning of the ground cover of forested areas was by no means restricted to the pine forests, but it was here that fire was the greatest agent in perpetuating the dominance of a specific tree species and in fostering the carpet of grass.[14]

The ground cover underneath the pine forest varied from one area to another and was made up of a number of plants. In the northern and western parts of the pine forests the most common plants were species of *Andropogon* or *Carex* (*Andropogon* includes the broomsedge and bluestems so well known in the South) while near the coasts, especially in Georgia, the wiregrasses (*Aristida*) and dropseed (*Sporobolus*) tended to be more common. These together with a few herbaceous plants, made up most of the ground carpet in the upland pine forests. They recovered quite well from the effects of burning and were used widely for cattle grazing by planters, farmers, and herders.

Supplementing this forage were the "canebrakes," dense patches of cane that occurred along many of the rivers and smaller streams of the South, especially in Alabama and Mississippi. They covered large lowland areas in parts of central Alabama not necessarily associated with streams, since the cane needed only fairly moist conditions to thrive.[15] These breaks were quite useful to the cattleman as they provided winter forage when the upland grazing were gone.

Inland at the higher elevations the species remained roughly the same except that the southern pines became much less common. They were replaced in the high mountains by other conifers such as the white pine (*P. strobus*) but except in the most elevated highlands, the white pine remained a relatively minor element of the plant associations. The chestnut was one of the more notable trees of what has been called "oak-chestnut" forest. Not only was it a large and imposing tree, but it bore vast quantities of nuts which supported a rich wild fauna as well as providing for the early white settlers and his hogs.

While the oak-pine and oak-chestnut forests did not offer the open appearance of the pine forests toward the coasts, they were not impassibly encumbered with undergrowth. Apparently the practice of periodic firing extended well into the mixed forest area with the result that understory growth was inhibited. In reminiscing about the area between Augusta and Wilkes County in Georgia one writer remarked:

> The grand groves of oak and hickory had not been felled save in occasional spots. The annual fires of the Indian had kept down all undergrowth, and the demands of the stock-raiser had still called for those annual burnings; so that grass and flowers and flowering shrubs covered the surface of the earth with a vesture equal to that of a regal park.[16]

The ground cover in the oak-pine and oak-chestnut forest probably had fewer grasses and a larger portion of herbaceous species, though the bluestems (*Andropogon*) and panic (*Panicum*) grasses still were quite common. Consequently, it probably offered poorer forage than the grass ground cover occurring in the pine forests.

Throughout the South there were many areas where trees were either scattered or completely absent. The most notable of these was the black belt or "prairie" of Alabama. The black belt is a crescent-shaped area extending from the Alabama-Georgia line across central Alabama and then northward to include a small area of northeastern Mississippi. A good portion of the soils are calcareous, dark in color and believed to have been formed under grass. However, the factors which led to the formation of the black belt are not clearly known since there is some question about the timing of its existence as a grassland.[17] On the other hand, judging from accounts written is the first half of the nineteenth century, it is difficult not to accept the fact that large portions of the area were essentially treeless at that time. It might well have been that Indian and white burnings had been so devastating that the prairie represented a Post-Columbian condition, yet the black belt, as well as other smaller prairies, certainly did exist in the antebellum period.[18] Whether they were part of a continuous treeless area or were relatively small, noncontiguous plots is not clear.

The use to which these prairie grasses were put also is hard to determine. With a widespread grazing system over much of the South during the early period it is tempting to speculate on their being for grazing, but specific references to grazing activities in the black belt are rare. It well may have been that these grasslands were sought out by prospective cotton growers so quickly that grazing had no time to develop.

Other aspects of the physical milieu that might have encouraged or inhibited food production are not so easy to assess. Obviously, both the surface configuration of the land and its drainage and soils were important matters to which any astute nineteenth-century agriculturist quickly became attuned. But, we must distinguish between the specific effects upon food production and the effects upon agriculture in general. Factors such as slope inclination and drainage certainly were important to the nineteenth-century agriculturist and they materially altered settlement patterns and density, but once settled, most areas that attracted agriculturists in large numbers were capable of producing most food crops that were grown in the area. Moreover, whatever deficiencies the soil might have had, it was much more apt to affect the growers choice of money crops that his attempts at subsistence.[19] The possible exceptions to this might have been the rice and sugar planters whose operations demanded specific locations not always suited to food crop production. This was especially true of the rice planter, since he was constrained to cultivating low-lying fields near tidewater, where irrigation water could be applied easily. Even so, one wonders whether poor soil drainage affected food production on rice plantations very much. Most plantations were very large, encompassing both floodplain and the better drained interfluvial land which could have been used for crops other than rice. It is true that the rice and sugar areas imported a larger percentage of their food than any other major regions, but it is also true that they had excellent trade facilities through which food could be brought in, they had a higher proportion of plantation-size landholdings, and also a higher proportion of their population was slave.

In summary, there is no question but that the southern natural environment had its effect (both positively and negatively) upon food production; to argue otherwise would be foolish. Yet, there is good evidence that the nonenvironmental factors had more to do with the southern food "problem" than did nature. In some cases, the environment may have affected the choice of one food crop over another, but the fact remains that many operators did produce their own food while their neighbors (in precisely the same environment) did not. In order to sort the matter out as carefully and systematically as possible, each phase of the southern food producing industry must be analyzed.

3 "All Kinds of Good Rations"

Any discussion of food supply in the South must include the distinctive character of southern food habits and diet. Nowhere in the nation has a culture trait become so outstanding nor certain foods so identified with a single area as in the South. While it is true that recent trends indicate a mass homogenization of American food habits, the notable food preferences of eighteenth- and nineteenth-century southerners and the persistence of these choices into the twentieth century have consistently distinguished the region from other parts of the country. Perhaps due to low production costs or ready availability of some food items, the area developed and maintained a strong dependence upon certain foods. Most southern food choices were not unique; indeed, many were frontier staples in other parts of the country. Yet, the South came to depend so strongly upon items such as pork, corn, turnips, sweet potatoes, okra and peas, that they often are regarded as "southern." This section deals with the development of southern food habits and describes foodways as they existed during the antebellum period. It also comments on the nutritional aspects of southern diet and the persistence of food preferences through time.

The scientific study of diet is essentially a post–Civil War phenomenon. Detailed information on food habits is not available for the antebellum period, leaving us the problem of extracting bits of material from scattered sources. Some information can be gleaned from the writings of travelers in the south who commented frequently on food they encountered while touring the area. More comes from the diaries and daybooks of planters and farmers. Finally, a number of studies published toward the end of the nineteenth century and in the early twentieth century indicate fairly precisely the food habits in a few specific areas.[1] From these rather scattered sources one can obtain some information about southern food habits and perhaps gain insight into those that existed before the Civil War.

The settlement years

The food habits of southerners during the antebellum period stemmed in part from those existing in the Atlantic Seaboard South during the late eighteenth and early nineteenth centuries and were tempered by frontier conditions and the availability of food items suited to conditions in the New South.

During the early years, food choices were dictated by frontier conditions and the state of agricultural development. Since settlement was not instantaneous, frontier conditions varied from place to place and from time to time. Parts of Georgia, central Alabama, Tennessee, most of Mississippi, and virtually all of Arkansas were considered wilderness and were avoided by all but the most adventurous travelers. Those curious enough to venture into the interior found that conditions changed markedly as they moved from the more settled areas into the back country. Before 1835 or 1840, many travelers reported an almost total lack of luxury items in the interior and often complained about the coarse food. On an overland trip from New Orleans to Charleston in the 1830s Thomas Hamilton described the food in the interior of Alabama: "We were now beyond the region of bread, and our fare consisted of eggs, broiled venison, and cakes of Indian corn fried in some kind of oleaginous matter." He reported this menu again and again, though at times there were no eggs.[2] In the back country there was a strong dependence upon game, and travelers found it wherever they went.[3]

The transition from wild to domestic food was gradual with most people depending less on forest and stream as their farms began to yield and as the supply of wild foods diminished. During the first year on a newly settled farm or plantation, practically everything was in short supply; even corn, the universal staple, had to be brought in from the settled areas or purchased from neighbors whose farms were already producing.[4] Most settlers, whether large or small holders, planted corn as soon as possible to provide food for the coming year. Usually, they also owned a few cattle and hogs, which were expected to increase and provide dairy products and meat.

Pork was the most common domestic meat during the early years. Brood stock was considered essential on all new holdings. It increased rapidly and even in remote areas salt pork competed strongly with venison as the staple meat. In discussing the South in the 1830s, Harriet Martineau complained that travelers found "little else than pork, under all manner of disguises." [5] One visitor complained about the toughness of Virginia chickens, but remarked that they would have been relished "in Alabama, where bacon and sweet potatoes constitute the only delicacies." [6] He described a meal offered him near Columbus, Georgia which, with the possible exception of the milk, probably represented the usual fare.

> In the middle of the table was placed a bottle of whiskey, of which both host and hostess partook in no measured quantity, before they tasted any of the dishes. Pigs' feet pickled in vinegar formed the first course; then followed bacon with molasses; and the repast concluded with a super-abundance of milk and bread, which the land-lord, to use his own expression, washed down with a half a tumbler of whiskey. The landlady, a real Amazon, was not a little surprised to see a person refusing such a delicacy as bacon swimming in molasses.[7]

A visitor traveling near Berrien, Georgia in 1837 reported the addition of rice to the usual "fryed middlin [sic], cornbread, and coffee." [8] Early settlers in Mississippi seldom could offer much variety to visitors as James Creecy complained:

> I have never fallen in with any cooking so villainous. Rusty salt pork, boiled or fried . . . and musty corn-meal dodgers, rarely a vegetable of any description, no milk, butter, eggs, or the semblance of a condiment—was my fare often for weeks at a time.

Again:

> But few, indeed, of the early settlers gave a thought to gardens or vegetables, and their food was coarse corn-meal bread, rusty pork, with wild game . . . and sometimes what was, most slanderously called coffee.[9]

Corn and pork were dietary mainstays and were the domestic food items most avidly sought, but other foods were added as soon as possible. A good crop for new settlers was turnips. Providing greens in only a few weeks, the plants were ideal for new clearings and were quite common on newly opened landholdings.

Even when the overseer of a new plantation or planter arrived at a site in late summer or fall there was always time for sowing turnips.[10]

As more land was cleared for farming, a greater variety of foods became available. A garden was planted, orchards were set out, the cattle and hogs increased, and poultry became more common. Moreover, the sale of cash crops such as cotton made possible the purchase of a few luxury items. Thus, the typical fare of new settlers underwent a gradual improvement in variety. During the first year there was a strong reliance on nondomestic foods supplemented by small purchases from neighbors. As the fields began to yield, other items such as pork, corn, sweet potatoes, turnips, and chicken were added. But most farmers had to wait a few years for beef and dairy products, until sufficient stock of animals was accumulated. Perhaps, by the third or fourth year, the fields and pastures began to yield adequately and by the fifth or sixth the orchard trees were bearing, but a decade might pass before the farm or plantation could offer a good variety of food. Even then, only the most foresighted could maintain an assorted fare throughout the year.

The antebellum period

While the more settled parts of the South underwent some change in food habits as the variety of foods increased, most farmers and planters retained a number of their frontier eating habits, keeping game, fish, and gathered food from the large areas of unimproved land on the table until the Civil War. Moreover, corn and pork remained the dietary staples in the South throughout the antebellum period and into the twentieth century.

Pork was the most important meat on American tables, but the total consumption of meat of all kinds was quite high in comparison with other countries. This heavy consumption of meat together with preponderance of pork tended to give European travelers the impression that Americans consumed little else. In commenting on food habits in America, Mrs. Frances Trollope remarked that "They consume an extraordinary quantity of bacon. Ham and beefsteaks appear morning, noon and night." [11] One estimate placed the per capita consumption of pork during the period at three times that of Europe.[12] In the South and West, the tendency was to rely even more strongly on pork, with most white people having it every day. One story has it that an immigrant Irishman wrote home that he commonly "took meat" twice a day. When asked why he prevaricated so outrageously, he replied that if he had told the truth and said "three times a day" he would have been believed even less.[13] In reply to a query sent out by the Patent Office in 1848, correspondents from a number of states estimated the annual consumption of meat for an adult in their area and their answers are shown in table 1.[14]

1. *Estimated annual meat needed per adult, by number of pounds.*

	BEEF	PORK	BEEF OR PORK	ANY MEAT; OR POULTRY AND BACON
Georgia	150	180	. . .	. . .
Illinois	. . .	. . .	200	. . .
Indiana*	65	250	. . .	. . .
Kentucky	. . .	. . .	150–200	. . .
Mississippi	. . .	. . .	200–250	. . .
New Jersey	100	100	. . .	. . .
New York	150	. . .	. . .	. . .
Pennsylvania*	100	100	. . .	340
South Carolina	50	150	. . .	. . .
Tennessee	. . .	. . .	. . .	100
Virginia	. . .	. . .	. . .	250

* Includes more than one example from the state

These estimates probably indicate ideal rather than actual conditions and are, therefore, much too high for some states, but they do suggest a very high total consumption of meat and a higher percentage of pork than beef in the southern and western states.

Within the Deep South, pork was the undisputed "king of the table." Olmsted stated that bacon "invariably appeared at every meal." [15] After observing southern culture for some time, Emily Burke concluded that

the people of the South would not think they could subsist without their [swine] flesh; bacon, instead of bread, seems to be THEIR staff of life. Consequently, you see bacon upon a Southern table three times a day either boiled or fried.[16]

Although cheapness may have been a deciding factor in its adoption as the primary southern meat source, considerable debate arose over the possible nutritive qualities of pork. Many people regarded pork as the ideal meat for working people. They recognized (correctly) that pork was packed with energy (calories) and regarded it as a "natural" for the hardworking slave. They also suspected that it was hard to digest, but mentally circumvented this minor disadvantage by attributing to their chattels unusual powers of digestion. Even though the prevailing opinion (and presumably taste) favored pork as the main meat, a few physicians were beginning to plead for less pork and more vegetables in the diet.[17] Dr. John S. Wilson of Columbus, Georgia, one of the most outspoken doctors in the South, frequently attacked the overuse of pork. In one of his numerous articles on diet and health he delivered a scathing attack on pork-eating and cooking with lard.

> The United States of America might properly be called the great Hog-eating Confederacy, or the Republic of Porkdom. At any rate should the South and West . . . be named dietetically, the above appellation would be peculiarly appropriate; for in many parts of this region, so far as meat is concerned, it is fat bacon and pork, fat bacon and pork only, and that continually morning, noon, and night, for all classes, sexes, ages, and conditions; and, except the boiled bacon and collards at dinner, the meat is generally fried, and thus supersaturated with grease in the form of hogs' lard. But the frying is not confined to the meat alone: for we have fried vegetables of all kinds, fried fritters and pancakes . . . fried bread not infrequently, and indeed fried everything that is fryable, or that will stick together long enough to undergo the delightful process . . . hogs' lard is the very oil that moves the machinery of life, and they would as soon think of dispensing with tea, coffee, or tobacco . . . as with the essence of hog.[18]

The dominance of hog meat led to a great deal of experimentation with production, slaughter, and preservation methods. The system of pork-packing that had developed in the Ohio River Valley was well organized by 1840 and, due to the dominance of large packing houses, exhibited considerable uniformity. With no organized packing industry in the Deep South, pork production was confined largely to farms and plantations; consequently, variety was the order of the day with each person having his own "pet" methods of slaughtering and curing. The most common curing method was dry-salting followed by smoking. The carcass was cut up into six or more pieces, placed in a meat box, and covered with salt. After a few weeks (sometimes as long as six) the meat was removed, washed, and hung in the smokehouse over a slow fire. Though not a universal practice, some producers preferred to sprinkle lightly with salt and let the meat lie overnight to "draw out the blood" before placing in the meat box.

An alternative to this method was pickling in casks filled with brine solution. Pickling offered advantages in that it permitted slaughtering in warmer weather without fear of spoilage and eliminated the laborious process of salting, hanging, and smoking. Moreover, awkward pieces, such as the head, could be preserved more easily than by smoking. While pickled meat was less likely to become spoiled than smoked meat, it required soaking in water to remove enough salt to make it palatable.[19] Moreover, most southerners much preferred the salt-smoke process since it produced, (to their tastes at least) better flavored meat. Consequently, it must have been the most commonly used method. Emily Burke reported from Georgia:

> Pork at the South is never to my knowledge, salted and barreled as it is with us, but flitches as well as hams are hung up without being divided, in the house built for that purpose, and preserved in a smoke that is kept up night and day.[20]

These general descriptions of pork processing hardly do justice to the myriad individual variations that existed. Such methods were employed commonly in making large quantities of pork, such as that needed for slave meat on large plantations, but meat destined for planter or farmer use received special treatment. The carcass was carefully cut up; the joints trimmed to shape; and the spine, ribs, and tenderloin were separated from the abdominal sides which were cured into bacon. Excess fat was rendered into lard while the lean pieces went into sausage, souse, or headcheese. The backbone and ribs, liver, tongue, and brains often were consumed fresh. The kidneys, heart, and lungs were eaten occasionally, but few southerners cared for them. Chitterlings (the large intestine), reputedly treasured only by Negroes, were relished by whites as well, and the traditional "chitlin supper" came to be an annual epicurean delight.

Curing techniques were matters of personal pride with each farmer or planter adding his own flourishes to the basic technique. Pepper, alum, ashes, charcoal, corn meal, honey, sugar, molasses, saltpeter, mustard, and a host of other seasonings were added, and each producer fancied his own meat to be "not inferior to the best Wesphalian hams." [21] The preferred cuts were the hams, shoulders, sausage and perhaps the tenderloin, but each part of the animal had its devotees and all were consumed, in one manner or another, through the winter and well into the summer. On occasion, the entire animal was roasted. Apparently, the famous southern barbecue was in practice before the Civil War as a young bride in North Carolina wrote her parents in New York:

> Not until you come here can you imagine how entirely different is their mode of living here from the North. They live more heartily . . . Red pepper is much used to flavor . . . the famous barbarque [sic] of the South . . . which I believe they esteem above all.[22]

The use of meat other than pork by the white people of the South is easy to underestimate. Such meats were commonly consumed but the total quantity was small. Beef was not relied upon very heavily because it was hard to preserve in a manner to suit southern tastes. Most beef was eaten fresh, but it was occasionally pickled and there is some evidence that it was also dried.[23] Except in mid-winter, fresh beef had to be consumed rather quickly in order to prevent spoilage. This was accomplished easily on a plantation with a large labor force since beeves were slaughtered one at a time and the meat divided among the families, to be consumed in a few days. Occasionally, planters and farmers formed cooperatives in which each family killed periodically and divided the meat among the participants.[24] Apparently, this became a common practice among the French in Louisiana.[25] In other cases, neighbors simply borrowed fresh meat and repaid later as their own animals were slaughtered.[26]

Because of the tendency to run short of pork in summer, there was probably a rise in beef consumption in that season. Cattle were fatter in summer and, after months of salt pork, beef was a welcome relief.[27] One southern writer, pleading for agricultural reform and higher pork production, cited planters who were forced to kill beeves so often that "the cows are afraid to come home at night." [28]

However, such comments must be regarded as propaganda supporting an impassioned plea for southern self-sufficiency in pork. Except for the herder, who kept large numbers of cattle, such frequent slaughtering was rare. It is unlikely that beef was eaten regularly, especially among the poorer whites. Among the more diversified farmers and better planters and especially outside the cash-crop regions, its use was more common. Most operators slaughtered one or two animals each year while the larger planters may have killed more.[29] Susan Dabney Smedes refers to beef used on the famous Dabney plantation as if it were common, and it is likely that beef-eating was the rule among the herders in the pine forest of the Coastal Plain.[30] Beef consumption by most southerners, however, must have been sporadic and the total amount small relative to pork. This might not have been true where cooperative slaughtering was practiced, but one questions just how widespread the cooperative system was.

Apparently, there were no regionally characteristic ways in which southerners prepared their beef. Travelers referred to "beefsteaks" but seldom with any hint as to their preparation.[31] In restaurants or hotels, beef was prepared in a variety of ways. Olmsted noted entrees on the menu of Commercial Hotel in Memphis which included a number of beef dishes—corned beef, Kentucky Beef (roasted), beef heart, and kidney.[32] Frying was a common cooking method and was well suited to situations where few utensils were available.[33]

Traditionally, southerners have not been considered consumers of mutton. In fact, in his monumental work on the history of southern agriculture, L. C. Gray concludes that "there was a strong prejudice in the South against mutton, a prejudice that must have been widespread, judging from frequent references to it."[34] Undoubtedly, mutton was a minor food on southern tables, but its use was not uncommon, and in many areas it was actively sought.[35] One visitor along the rice coast remarked, "so far from mutton being despised, as we have been told, it was much desired."[36] In Louisiana, mutton was well liked, and even in the interior of the South there was a sizable demand.[37] In fact, some evidence indicates that southern sheep were kept *primarily* for their flesh rather than for wool. Solon Robinson met a planter in Louisiana who kept 200–500 sheep to feed his slaves, and he hinted that the practice was common along the Mississippi.[38] In writing to the Patent Office in 1849 a Mississippi agriculturist revealed a surprising concern for mutton sheep: "Few planters keep more sheep than enough to supply their own tables with that most excellent dish, a saddle of Mississippi mutton." [39] Another wrote:

> I do not think it an object with our planters to increase their flocks to a greater extent than to supply their family wants. The sheep is valued with us more for his flesh than for his fleece. The mutton, we think is quite equal to any in the world.[40]

Undoubtedly, lamb and mutton were more common among the affluent than among the poorer whites and slaves. The larger farmers and planters were more likely to keep sheep, and most planned on slaughtering several each year, a practice that resulted in mutton becoming a periodic supplement to the meat supply.[41] Some planters, however, kept sheep enough to have lamb or mutton quite often. Fanny Kemble, while visiting along the Rice Coast, remarked that "we have now not infrequently had mutton at the table, the flavor of which is quite excellent.[42] A Mississippi planter butchered as often as twice a week during spring and summer, and on "Rosedew," a Georgia coastal plantation, lambs were slaughtered weekly and sent to market, indicating a demand in urban areas.[43] It is entirely possible that there was a relationship between the fondness for lamb and the high rice consumption in coastal Georgia and South Carolina, since the two make excellent table companions.

Although mutton and beef offered periodic respites from pork, poultry served as a regular, though supplementary, meat dish throughout the year. Chickens and turkeys were kept on virtually all southern landholdings, and were important elements in the white diet, possibly more than either beef or mutton. Even if the total quantity of poultry did not equal the amount of beef and mutton consumed, it was available more regularly and was therefore more important in breaking the monotony of the meat routine.

Poultry was regarded as a semiluxury item and the implications of the term "chicken on Sunday" probably were accurate. The more astute farmers and planters were able to have poultry frequently, and the visitor was plied with either chicken or turkey.[44] Most planters had their own flocks and some supplemented this supply with purchases from their slaves who kept poultry. The smaller landholder had fewer fowls, but he still depended upon poultry for special occasions. Southern pots often were filled in expectation of the preacher or other special guests. For example, Olmsted's request for breakfast in northern Mississippi was fulfilled promptly after a group of Negro children chased and caught a hen in the backyard.[45] The occasional visitor, the family get-together on Sundays, or the periodic visits by the preacher were times for slaughtering a fryer or nonlaying old hen. A favorite story in the rural South portrays barnyard fowls becoming so "educated" to the Sunday slaughter that when a "genteel-looking" person approached the house they fled to the woods.

The preparation of poultry meat was simple with few southern flourishes added. The most notable dish was fried chicken, but frying required a young bird which was not always available. Those too old and tough for frying were roasted or boiled until tender, and leftover chicken or turkey carcasses were converted into pies with large dumplings made of wheat flour.

While poultry flesh helped relieve the monotony of a diet dominated by pork, eggs added even more variety. Commonly used as ingredients in breads, cakes, and pies they also were used as food items themselves and were surprisingly common as food for travelers.[46] Though the quantity of eggs consumed is not known, they must have been eaten regularly during summer by most white families, but the seasonal character of egglaying meant a dearth in winter.

Southerners took game of all kinds throughout the year, but fall and winter were the preferred hunting seasons. This provided game during the period when poultry and eggs were least abundant. Wild turkey, rabbit, and squirrel tended to replace domestic poultry and eggs in the diet during winter. The cooking of game was similar to that for domestic meats. Frying was a favorite method of preparing young rabbit, but older animals were boiled.[47] Squirrel meat was tougher than rabbit and required more cooking, but the results were considered superior to rabbit dishes. Squirrel broth or pie with dumplings were considered delicacies.[48] Opossum certainly was not confined to the Negro diet. Most whites ate the animal and many sought them eagerly. Young ones could be fried, but the preferred method was roasting and serving with sweet potatoes. An ex-slave commented on their gastro-

nomical worth: "but verily there is nothing in all butcherdom so
delicious as a roasted 'possum." [49] Perhaps the game most sought
were the various kinds of fowls. Along the Atlantic coast and Mississippi flyways waterfowl were numerous and they provided excellent food. However, wild turkey was the favorite since it
abounded throughout the area.

Like game, fish and seafood were important minor foods in
much of the area, but near the coasts and in the larger rivers they
were relied on quite heavily. The oyster was the easiest of the marine foods to harvest, but other kinds were taken easily by nets
and seines in large quantities. Shrimp and mullet were favorites
along the coast. Farther inland, catfish became the prize catch.
They were found in all major rivers, were easy to catch, and many
were large enough to feed an entire family. Frying was the most
common method of preparing fresh fish and, no matter what the
species, the fish was rolled in cornmeal and then fried. Saltwater
fish were treated in the same manner. Near the coast shellfish,
too, were so prepared, though often they were roasted unshucked
over an open fire or made into a stew.

As mentioned previously, corn was the companion food to
pork and in many respects it was more important. Corn was utilized in myriad ways. During early summer, while still green, it
was boiled on-the-cob, cut off the cob and creamed (called "fried
corn"), and roasted in the shuck.[50] After the ears had ripened and
dried there were many other ways it could be prepared. The most
common was to grind it into meal from which an almost endless
variety of breads were concocted. Corn bread was the most common which, in its simplest form, was baked cake or "pone" made
from meal, salt, and water. Variations upon this included the addition of milk, buttermilk, shortening, or eggs. After hog-killing,
bits of crisp "cracklings" left over from the lard-rendering process
were added to make "crackling bread." The variations were legion
and, even today, one encounters dozens of recipes for southern
corn bread.

The dominance of corn bread as *the* bread for the South is
unquestionable. Whether in the mountains or near the coast,
Olmsted constantly commented about being fed corn bread, and
apparently, it was the bread he encountered most often.[51] U. B.
Phillips refers to corn as the food of the "plain people," but there
is little to indicate that corn bread was exclusively a poor man's

food. It is true the more affluent could afford wheaten bread, but most did not abandon corn bread as they "moved up" to the use of other cereals. Charles Lyell found that even in "some rich houses maize, or Indian corn, and rice were entirely substituted for wheaten bread.[52] Harriet Martineau, in describing a fantastically sumptuous plantation menu, lists "hot wheat bread . . . corn bread, biscuits" as if both corn and wheat breads were commonly served together.[53] Phillip Gosse, while visiting in Alabama, concluded that it was "even preferred to the finest wheaten bread." [54]

The popularity of corn bread is not easy to explain. Its use for slave food presumably was due to the cheapness of cornmeal compared with wheat flour, but one wonders why it was so well liked by all. It was very easy to make but, unlike most European breads, did not remain fresh very long. This is probably the reason why southern housewives came to think of hot bread as an essential element of every meal. In the absence of other reasons for its popularity one can only conclude that southerners learned to like the taste of corn bread when it was all they had and continued to demand it though they might well have afforded wheaten bread. However, such persistence has not necessarily been the case in other areas where corn was the principal "frontier" cereal.

Cornmeal was used to make a number of other items besides corn bread. Some, such as corn dodgers, hoecake, corn muffins, and egg bread, were simply variations of corn bread while other dishes were quite different.[55] Often cornmeal was made into mush (porridge), griddle cakes, or waffles.[56] Sometimes it was mixed with wheat flour and occasionally with rice to make bread. On occasion, cornmeal was mixed with milk or water, put in a warm place to sour, and made into "sourings" which served as bread.[57]

In addition to the use of corn as meal, southerners converted it into hominy and grits. Both were made from corn but the grains went through a soaking process which removed the husk (not the shuck) from the grain. Hominy consisted of whole grain corn boiled and eaten as a vegetable. When hominy grains were dried, ground into a coarse meal, and boiled, the dish was called grits. The preparation of grits varied depending upon personal preference but they usually were cooked into a thick porridge. On occasion, both hominy and grits were subjected to further refinement by immersion in hot grease and fried. Contrary to popular opinion, neither grits nor hominy ever came close to being universally used in the area prior to the Civil War. Both were common but, compared to other uses to which corn was put, they were certainly subordinate. In the twentieth century grits has come to be a common complementary dish to ham, sausage, or bacon and eggs for breakfast, but there is a little evidence that grits were used nearly as much as corn bread during the antebellum period.

Other cereals have had much less notable places in the southern diet. Buckwheat, rye, oats, and other cereal grains have never been particularly liked and seldom were used. Wheat and rice were the most common minor cereals. Southerners always have liked wheat bread, but the relatively low production of the grain within much of the area and the high cost of imported flour tended to cut down wheat consumption. Travelers often complained about the lack of wheat bread, and when available some considered it "doughy" because of the addition of too much shortening (hog lard, of course).[58] Wheaten bread undoubtedly was more commonly used in the older states of the South than in the later settled areas. More wheat flour was consumed per capita in Virginia and North Carolina than in Georgia and more in Georgia than in Mississippi or Alabama. Wheat bread and other wheaten items certainly were not rare, but among the less affluent people they were "something special," available perhaps on Sundays or two or three times each week. The day-to-day bread was corn bread. Moreover, much of the wheat flour was used for pastries, cakes, waffles, and pancakes rather than for bread.

Rice consumption was quite high along the Carolina and Georgia coasts, yet outside the "rice area" rice was a minor item. In a few counties along the Georgia-Carolina coast extremely high production and correspondingly low costs—especially for the less marketable kinds—made it a staple in the diet of both blacks and whites. Charles Lyell noted that rice, together with corn bread, took the place of wheaten bread in the rice area of South Carolina.[59] Olmsted commented quite favorably upon a breakfast roll made with rice flour.[60] Another visitor noted it was one of the principal dishes: "I always eat from this dish of rice at breakfast because I know it to be very wholesome. People generally eat it with fresh butter, and many mix with it also a soft-boiled egg."[61] The high consumption of rice in limited areas of the South is an excellent example of a food preference being determined by the ready availability of an item. Though rice is no longer grown in coastal Georgia and South Carolina, the local preference for rice has persisted. In some parts of South Carolina today, the typical housewife would never think a meal complete without a dish of rice. It replaces grits as the breakfast "filler," and potatoes at the remaining meals.

The favorite southern vegetables were sweet potatoes, turnips, and peas. More than any others, these were the items to which southerners turned for vegetable food. The sweet potato (commonly and confusingly referred to simply as "potato") was useful in that it was highly nutritious, kept well during winter, and could be cooked a number of ways. Baking or roasting in ashes was a common method of cooking and the result was quite suitable for hunting trips or for snacks (this writer often has carried a bag of baked potatoes to serve for lunch on daylong hunts in Georgia). Olmsted noted both Negro and white boys roasting potatoes in the ashes of a campfire at a religious service; later the children crawled around on the church floor carrying "handfuls of corn bread and roasted potatoes about with them." [62]

Turnips were grown for the roots and greens and both were eaten in large quantities. Both were invariably boiled (seemingly for hours) and southerners preferred the greens boiled with a large "chunk" of bacon in the pot. Cabbage, collards, other greens, beans, and peas (field peas or cow peas) all were cooked in this manner. A by-product of this process of boiling with a piece of bacon was the "pot-likker." This was a concentrated broth combining juices from both the vegetables and meat and was eaten with corn pone crumbled into the dish and mixed with the "pot-likker." Although this practice might not appeal to today's discerning tastes, it was extremely important that the highly nutritious juices were consumed rather than discarded. In addition to boiling, many vegetables were fried, including white potatoes, eggplant, okra, squash (southerners preferred the yellow summer squash), and even sweet potatoes, sliced and rolled in meal.

Fruits and melons were popular during season and were easily preserved for winter use.[63] For desserts, fruits were made into pies or served fresh. Surplus fruits were either dried or preserved by some sugar process. Dried peaches, apples, and other fruits were served in winter while apples, peaches, various kinds of grapes including scuppernongs and muscadines, blackberries, strawberries, and even watermelons were converted to sweets for off-season use. Additional sweetening came in the form of molasses, syrup, and honey (both wild and domestic).[64] The molasses and syrup used in the South was of two basic kinds. In areas near the South Atlantic and Gulf Coasts, especially in Louisiana, the most common syrup was molasses made from sugarcane. It was an important trade item and was the sweetening most frequently issued to slaves. The major sources were Louisiana or the West Indies. On landholdings not producing sugar, syrup was made from sorghum cane and was referred to as sorghum, ribbon cane, cane syrup, but occasionally as "molasses" too.

The southern attitude toward beverages has changed markedly since antebellum times. While there was a small temperance movement before the war, the great, almost universal, condemnation of alcoholic drinks came in the late nineteenth and early twentieth centuries. During the antebellum period whiskey and wine were consumed in huge quantities by all whites who could afford them with whiskey being preferred by the less well-to-do.[65] Wine was very common among the affluent. A number of visitors noted its use and it appears that claret was the favorite.[66] This preference for claret is further confirmed by the statistics for wines imported into the country which show the major part of the claret moving into New Orleans.[67]

Nonalcoholic drinks included coffee, tea, and milk. Coffee was a favorite but tea was fairly common. Milk was consumed fresh, sour (curds), or made into buttermilk. Both sour milk and buttermilk were quite popular and, even today, a favorite dish is corn bread crumbled into buttermilk to make a soupy mixture.[68] It was common to serve plain water at meals and, between meals, a gourd of cool spring water was a summer treat invariably offered to visitors.

Many towns and cities, notably New Orleans, Mobile, Savannah, and Charleston, offered a variety of luxury foods not available in the more remote rural stores. The inland towns functioned much as did the coastal cities but on a smaller scale. Raleigh, Columbia, Augusta, Macon, Milledgeville, Columbus, Montgomery, Selma, Florence, Decatur, Jackson, Vicksburg, and Natchez were centers where luxury foodstuffs were available. Stores, restaurants, and hotels as well as factors handled imported wines, liquors, spices, cheese, and other items for the more affluent. Lewis Atherton's study of country stores in the South revealed a surprising variety of goods available in many rural areas as well. All stores carried sugar, coffee, tea, salt, and whiskey, but a number went far beyond this simple list. A wholesaler in Athens, Georgia listed an almost unbelievable array of gourmet items, and a house in Huntsville, Alabama advertised "loaf and lump sugar, pineapple cheese, allspice, ginger, pepper, raisins, almonds, nutmegs, mustard . . . tea, and wine." In Talladega, Alabama a store advertised "liquors, brandies, wines, whiskies, ale, porter." Furthermore, many towns had confectioners where "candies, cordials, fruits, cakes" were offered.[69] J. S. Buckingham noted (even in the 1840s) that Columbus, Georgia had "more than the usual number of . . . 'Confectionaries,' [*sic*] where sweetmeats and fruits are sold." He apparently found a similar situation in Alabama but noted that the cordials were alcoholic and that some confectioner's shops were only gentlemen's bars.[70]

Perhaps the most notable innovation affecting popular nourishment was the availability of ice. It became available in port cities early in the century and by the 1850s had penetrated the interior as well. Ice was sold in Selma, Alabama in 1840 and by 1855 had reached most urban places located near rivers or on railroads. In the major ports the ice was of New England origin, but many westerners began floating ice down the Mississippi and at New Orleans it often sold quite well.[71] The availability of ice increased the variety offered by the confectionery and the true soda fountain came into being. Just prior to the war an Alabama store advertised:

> The subscribers have put up a soda fountain in their establishment, and have arrangements to be supplied with ice. . . . The syrups will be of the richest and most choice variety, consisting of rose, lemon pineapple and strawberry, vanilla, sarasparilla, sassafras, ginger, almond, and peach.[72]

As ice became available the year round, ice cream making became possible. It was made in the area before the 1840s, but few machines were in use. A freezer, roughly the same as the freezer now used, began to be marketed during the 1850s and presumably some moved into the South.[73]

With such items available, the urban inhabitant as well as

planters and farmers living nearby had opportunities to vary their food intake with unusual or exotic goods. It is unlikely that people indulged in such luxuries very often, but there must have been special occasions when even small farmers purchased a few special items. The occasional trip to town, the birthday, or the trip to take a son away to the academy, were occasions calling for treats which offered a welcome variety in the day-to-day fare.

The availability of these items together with a disparity of wealth among southerners led to variations in food habits among economic classes. Unfortunately, most detailed menu descriptions come from the pens of affluent planters or writers who visited the larger and better managed plantations, most of which were in the old or more developed settlements such as the Georgia-Carolina Coast or lower Louisiana. Such descriptions reveal an almost unbelievable opulence. At one meal on the Alston plantation along the rice coast a sumptuous table was laden with

> turtle soup at each end [and] two parallel dishes, one containing a leg of boiled mutton and the other turtle steaks and fins. Next was a pie of Maccaroni [sic] in the center of the table and on each side of it was a small dish of oysters. Next . . . were two parallel dishes, corresponding with the two above mentioned, one of them turtle steaks and fins, and the other a boiled ham. When the soups were removed, their place was supplied at one end by a haunch of venison, and at the other by a roast turkey. . . . [a second course included] bread pudding . . . jelly . . . a high glass dish of ice cream . . . [and] a pie. . . . [After the second course came] . . . two high baskets . . . one of bananas and the other of oranges. One larger . . . of apples.

During the meal Madeira, sherry, and champagne were served and, after dessert, Hermitage, Madeira, and cordials.[74] John Grimball describes another meal for eight with four courses that included two soups, ham, turkey with oyster sauce, a leg of mutton, a haunch of venison, three wild ducks, turtle steaks and fins, four vegetables, apple pudding, custards, cheese, and bread. All this was followed by dessert.[75] Apparently overindulgence was not unknown as he complained of another meal:

> Dined yesterday with Mr. Vanderhorst . . . the table absolutely groaned under the load of meats . . . the wines were good . . . I mixed the wines and drank more than my stomach would bear, and when I came home was made quite ill.[76]

The tables of the less wealthy were not so abundantly supplied, yet it was common to have more than one meat at a single meal. A traveler through Mississippi in the 1850s described a table: "Here we have excellent ham, boiled whole, a surloin [*sic*] of Venison, and dainty steak from 'Old Bruin.'" [77] Small planters and farmers served abundant and wholesome but not sumptuous meals. In Virginia a traveler was fed soup, cabbage and bacon (boiled together), fowl, both wheaten and corn bread, potatoes, green corn, and apple dumplings for dinner. Breakfast was made up of "coffee, small hot wheaten rolls [probably biscuits] batter bread, and hoe-cake . . . milk, eggs, and rashers of bacon." [78] But, even these modest meals were not available to all whites. Many southern tables saw only pork, corn bread, and a vegetable or two day after day, week after week. This was particularly true in winter when vegetables were fewer and there was a strong dependence upon cured meat and semiperishable cereals and vegetables.

Feeding the "people"

There were many similarities between the diets of Negroes and whites, but the basic differences in their social, legal, and economic positions led to marked differences in the kind, quality, and (possibly) the quantity of foods consumed. To be sure, there were many slaves who received the same foods as whites—even dining at the same tables—and many whites lived little better than slaves; yet one must recognize the fundamental fact that whites had greater opportunity to vary their diets as food availability and economic means might have permitted. Living in close proximity and often subsisting on the same kinds of foods, both blacks and whites developed the same likes and dislikes, yet there seems little doubt that most whites had a much better and more varied diet than the great bulk of the slave population.

The simplicity of the slave diet coupled with the numerous contemporary references to slave food make it relatively easy to describe slave food habits. In fact, a great deal more is known with confidence about slave food consumption than that of the white population. There are still blanks in our knowledge but, on the whole, the picture of slave diet is much clearer than that of southern whites during the same period. [79]

The slave had three primary sources for the food he con-

sumed. The bulk of it came as daily or weekly rations issued by
the master, consisting principally of a regular allowance of corn
and pork supplemented by periodic doles of sweet potatoes, vegetables, and fruits. Occasionally, molasses, salt, coffee, and a few
other items were added, but the basic ration was comprised of
corn, pork, and vegetables. The second source was the food raised
by the slave himself, either by keeping animals or growing vegetables in his own provision plots. The third major source was
gathering, hunting, and fishing. Not all slaves could exploit the
last two sources, and the extent to which each was utilized depended upon the location of the plantation, the attitude of the
master, and the resourcefulness of the slave.

The slave ration (usually doled out weekly) almost invariably contained corn which, in some cases, was unground, but
most planters preferred to issue cornmeal since it saved the time
required to grind the corn. The usual ration was a peck to every
hand each week. Cornmeal was a major segment of the slave's
diet and, in most cases, the recommended allowance was followed
carefully, but some planters allowed unlimited access to the meal
bin. It was consumed primarily in the form of corn bread, but
from time to time mush was made. Occasionally, grits and hominy were issued but by far the most common was cornmeal.

Although the slave's cornmeal supply usually was ample, the
pork allowance was another matter. Masters varied in their notions of what constituted a proper meat ration, and there was
always a possibility that it would be discontinued if supplies ran
short. The usual ration was from two to five pounds each week.
This was not universal, however, and many operators varied considerably both above and below these figures depending on the
slave's age, condition, work load, and season of the year. As mentioned earlier, Negroes were thought by many to require large
amounts of pork while laboring heavily and were more gener-
ously supplied with meat during the working season.

The kind of hog meat commonly issued to slaves is not an
easy matter to determine. Most references describe it as either
"pork" or "bacon," but precisely what is meant by these terms is
not absolutely clear. The common assumption today is that bacon
was cured middlings (the relatively fat abdominal walls, commonly called "fatback" or "sowbelly") and that such meat made
up the bulk of the slaves' meat ration. When purchased meat was

used or when both whites and Negroes were fed from the same source, the slave undoubtedly received the middlings and poorer cuts. For example, on small holdings, a slaughtered animal might be divided between slaves and whites in which case the better meat cuts (or at least a large portion of them) went to the whites. In some cases, planters living off the premises left orders for a certain amount of choice meat to be sent to them.[80] Apparently a surfeit of such choice items was not unknown as an overseer of the Telfair plantation in Jefferson County, Georgia wrote his master concerning leftover hams:

> After sending the usual Quantity of hams to Savannah I gave the ballance [sic] out to the Negroes in the Early Part of the season while they were good as I did not expect you would wish any of them sent down in the fall season.[81]

Although *fat* pork and bacon were used commonly as slave food, it is extremely difficult to imagine the majority of slaves living off "fatback" the year round. For one thing, there simply was not enough side meat produced from the hogs slaughtered on each landholding to feed the slave population. Apparently, many operators maintained a supply of "meat hogs" for the use of the slaves and a few special hogs kept for family use in which case the two meat supplies were separate. Furthermore, on plantations that were overseer operated (often he was the only white on the plantation), the great majority of the hogs were killed and made into pork for the slaves. With an annual slaughter of fifty to one hundred hogs, it is almost certain that the entire part of nearly all the hogs was consumed by the slave force.

Where written records of slave rations are examined, the usual reference is to "bacon" or "pork" and it appears that the terms did not refer exclusively to the sides but to all or most of the hog. Frequently, the meat was described as "good clean bacon" or "clean meat" or "clear meat" or "bacon-clean of bone" with an implication that the term did not always mean simply side meat.[82] In fact, some planters varied the weekly ration depending upon the kind available, especially since some thought fat pork was better for working persons, Negroes in particular, than the leaner meat.[83] Records from a number of sources support this observation. A Sumter County, Alabama planter fed his hands one pound per day while feeding the "boney parts" (presumably the backbone and ribs, feet, head, and neck), four pounds a week while feeding joints (hams and shoulders), and three and one-half pounds when feeding middlings.[84] A perennial contributor to antebellum southern agricultural periodicals, *Agricola,* states that he allowed three and one-half pounds of bacon if middlings were issued and four pounds if the allowance was of shoulder.[85] Apparently, these people shared the notion that fat meat was more nutritious than lean and increased the allowance accordingly.

Therefore, the terms most commonly used, "bacon" and "pork," referred to more than simple pork sides and must have included at least the shoulders and, on occasion, all the joints. Meat that was labeled "pork" could have been either salted or pickled meat but that referred to as "bacon" underwent an additional smoking process which took several weeks.[86] Apparently, these terms applied in the packing plants in the West as well. Charles Cist described the Cincinnati packing industry's output:

> The different classes of cured pork packed in barrels, are made up of the different sizes and conditions of hogs—the finest and fattest making clear and mess pork while the residue is put up into prime pork or bacon.[87]

Part of the output of the packing houses was sent to smokehouses to be cured into bacon. Usually, bacon was made up of most parts of the hog, but the individual parts must have been put up separately since it was possible to buy "bacon sides" or "bacon hams." According to Cist, prime pork was the class most often shipped south for plantation use and this consisted of: "Two shoulders, two jowls, and sides enough to fill the barrel." [88]

In answer to the question originally raised, it appears that pork issued slaves varied depending upon the situation. Where the pork was made on the plantation, the slaves most likely were fed the entire animal. On smaller holdings where the proportion of white inhabitants to slaves was relatively high, the better cuts went to the whites. And, when meat was purchased, it probably contained some joints, although much of it was bacon sides.

While pork made up the great bulk of the slave's meat supply, on occasion he received beef and mutton. Considering the large numbers of cattle in the area, it is surprising that beef was on the menu so infrequently. Apparently, it was because beef was considered harder to cure and, when fed, was believed to be nutritionally poorer than pork. For this reason, when beef was fed to slaves the allowance was generally higher than that of pork. On rice plantations, where beef was more commonly issued, the usual ration was "one pound of pork or two of beef." [89] A Mississippi planter issued three pounds of fresh beef a day (this would amount to twenty-one pounds per week).[90] Another factor in the low consumption of beef may well have been that the Negroes simply preferred pork to beef. Solon Robinson, in discussing southern pork production, cites Negro prejudice as the reason for the little use of beef.[91] Apparently, a century has not changed this taste as the Negro of the rural South today is not very fond of beef. Given a choice, most will take pork over any other meat. There were, of course, individuals who advocated feeding beef, mutton or even goat in order to get away from the heavy dependence upon pork, but few southerners were convinced that pork was anything but the best possible slave meat.[92]

Beef and mutton seldom were relied upon as steady meat sources for slaves but usually were reserved for special occasions such as holidays and weddings. Apparently, a common practice was to celebrate notable occasions with a barbecue. Some planters had annual affairs toward the end of the season where pigs, beeves, lambs, and goats were roasted over coals.[93] Such occasions were the delight of the participants, of course, and were important interruptions in the slave's routine, yet they were relatively infrequent and short-lived. More important to the overall slave diet was the practice of slaughtering one or more beeves periodically to be divided and issued as fresh meat. For example, on the Telfair plantation in Georgia there was a standing order to kill in July, August, and September.[94] On other plantations, beef or mutton was slaughtered weekly and where practiced, such a system could easily yield several pounds of meat per family at each occasion.[95] Mutton and beef may have been issued more commonly on holdings near the Atlantic coast than on cotton plantations. Apparently, the daily ration of cured pork was not the rule on most rice plantations with the meat supply coming primarily from periodic slaughterings of either hogs, cattle, or sheep.[96]

Estimating the importance of poultry consumed by slaves presents a problem. It is known that slave-owned poultry was fairly common, but the practice of selling or trading their own poultry and eggs must have reduced severely the amount actually consumed by the slave. For the same reason one must question the general use of slave-owned swine as food for the slaves. It was very common for slave-owned pigs to be sold rather than eaten; in fact, many slaves never thought of eating their own animals but kept them solely for ultimate sale either to merchants or to a planter to augment his supply of pork.[97] It is conceivable, of course, that the slave's own swine might have been slaughtered and issued back to him as a part of the weekly ration.[98]

While the staple ration for the slave was corn and meat, most slave owners attempted to provide vegetables as well. This was probably due more to the desire to cut down on costly meat consumption than any recognition of their nutritive qualities. The variety of vegetables was limited. Apparently, the plants were chosen for their yield and ease of cultivation. The most common were turnips, sweet potatoes, peas, cabbage, collards, and pumpkins. Others, such as onions, okra, and squash, were known, but most operators concentrated on the items most common in the area. In fact, where the slave had his own garden he usually planted the same items as he was regularly issued (peas, turnips, and sweet potatoes). Most slaves usually could count on some kind of garden vegetable as a regular ration, but he did not always receive a variety at one time nor were vegetables available every meal. Slaveowners attempted to provide vegetables daily but may not have been able to do so consistently.[99] Most slaves probably had at least one vegetable each day, but the limited variety with perhaps only one or two available at a given season led to a monotonous routine. During late summer and fall, sweet potatoes were relied upon quite heavily; in winter, turnips and greens served as staples; but by spring and summer a few more items were available. Peas, either fresh or dried, could be had the year round.

The consumption of fruit by slaves was fairly common. Recognizing their nutritive value, most planters provided some fruits, mostly peaches, for their hands.[100] Hugh Davis planned and planted a large orchard at Beaver Bend plantation in Alabama, and M. W. Philips of Mississippi was noted for his fruit culture. Philips constantly wrote articles about fruit growing and boasted that he had "more fruit to the number of persons, than any man in Mississippi." [101] Although generally critical of the slave's fare, a temporary resident on an Alabama plantation observed that the orchard "affords them [the slaves] considerable help." In commenting further he remarked: "Peaches are now ripe. . . . So highly is the fruit esteemed, that every farm has large tracts planted with it, as orchards, to one of which the slaves have liberty of access when they please." [102] Fruits were cooked on occasion but the great bulk probably was consumed raw. Many, both wild and domestic, served as snacks between meals, with the watermelon being the odds-on favorite.

Slaveholders issued molasses and syrup periodically. The exact amounts are difficult to determine, and the practice was by no means a universal practice. On some plantations a molasses ration, such as a quart each week, was regularly issued but on other holdings it was considered a special treat.[103] Other planters purchased molasses by the barrel in which case it was used as the slaves pleased.[104] Other minor items were occasional dabs of coffee, tea, and whiskey. Salt was the only seasoning the slave saw regularly; other condiments were unknown.

Although the food habits of whites and slaves were similar in many respects, one of the greatest differences was in the relative amounts of dairy products consumed. Some masters attempted to provide milk for their slaves but the total amount must have been very small. When dairy products were consumed by slaves, it was most often in the form of buttermilk. Whole milk was occasionally given, but butter seldom and cheese almost never.[105] The primary reason, of course, was the extremely low milk production in the area. Almost all farmers and planters kept lactating cows during summer, but the production was never enough to provide substantial quantities for the hands. Where a small milk surplus was produced, it usually went to the slave children.[106]

In many respects, the preparation of slave food was quite like that of whites, the primary difference being in the variety of food available, the utensils used, the time taken to prepare food, and the knowledge of cooking methods. With the same basic foods with which to work, and living under the close supervision of white masters, it was almost inevitable that the slave would develop similar, though much less varied, cooking methods. Where cooking was done individually, a lack of utensils and cooking knowledge hampered the cook; where communal cooking was the rule, the necessity for cooking large amounts inhibited any great variation. The dearth of utensils (a complaint common to most frontier areas) often necessitated cooking several items together and may have been the factor which led to the southerner's (both white and Negro) liking for his meat and vegetables cooked together. While the southern white has been notable for his odd food combinations, the Negro had an even greater reputation for seemingly incongruous mixtures, and this tendency probably was due to his having to cook and eat with a minimum of equipment.

Vegetables usually were cooked in a large pot with pieces of meat while corn pone was baked on the hearth or occasionally in a pan. If communal cooking was employed, there was probably an oven for baking bread.[107] Apparently, toward the end of the antebellum period the communal kitchen came to be the preferred, though not universal, place of cooking. This probably grew out of an attempt to cut down food waste and increase the efficiency of the field hand's labor. There seemed to be a growing realization that the employment of a few plantation cooks allowed field hands more working time in the field and more rest at night. Furthermore, some masters felt that slaves seldom had time to prepare their food properly. There was a strong feeling that some foods, especially vegetables, should be cooked a long time and a well-supervised plantation kitchen was a means of insuring against poorly cooked food.[108] One Georgia planter showed a surprising concern for the slave's food as he gave orders in a letter to his overseer to "look into the cook pot to see if the victuals are well cooked and [the] utensils clean." [109] This insistence on "well-cooked" food has remained with many southerners and may be partially responsible for overcooked vegetables and the coolness toward some raw vegetable salads in the rural South today.[110]

Foodways and nutrition

Though peripheral to the main theme of this work, it seems useful to raise a few questions about the nutritional adequacy of southern foods and speculate on the overall quality of southern diets. It is certain that a strong obstacle to good nutrition in the South (or any other part of the country at the time) was the lack of detailed knowledge about human physiology. The study of nutrition was poorly developed prior to the Civil War, and not until the late nineteenth century were any detailed dietary studies done in the South. Apparently, there was a marked improvement in the quality of diet in the nation after about 1840, but this was due primarily to greater food availability and a higher standard of living rather than any significant development in the science of nutrition.[111] Most planters (and perhaps many doctors) felt that the southern foods commonly used were quite nutritious and adequate for human health. For example, pork was believed to have been difficult to digest, yet it was favored for persons doing heavy labor. It was ideal for the slave who was considered a "low heat producer," but was looked upon as the worst possible food for the "delicate" southern white female.[112]

Even if not very soundly based in theory, it must be said in defense of the antebellum physician that his food recommendations were not wholly inconsistent with today's practices. His explanations for prescribing certain foods may not have been sound, but had planters and farmers listed to his advice and adhered more closely to his recommendations, they and their chattels would have fared much better. Most doctors recommended meat, bread, vegetables, fruit, milk, sugar, and molasses which, if abundantly supplied, would have provided a fairly decent diet.[113] It appears, then, that the lack of knowledge about nutrition was only one of the factors which led to poor diet. In addition, there was often an inability (or lack of concern) on the part of the planter to provide an adequate supply of the foods commonly recommended. Furthermore, it is probable that the variety of foods, particularly fruits and vegetables, was so limited that many nutritionally desirable items such as yellow vegetables (supplying vitamin A) and citrus fruits (vitamin C) were missing.[114]

There seems little doubt that the predominance of pork contributed to a high energy diet with less protein than had other meats been used. Where fat sidemeat was predominant the protein intake was probably one-third that of a beef diet. Where more lean pork was included, the protein increased but did not reach the level that beef would have provided.[115] This protein deficiency may not have been critical among whites but some slaves, whose supply of meat was low or irregular, almost certainly suffered critical protein shortages during a part of the year. The large quantities of corn consumed probably did little to help since some of the animal proteins are essential to good health and cannot be replaced by cereal proteins. Whites had advantages over Negroes in securing these animal proteins in that they had more milk, eggs, and beef and often had access to the larger game. The use of pork did, however, provide a high energy diet. This was especially true where fat pork was used since fat yields considerably more calories per pound than does either protein or carbohydrate.[116]

Corn provided considerable bulk in the diet as well as the major part of the carbohydrates. Where meat consumption was low it also provided much of the energy. Corn supplied few vitamins, however, and little protein. To make matters worse, southerners preferred white corn which, unlike yellow corn, has virtually no vitamin A.[117]

Garden vegetables, when consumed in sufficient quantities, provide many of the essential minerals and vitamins needed for adequate nutrition. Shortages of these essentials probably occurred among the slave population fairly frequently, especially in winter, and on occasion among whites. It is probable that the deficiencies were severe enough in winter to cause pellagra and other related deficiency diseases. After studying plantation records and diaries of planters, William Postell concluded that notations suggesting such diseases were most common during the time of the year when vegetable consumption was relatively low.[118]

An additional unfortunate characteristic of the southern diet was the frequent omission of green and yellow vegetables. Turnip greens and cabbage were common but when supplies ran short, there were few other green vegetables to replace them. Furthermore, those people not engaged directly in farming, such as urban dwellers and laborers, probably consumed a disproportionate amount of cowpeas and potatoes (items more often offered in markets than green and yellow vegetables). Such food choices easily could have led to deficiency diseases, since they were lacking in the antipellagra factor (niacin) as well as other essential vitamins such as vitamin A.[119] Table 2 lists some of the more common southern foods with comments on their nutritive qualities.

Dietary studies made in various parts of the South in the late nineteenth and early twentieth centuries provide some clues about southern nutrition and, while there certainly had been some dietary change in the half century or more since antebellum

2. General characteristics of some major southern foods.

	NUTRITIONAL CHARACTERISTICS	REMARKS
Beef and Mutton	High in protein.	Too little consumed, especially among slaves.
Pork	A good protein source if not too fat. High in energy.	Made up a disproportionate part of most diets.
Fish	Excellent source of many nutrients.	Too little available. However, it may well be that fish and seafood were the major sources of protein along the coasts and rivers.
Game	Good source of many nutrients.	Much more important for whites than slaves. In many areas probably replaced beef.
Poultry and Eggs	Excellent source of many proteins. Easy to kill and eat. No preservation problems.	May have been very important for whites. Negroes, unfortunately, sold much of their poultry and eggs.
Turnips (roots and tops)	Rich in vitamins and iron.	A very good source of vitamins. Might well have saved many from serious deficiency diseases.
Sweet Potatoes	Very high in many nutrients. Good vitamin source.	An excellent food choice combining ease of production and preservation with good nutrition.
Molasses	Rich in energy, calcium, and iron.	Together with sweet potatoes and turnips was the "savior" of many southern diets.
Peas	High in energy, fairly high in protein and some vitamins.	Many were eaten green but large quantities were dried for later use.
Dairy Products	High in calcium, protein, and fat.	Too little consumed, especially by slaves. White consumption was low but probably not critically so.
Fruits	Rich in vitamins. Dried fruit high in energy.	Especially rich when dried. Whites had a fair amount; slaves probably had less than they needed.
Corn	Provided adequate bulk, carbohydrates, and energy. Low in protein and some vitamins.	

times, the studies have general applicability. In an Alabama study
done in the 1890s the most common diet was found to have been
very high in energy but deficient in protein.[120] Studies in Mississippi in the 1920s revealed similar diets. They found few Negro
diets to be substandard in calories but many that were deficient
in iron, calcium, phosphorus, and protein (in that order).[121] In
Georgia, the same general pattern was found, though the deviation from the accepted "norm" was much less. In general, the
intake of meats, eggs, dairy products, fruits, and vegetables was
low while that of fats, sweets, and cereals was high.[122]

The use of these late nineteenth- and early twentieth-century
dietary studies to explain conditions a half century or more earlier
has its limitations, but it is tempting to speculate on the similarities between the two periods. There is little doubt that many
of the food preferences existing during the antebellum period
were carried over to the twentieth century and survive as relics in
the rural South today. On the other hand, gradual dietary changes
accompanying the rise of sharecropping after the war may have
made the typical southern diet around 1890–1920 significantly
different from, though not necessarily superior to, that of the
1850s. The rise in sharecropping, in particular, may have had a
detrimental effect upon diet in the years following the war. The
effects upon the Negro population undoubtedly was greater than
upon the whites who remained landowners. Nevertheless, some
deterioration in diet occurred as a consequence of the decrease in
standard of living accompanying the process by which landown-
ing whites became croppers. The restriction to certain small plots
of land, the encouragement to grow as much cotton as possible in
order to raise cash, the rise of the "furnish" system with its accompanying "crop liens" leading to increased credit buying at the
local or plantation store, all led to a system that decreased the
amount of home raised foods resulting in a diet poor in variety
and nutritive quality. Negroes suffered the same as the white
croppers but, having lived under the protective aegis of slavery,
they were handicapped further by less knowledge about food production, preservation, and cooking, as well as nutrition.

The total meat consumption in America remained fairly
high after the Civil War, but it is likely that there was a gradual
decline in the amount of meat consumed during the period 1860–
1920.[123] However, while the remainder of the nation shifted away

from a heavy consumption of pork, much of the South may have actually increased the proportion of pork in the diet. It is true that the beef industry in the South has increased markedly during the twentieth century, but this increase is primarily a post-World War II phenomenon and little of it was reflected in the diets of share-croppers or tenants (white or Negro) prior to 1940. Moreover, there is good reason to suspect a higher intake of lean meat prior to the Civil War than in the 1890–1930 period. Considering the relatively small and lean southern hog of the 1840s and 1850s in comparison to the larger (and fatter) animal of the early twentieth century, it is difficult not to conclude that fat meat consumption increased during the 1860–1930 period. Furthermore, there was probably an increase in the proportion of purchased meat (as opposed to home cured) by tenants, which by 1890 or 1900 almost invariably meant side meat or "sowbelly." [124]

Other items in the diet may have been altered materially from the antebellum period up to the time of the Atwater, Woods, and Dickins dietary studies. Plantation orchards, while scarcely adequate before the war, must have deteriorated rapidly as plantations became fragmented by the granting of share-plots or, in many cases, became restricted to the owner and his family. Gardens, too, probably suffered more for care after the war than before; in fact, a common fault of the cropping system was that it encouraged the cropper to produce as much cotton as possible, often leaving little time or space for gardens. Before the days of acreage restrictions an outstanding characteristic of the cotton belt landscape was the absence of gardens around cropper's cabins. The usual pattern was for croppers to work as much land in cotton as possible—often right up to the back door of their cabins—leaving little room for gardens. Felice Swados concluded that fresh vegetables were probably a more common part of the Negro diet before 1860 than in the early 1940s and there seems little reason to quarrel with his observation. [125]

Conclusions regarding southern diet and food preferences during the antebellum period can never be precise. The inevitable loss of information involved in the passing of a century casts doubt on the knowledge of both quality and quantity of southern foods. Considered in the light of nineteenth century customs, habits, and technology, it is very unlikely that many whites in the South were underfed. The lack of methods of food preservation and an apparent unwillingness to accept and encourage the production of a wider variety of foods, however, led to relatively monotonous foodways with less variety than was the rule in the remainder of the nation. The slave diet was characterized by the same monotony but, in addition, was frequently nutritionally inadequate. Part of the blame for these diets, which ranged from "tolerable" to "inadequate," must go to the lack of information about human nutrition. Additional blame can be placed on a cotton monoculture in which food crops were often neglected. Finally, the institution of slavery itself must be held largely responsible for the poor Negro diet and may be further indicted as being partially responsible for the continuation of the low dietary standards which were characteristic of southern Negroes during the postbellum period—since it in no way encouraged either a variety in the foods they grew or imagination in the way food was prepared.

Perhaps the most significant aspect of southern foodways is the persistence of food preferences once they were established. The most obvious characteristic of southern food habits was the strong dependence upon corn and pork which persisted throughout the nineteenth century and, indeed, well into the twentieth. During the colonial period both were staples all along the Atlantic coast including New England. Both were staples in the South and West during the first few decades of the nineteenth century. But by the 1830s and 1840s food habits in the East and West were undergoing significant changes. There was a general rise in standard of living after about 1840 with a consequent change in food habits. Better methods of food preservation and transportation increased the variety available to the consumer. At the same time, waves of immigrants from all parts of Europe introduced new food habits into the increasingly complex cultures of the East and West. The South, on the other hand, shared little in these changes. Instead of being strongly affected by these factors, it became increasingly isolated during the years prior to the Civil War. Perhaps even more important was the continuation of these processes after the war. Emancipation did little to alter the economic position of the Negro, nor did it greatly alter the agricultural commodity emphases. If anything, there was an intensification of the cotton economy. Moreover, the effects of sharecropping reduced many former white landowners to tenancy and a lower level of living. Without the cultural "shock" of immigrants moving into the South and handicapped by a lower level of living than other regions, many elements of the southern diet persisted through the nineteenth and well into the twentieth century. Thus, the traditional southern foods have survived the settlement years, a civil war, and more than a century of time to become a frontier "relic" in the midst of twentieth-century American life.

4 The Forests, Streams, and the Sea

The story of the eighteenth- and early nineteenth-century pioneer has been, at least in the layman's mind, one of the rugged individualism, isolation, and dependence upon nature for sustenance. Sketches of settlement in the east during the early colonial period, and penetration into the Appalachian hill country, the Mohawk lowlands, and the Lake Plains north and west of the Ohio River during the early nineteenth century are replete with stories about the "bountiful wilderness" upon which the immigrant settler depended for food. On the other hand, the South has been the subject of such frontier interpretations less frequently. Perhaps it was the presence of the plantation and slavery or the commercial nature of southern agriculture, but recognition of the area as a host for the true "frontiersman" has been slower than for other parts of the country. Yet, when one considers the southern settlement process with the great expanses of unimproved land and the varied and abundant flora and fauna of the area, it is difficult to imagine the dependence upon nature as having differed greatly from other parts of the country. Moreover, the rather loose and extensive nature of southern agriculture with its low ratio of cleared to uncleared land provided excellent wildlife habitat throughout the antebellum period. This, together with the relatively dense network of fishbearing streams and the lengthy coastline with its rich store of seafood, provided a strong environmental potential for a substantial production of fish, game, and gathered food.

Unfortunately, for our purposes, the extent to which early settlers utilized this reservoir of non domestic foods is not clear. A sketchy picture of southern subsistence can be obtained from the existing written accounts of early settlement, but much more is to be learned by applying present-day knowledge of wildlife habitats, the biotic potential of certain game animals, and the effects of fire and agriculture on vegetation to the problem of interpreting the role of nature as a food supplier. There is no question but that man often depended upon wild foods for his sustenance, but the degree to which he looked to nature for food and the shift from wild to domestic foods as wildlife declined are important elements of the southern food system that must be examined. Furthermore, we need to know more about the effects of man as a cause in the decline of wild food production in the area, and establish the details of his changing levels of subsistence as settlement progressed.

Game and hunting

Hunting is certainly one of the most extensively and land-using types of human occupance. Wildlife requires not only an adequate supply of food, but many animals need large, relatively contiguous areas of protective cover in order to elude their foes, mate, and reproduce. In general, though not always, this is related to density of human population with the sparsely populated areas being most hospitable for wildlife.

Of the limiting factors operating against the maintenance and increase of wildlife numbers, none has been as devastating as man and his activities. In addition to the obvious effects of man as a predator, he also acts as a competitor in that he seeks to raise his own domesticates on land already supporting wildlife. Indeed, his greatest effects come not from direct action, such as killing, but from destruction of wildlife habitat, e.g., cover and feed. Even if no game had been consumed for food, the mere fact of an agricultural people existing in rather large numbers in an area would have limited severely the amount of wildlife available.

On the other hand, some effects of man and his agricultural exploitation improve wildlife habitat and increase wildlife populations. Some animals learn to "live with man," that is, feed off his agricultural produce, reproduce under limited cover conditions, and exist in close proximity to him. In this sense deer, quail, rabbit, and opossum have become quite at home and, with reasonable protection, maintain themselves quite well.[1] Furthermore, some activities of man, such as lumbering, materially benefit wildlife habitat by removing some sizes and species of trees allowing a growth of browse-size plants that offer better food for deer or other animals. Moreover, the extensive nature of southern agriculture (or most early nineteenth-century agriculture for that matter) with its noncontiguous field patterns and associated bush, briar, and weed patches, created a number of microhabitats well suited to animals such as deer, rabbits, and quail.[2] Thus, one can visualize a dual set of processes operating on the land, one of which (the increase in population and its associated expansion of agriculture) worked toward the decrease in habitat area and a decrease in wildlife numbers, while the other (the alteration of existing vegetation to provide special habitats catering to certain animals) worked to slow the process of habitat destruction and alter species ratios, thereby increasing the production of selected species. For the most part, these habitat changes were detrimental to bears, bobcats, wolves, mountain lions, and pigeons while they either encouraged or permitted existence of deer, raccoons, opossums, rabbits, squirrels, quail, and doves. Ducks, geese, snipes, and other water and shorebirds probably decreased in numbers though the primary causes may have lain elsewhere, in the nesting grounds and along migration routes to the north. The added benefit from this process of species selection was that it discriminated against a number of predatory species thereby insuring higher survival rates and larger numbers of other, more desirable, game animals. This fact was recognized by some even before the advent of modern wildlife management. William Elliot of South Carolina, writing in the 1850s, remarked:

> If my observation serves me faithfully, I should say, that unlike . . . other game, they [quail] have increased instead of diminished with the clearing of the country. The extensive grain fields furnish them with ample subsistence.[3]

During the period of Indian occupation, game must have been generally abundant and, while yearly fluctuations occurred, the southeastern tribes probably depended to a large extent upon game for food. The southern habitat could hardly be called "natural," since the Indian had occupied the area for centuries and was a significant modifier of the area's flora and fauna.[4] His practice of burning the forest to facilitate hunting and his rather rudimentary but widespread agriculture had created large areas of second-growth vegetation favorable for animal sustenance.

Though the details of Indian agriculture are not known accurately, it is probable that most crop production involved three stages. First, the forest was burned to obtain a small clearing, the plots then were planted to Indian crops such as maize, beans, or squash, and after years of cropping, villages were abandoned and the fields allowed to reforest themselves. Where practiced, such a system created excellent habitat for a number of animals.

The agricultural practices developed by southern whites were, in many ways, similar to those of the Indian. The extensive cultivating methods with the resulting "brushy" fields, and semi-abandoned or bush-fallowed fields were closely akin to the Indian system. The white system differed from that of the Indian primarily in the amount of the area involved, its intensity of cultivation, and the population densities it supported.

Due to increased hunting pressure, the numbers of animals available for harvest may have increased in the interim between Indian removal and white settlement. However, on the better Indian lands of the southeast the transition from Indian to white tenure was almost immediate with no significant "break" between Indian and white settlement. In any case, as settlement became more dense, increased hunting pressure and decreasing habitat began to reduce the number of available animals with the amount of harvested wildlife varying from one stage to another.

Since white settlement was prolonged with some areas being opened before others, the better lands were taken first leaving the remaining areas unclaimed and uncleared for many years. This process occurred on a regional basis with places such as the Carolina Piedmont, central Georgia, the black belt of Alabama, and the Tennessee and Alabama River valleys being sought out relatively early leaving large unsettled areas elsewhere. This selection process also operated at the local level with smaller areas within the counties remaining unsettled throughout the antebellum period.[5] Frank Owsley makes a strong case for much of the South being "frontier-like" until after the Civil War.[6] In fact, much of the coastal South has never seen the plow, only the blade of the "rosen" (naval stores) and lumber men.

A large portion of the 385,000 square miles in the area remained unimproved as late as 1860. Only 57 percent of the entire area was not even in farms in that year, and in 1850 this figure had been only some 43 percent. In addition to such a high proportion of land not in farms, a large part of the acreage "in farms" was unimproved. Together nonfarm land and unimproved farmland added up to an almost incredible 87 percent of the land area in 1850 and nearly 82 percent even in 1860. Compared with the East and the states north of the Ohio River, the South had much lower percentages of its total land improved.[7]

Of the game animals, it is almost certain that the deer was the most important in terms of pounds of flesh utilized for food. It provided a number of useful products for the aboriginal population and offered both meat and hides for white settlers. Indian hunting pressure on southern deer herds is not known in detail, but it is likely that by 1800 or so the southeastern tribes were taking large numbers of animals. The prolonged contract with whites had led many Indians to discard their primitive weapons in favor of firearms, and the fifty to seventy-five thousand Indians living in the area must have consumed at least that many deer annually, and probably several times as many. Game may have been scarce on occasion, but quite likely it was a local matter and not very widespread.[8]

As white settlement began to advance, the deer kill increased proportionately to the demands of population. As mentioned earlier, there may have been an interim period between Indian and white occupation that allowed deer number to increase, but even if it did exist, the rapid increase in white population soon began to take its toll and the large expanses of continuous cover and forage were doomed.

Except for the relatively densely settled parts of Virginia and the Carolinas, deer were ubiquitous during the first few decades of the nineteenth century. Early settlers had as much venison as they desired; often it served as the chief meat for pioneer farmers. Frequently, planters opening up new operations in wilderness areas depended upon venison until enough hogs were accumulated to provide adequate meat.

Even during the second quarter of the century there is ample documentation of the widespread existence of deer throughout the area. From the Carolinas to Louisiana they undoubtedly were numerous and in much of the area "as late as the fifties deer were still right common."[9] Travelers were plied with venison until they tired of it.[10] Even in the well-settled areas, some people depended heavily upon game. Fanny Kemble, while resident on the

Butler plantation in Georgia in 1838 and 1839, stated that their "living consists very mainly of wild ducks, wild geese, wild turkeys and venison."[11] Tyrone Power described the Mobile market as "abundantly supplied with provisions, fish, and game of every variety."[12] New Orleans markets were similarly stocked with "game of all kinds, venison, woodcock, pheasant, snipe, plover, etc."[13] Apparently, there was a lively game trade as people in the piney woods of Mississippi and Louisiana sent both meat and skins to market in Mobile and New Orleans.[14] As late as the 1840s, thirty-five bales of deerskins were shipped out of Mobile.[15] The *Southern Cabinet,* after describing the Charleston market as being "abundantly supplied with game . . . as in former years," went on to discuss deer:

> This fine animal, which, in all newly settled countries, is food for thousands . . . appears in some parts of our lower country to be on the increase, although it is fast diminishing in the more thickly settled districts of the upper country. Our large tracts of pine barren, and our interminable swamps . . . and our island along our coast will, for many years, serve as a harbor for deer. Thousands are annually slaughtered, but still they are so prolific; that the race has been preserved. In our markets, we one morning counted twelve exposed for sale, and frequently five or six.[16]

Olmsted found deer plentiful in South Carolina. While in the up-country he referred to a farmer who had "lately shot three deer," and near Charleston the sons of his host returned from a night hunt "with a boatload of venison, wild fowl, and fish"; he added that "the woods and waters around us abound . . . with game."[17]

After midcentury the scarcity of venison showed up only in some areas. Charles Lanman reported in the 1850s that Mississippi was still a haven for wildlife. Night hunting was a favorite means of taking deer and thus great numbers were slaughtered. He reported as many as one hundred being killed by one hunting party.[18] In Alabama the situation was similar in that "deer, wild hogs [feral swine], and turkeys, with smaller game were bountiful . . . the deer were so close that [one] . . . would have time for a drive [hunt] before or after school."[19]

As stated in the preceding chapter some planters relied upon venison for meat. Often the planters themselves provided the game but, on occasion, slaves were allowed to hunt. Usually permission was given to hunt smaller animals which could be taken without firearms, but there is evidence that slaves did obtain and use guns.[20] Joe Taylor, in his study of slavery in Louisiana, concluded that many Negroes obtained guns and, despite the strict laws against such a practice, hunted large animals such as bear and deer.[21] A number of planters allowed or even encouraged the older and more trusted slaves to hunt deer, providing meat for both master and slave.[22]

Apparently, hunting with a gun was the most common means of taking deer, though the method of getting close enough for a shot varied somewhat. Where cover permitted, hunters stalked the animals. It required great skill and, since stealth was the key to success, was most successful after a rain or in areas devoid of dry leaves. Some hunters learned deer habits quite well and knew the game trails used most frequently. Stationing themselves in "stands" nearby, they remained motionless until the deer came close enough for a shot. Stand hunting is still the preferred means of hunting deer in much of the area, though it is (and was) aided frequently by trained deer hounds who flushed the quarry out of the thickets and swamps.

Perhaps the most successful means of hunting was "fire hunting" involving the use of fire to reflect the animals' eyes at night. Hunters used a pan filled with burning coals which, if kept in the proper position reflected the deer's eyes giving the hunter a chance for a still shot. Since most animals are usually transfixed by the appearance of a light at night, they were easy targets. (Night hunting with lights is banned in virtually all states today, an indication of its effectiveness.) A hunter in Liberty County, Georgia described in his journal the use of coals in hunting both deer and wolves. "Booth and I go fire hunting tonight . . . I have [sic] 3 shots in the course of a few minutes." Later, after hearing wolves howl, he "seized my gun and firepan and went alone in pursuit of them."[23] Probably the most rewarding of all the various methods, fire hunting was a means whereby large numbers of animals were taken.[24]

There seems little doubt about deer being widespread in the area before 1830 or 1840. Moreover, it is likely that they were well utilized by the entire population, Indian, Negro, and white. The question that arises is whether good habitat conditions and large numbers of animals remained in existence during the last two decades of the antebellum period. There is no doubt about the ultimate decline of deer in the area; the question is whether it occurred before 1860 or in the post-1860 period.

With the expansion of agricultural land and population after the Civil War came a decrease in proper habitat and an increase in the number of people preying on the herds. Moreover, the improvement in firearm accuracy and firepower increased hunting effectiveness. All these factors worked to reduce deer numbers over the entire nation. Cut up into small herds and surrounded by encroaching agricultural land, deer dwindled in numbers until they reached a low point of less than a million animals around 1900 or 1910. The most important fact is that the nadir in deer numbers was reached at about the same time the nation's agriculture approached its greatest areal extent. Moreover, it is almost certain that most of this decline occurred after the Civil War.

Though accurate estimates of populations, carrying capacities, and numbers harvested annually cannot be made, it is interesting to speculate on the probable numbers and production of deer in the area. The large reservoir of unimproved land usually was good deer habitat. Moreover, where timber cutting, burning, or patch farming had been practiced, it is likely those conditions for the animals were improved somewhat over those of the pre-Columbian period.

The number of animals available during the antebellum period varied, of course, from one area to another, yet it is probable that they were not appreciably diminished from those of the presettlement period. Estimates on the number of whitetails at the end of the pre-Columbian period run as high as forty million animals.[25] The area included in this estimate comprised the eastern two-thirds of the United States and Canada. If such numbers did, in fact, exist this would have amounted to about twenty animals per square mile and, within the area included in this study, about eight million animals. Actually, such figures are not at all unreasonable and, based on present knowledge of deer habits and possible populations, may be quite conservative. Moreover, when considering the South with its Indian agriculturalists, who practiced forest burning and rudimentary agriculture, the figure could perhaps be raised or even doubled. One estimate of population densities in Wisconsin under pristine conditions placed the figures at approximately ten deer per square mile in the northern coniferous forests and twenty to fifty per square mile in the southern part of the state where deciduous forests and oak openings were common.[26]

Except where agriculture was well established, there is a good case for at least comparable forage conditions in much of the southeast. Moreover, southern deer herds suffered few winter casualties and were not hampered by lean years following severe winters. Thus, they were more sensitive to favorable changes in habitat, and if conditions were improved could "rebound" faster than herds farther north. However, by 1850 there might have been enough hunting pressure to have been felt. If allowance is made for those factors it is reasonable, then, to expect a population of from fifteen to twenty-five deer per square mile. In places where improved land made up a substantial proportion of the total area, densities were lower. But since most of the land was unimproved even in 1860, it is likely that the entire area supported a deer herd which varied from about six million to better than ten million animals. Allowing an annual kill of from 20 to 30 percent, the total annual harvest would have varied from about one and one-quarter millions to about three millions. As would be expected, the wide variation in suitable deer habitat resulted in the dependence upon venison varying considerably from one area to another. Where human population densities were low, there might have been several kills per family per year; in the older, more settled areas venison probably was tasted only infrequently.

While venison was the major large game animal, the wild rabbit was the unquestioned favorite among the small game. Though quite small in size the cottontail was virtually ubiquitous, making it especially useful in areas where deer were scarce.[27] Being smaller and more numerous than deer, it was used for food more frequently. It served both whites and Negroes, but being easily taken without guns was especially important in the slave diet. Only a person who has lived in the rural South can appreciate the usefulness of the cottontail. Being somewhat dependent upon the farmer and planter for food and protection, the cottontail is most numerous on agricultural land. The careless cultivating practices of southern agriculturists with their semiabandoned fields and noncontiguous patches created ideal rabbit habitat. Moreover, rabbits were harvested easily with a number of trapping devices. When available, both dogs and guns were employed, but for those who preferred not to waste powder and shot, the trap or "box" was the most common method of taking them.[28] Five or six "boxes" set in good locations could keep a family in rabbit meat all winter. Many hunters sharpened their hunting prowess to the point where they could spot cottontails in their "beds" (forms) and club them with a heavy stick before they flushed. Phillip Gosse, a schoolmaster employed in Alabama, complained about his students who "handle the long rifle with more ease and dexterity than the goose quill, and who are incomparably more at home in 'twisting a rabbit,' or 'treeing' a possum, than in conjugating a verb." [29]

Like venison, rabbit was an item of trade and entered local trade channels. The game and fish market at Charleston, praised by travelers as being well supplied, had rabbits along with a variety of other game, and Olmsted found barbecued rabbit on the menu of the Commercial Hotel in Memphis.[30]

Because of disease, rabbit populations can fluctuate widely from year to year, yet their biotic potential is high and they "rebound" quickly from such disasters. During good years, rabbit population densities reached astounding levels; on a small farm of 100 to 150 acres, literally hundreds may have existed. Undoubtedly, rabbit appeared on the tables of both blacks and whites frequently; most families probably consumed dozens each year, while others may have consumed hundreds.[31]

Like rabbit, squirrel was a common food animal, and it was tenacious enough to survive in large numbers in most of the area throughout the antebellum period. Squirrels were common wherever adequate food could be found, and the woodlot or forested stream course that was a part of every southern landholding provided as many animals as one might wish. Gray squirrels abounded throughout the area and were especially numerous in the deciduous forests. In the Coastal Plain and Mississippi Valley the much larger fox squirrel also was found. Both were relished by whites and slaves though squirrel may have been less common in the slave menu than rabbit since it usually was obtained with firearms. But it is certain that many white farmers, particularly the smaller ones located in the oak-pine, oak-hickory, and chestnut forest areas, had as much squirrel as they desired.

While rabbits and squirrels dominated the daytime hunting activities, the nocturnal opossum and raccoon were the prey of the night hunter. Of the two, the opossum was easier to obtain, more numerous, and more easily taken without guns. Moreover, it was considered by most to be more palatable than the tough and stringy "coon." Both usually required dogs to hunt them, though such hounds needed little training to teach them to "tree" properly. Both Negroes and whites relished the animals, and it was not uncommon to bring home a "sackfull of possums" to be slaughtered or fattened. Since it is a scavenging omnivore, often eating dead flesh, most southerners preferred to fatten or "clean out" the animals by penning and feeding them for several days on milk and bread or roasted sweet potatoes. Such animals were considered delicacies (even today they are prized) and were hunted eagerly. One can imagine the satisfaction of the southern hunter who proudly entered in his diary the results of a night's hunt: "Caught three fine possums last night." [32] Such unlikely animals were even seen in the markets; William Russell noted them on the menu in a Montgomery restaurant, and Charles Lyell remarked:

> In the course of all my travels, I had never seen one opossum in the woods, not a single raccoon, their habits being nocturnal, yet we saw an abundant supply of both of them for sale in the market here [probably Savannah]. The Negroes relish them much.[33]

In addition to mammals used for food, many southerners turned to a host of birds to add culinary variety. The one most widely and avidly sought was the wild turkey, which was second only to deer and rabbit in popularity. The birds' desirability is understandable since it yields meat enough to justify the time needed for the hunt and has very delicious meat. It may well have been as important as deer and rabbit in some areas, and was certainly celebrated by travelers as being quite palatable.[34]

Turkeys were taken in several ways. Perhaps the most successful was trapping. A trap could be erected quite easily. It consisted simply of a pen built out of rails with an opening in one side in the form of a small trench dug so as to allow a bird to enter underneath the rails. It was baited with a "trail" of corn from the outside through the trench and into the trap. The birds, while eating the corn, entered the trap with their heads down and once inside, tried to escape through the top which was made of slats or rails laid a few inches apart. Somehow they never quite got the idea to go back through the trench opening, and many birds could be caught at one time.[35] The gun was indispensable if the trap was not used, and many hunters became adept at "calling" a flock by means of a turkey-bone caller. Night hunters located their roosts and shot them out of the trees; others used dogs to flush them so the hunter could get a shot.[36]

Since the turkey was prized by both whites and slaves, it was hunted avidly and taken in large numbers. Charles Lanman thought turkey plentiful enough to be considered "an important item in provisioning a family." He added that venison and turkey generally took the place of beef.[37] Fanny Kemble describes the Butler plantation as being very dependent upon game, turkey included.[38] This strong dependence on turkey is indicated by the daily entries of a South Carolina diarist who waited for the birds with eager anticipation.

March 21, 1857:   I have heard of no turkey gobling [sic] yet but I think I shall soon.

March 28, 1857:   This morning I went to the woods to listen for a gobler [sic] but did not hear one.

April 6, 1857:   Heard the first wild turkey goble [sic].

Apparently, he was an avid turkey hunter as the following year saw him still enthusiastic over the thoughts of a turkey feast: "Today I saw a lot of wild turkeys . . . among the others was one fine old glober [sic]; I have marked him as mine—and if he does not leave the neighborhood I will be sure to eat him." [39] One observer in the late 1850's felt that South Carolina turkeys had survived rather well and were "not very sensibly diminished in numbers." [40] It seems probable, then, that turkeys remained fairly important as game through the 1850s. Just how important they were in each family's food supply is another question. A Coosa County, Alabama man recorded catching nine birds during 1867, but whether this was representative of many families is another question.[41] Apparently, turkeys were common even in the post-bellum period as the birds were extremely wary, surviving in many areas throughout the nineteenth century.

Parts of the South were in an excellent position to take advantage of the wintering habits of American waterfowl. Millions of ducks, geese, snipes, plovers, and a host of other shore and water birds served hunters from Canada to the Gulf. They were slaughtered for food by the thousands to be consumed by rural inhabitants and sold in the urban markets. Where waterfowl occurred, they were abundant and were slaughtered in numbers for food. Unfortunately for many people in the South, however, waterfowl occurred primarily in certain areas which lay, for the most part, outside the major populated areas. The two major flyways skirted the core of the cotton belt, but the birds passed over much of the Carolinas and the Georgia coast in the East as well as the Mississippi Valley area in the West. During migration, waterfowl were seen outside these areas. In fact, small flocks were common throughout the South, but their numbers were small and without sizable concentrations large-scale hunting was impractical. Near the coast and along the rivers, however, waterfowl abounded and were taken in large numbers. The Charleston market was abundantly supplied with snipes and ducks, and in Louisiana ducks were common market items.[42] Timothy Flint enjoyed "duck-pies" in Louisiana at both supper and breakfast after which he washed them down with the common southern wine, claret.[43] When properly prepared, waterfowl made an excellent meat dish. Mrs. Francis Trollope, one of the more critical of the British travelers through America, spoke highly of waterfowl and regarded the canvasback duck as superior to "the black cock" which to her was the last word in culinary excellence.[44]

It is not clear whether large-scale methods of taking waterfowl were ever devised, such as the punt gun of England (a large-bore shotgun fixed on a swivel in a punt) or the nets used in parts of the Middle East and Asia, but it is likely that most waterfowl were taken by firearms. The simple, terse diary entry by a Mississippi hunter seems to bear this out: "went duking [sic] killed ½ dozen." [45] Even so, large numbers fell prey to the numerous market hunters, and near the coast were as important food item.[46] Unfortunately for the majority of southerners, the birds' limited range kept them from being utilized more fully throughout the area.

Quail and pigeons were perhaps the most important small birds in the South. Usually associated with the Deep South, the quail has become its traditional game bird. Quail are gallinaceous and have habits similar to grouse and turkey. Small even when mature (less than one pound), they must be taken in large numbers in order to be a significant supply of meat. Some hunters were able to locate the coveys (a family of eight to fifteen) on the ground and kill several with a single shot. Another method of obtaining large numbers was to use the trap—a scaled down version of the turkey trap—in which many could be taken at one time.

During the first few decades of the nineteenth century, wild pigeons abounded in most of the eastern United States. They occurred in the South and were noted by travelers and others who commented about game. At one time, large flocks were common in the mountains as well as in parts of the cotton belt. Pigeon roosts were frequented by Indians during the very early years, and some flocks must have survived until the antebellum period.[47] Although pigeons were sighted frequently throughout most of the area, they probably were not as numerous in the Deep South as in the mast-producing deciduous forests of the Appalachians and Lake Plains. Accounts of the settlement period in the Old Northwest are embellished with stories of the millions of pigeons "darkening the skies" and how they were hunted and killed, yet one finds relatively few such accounts concerning the Deep South. William Elliot, in his *Carolina Sports*, gives the pigeon a scant four lines. He said, "[*it*] makes us but occasional visits, only I suppose when it has devoured the mast and other food, which in ordinary seasons it finds in more northerly latitudes." [48] Undoubtedly, the pigeon was found in the South, but it did not occur in such numbers as were reported in other areas.

Fish and other marine products

Though the South had no commercial fishing industry comparable to that of New England, southerners developed a liking for both fresh and saltwater products. The long and deeply indented coastline with extensive tidal flats created huge areas hospitable to shellfish as well as a number of fish. Moreover, the inland South contained a dense network of streams and rivers capable of supplying substantial quantities of freshwater fish, though the variety was less than that of the coastal waters. From Chesapeake Bay to Texas, a variety of fish and shellfish awaited the person diligent and skillful enough to take them, and, judging from the documentary evidence, their use was common.

The easiest of the seafoods to harvest was the oyster. Found

on almost all the tidal flats of the area, it offered an abundant
source of food for the taking. Along the estuaries oysters are
found all the way from the high-tide mark out into water several
feet deep at low tide, and during a single low tide one could easily
fill a small boat with several bushels. Taken ashore they could be
"shucked" for table use or simply boiled or roasted in the shell.
In many cases, they were simply eaten raw.

Oyster beds covered fairly large expanses and, where the
shoreline consisted of islands, estuaries, inland channels, and
extensive mud flats, the area supporting oysters was very large.
The Chesapeake Bay area, of course is the famous oyster producer, but much of the coast from Virginia to Texas offered comparable conditions. For example, the sea island area of Georgia
covered hundreds of square miles and provided excellent oyster
habitat. Emily Burke noted that the Georgia oyster banks were
numerous, "rising out of the rivers like a ledge of rocks." and that
slaves often harvested them.[49] William Russell described the slave
cabins on coastal plantations as littered with junk and "heaps of
oyster shells." [50] Often planters designated one or two older slaves
to harvest oysters for the entire plantation, in which case they
were given a small skiff and time off from other work.

In the Chesapeake Bay area, a lively trade in oysters supplied
the nearby markets and some moved into the large eastern urban
centers. First dealing in fresh products, the industry developed
"pickling" and canning as a means of preservation, and by 1850
canned "cove" oysters had extended the trade deep into the interior.[51] Both Maryland and Virginia capitalized on the resource
and one source reported on annual harvest of twenty million
bushels in Virginia.[52] Though the Virginia trade was well known
and reported, a similar but smaller trade linked the South Atlantic and Gulf Coast cities with their hinterlands. Seafood moved
inland to Montgomery, Macon, Augusta, and other inland cities.[53]
Olmsted was amused by an inhabitant of inland Georgia who
described an oyster supper at which he found it difficult to consume the "nasty things." [54]

The oyster was the easiest of the marine foods to harvest,
but others fell prey to the hook, net, and seine. Shrimp and mullet
were taken with "cast nets" and the skillfull fisherman could land
large quantities in a few hours casting.[55] One source describes a
bachelor South Carolina planter who owned five or six slaves and

lived off fish, shrimp, potatoes, and game. Apparently, he spent "half of his time hunting and fishing and the rest in making shrimp nets and fishing tackle." [56] Though shrimp and mullet were the most common varieties netted, crabs and other fish also were taken. Crabs were especially prized for food, but also were used as bait for the spectacular drum which Emily Burke described as "large as swine, weighing four or five hundred." [57] Such fish were taken often, and planters designated fishing parties to fish for these monsters. Obviously, a single fish would supply food for an entire plantation for several meals.[58] Other fish frequently sought were grouper, whiting, catfish (both fresh and saltwater), sheepshead, flounder, bass, red snapper, weakfish, and trout.[59]

Since few records were kept, estimates of the amount of seafood consumed are difficult. Nevertheless, one suspects that it constituted a major segment of the diet, especially by those whose landholdings were near enough to a stream or channel that provided access to the sea. Moreover, the numerous references to the "well supplied" urban markets suggest that those living in cities strongly favored such foods. This dependence, however, decreased rather markedly as distance from the coast increased; seafood did enter the commercial trade and often was found in the interior but its importance was more limited.

While the coastal inhabitants availed themselves of the great quantity and variety of marine food available, inland dwellers had fewer opportunities. The interior streams offered a more restricted variety of food than the coastal waters and, in addition, were less accessible to large numbers of people. River plantations frequently utilized nearby streams that offered relatively fertile fishing grounds, but those located on the interfluves farther away from the streams were in a less advantageous position, having either to travel several miles to fish or do without. The smaller streams offered fish, to be sure, but the variety and quantity were inferior.

The most important food fish in the interior was the catfish. At least one of several species inhabited virtually every stream deep enough to wade in, and many "river cats" reached gigantic proportions. Not confined to any single area, they were found in all streams including the waters of the Tennessee, Mississippi, Alabama-Tombigee and the Atlantic flowing streams. Catfish are easy to catch with a number of devices, and many were large enough to provide food for an entire family meal. Undoubtedly, many people expresed disgust upon seeing their first slimy, be-whiskered cat, but their reservations disappeared when con-fronted with steaming platters of fillets or steaks. Both whites and Negroes came to love catfish and, indeed, it has become the fish most commonly identified with the South. Methods to take them in large quantities were devised and catches could be quite large. On the Davis plantation in Alabama, several dozen were caught daily and, on occasion, large ones were caught weighing 30 to 40 pounds.[60] In the channels and tribuatries of the Missis-sippi, they were even larger; on one plantation two were caught that weighed 104 and 108 pounds.[61] Set hooks, trot lines, nets, seines, and baskets all were used to catch catfish. The basket, or "trap," was particularly useful, since the angler wasted little time tending them, only that needed to empty them daily or semi-weekly. Trot lines and set hooks could be left untended, too, but most fishermen preferred to "work" them every few hours during the night to keep down depredations by gars and alligators. These methods were particularly suitable for slaves, since their main-tenance did not interfere materially with the slave's daily tasks.[62]

Other fish that fell prey to baskets were buffalo, sucker, perch, eel, bass, pickerel, and carp, although many of these could also be caught with hook and line. J. S. Buckingham reported a great number of fish taken at Wetumpka (upriver from Mont-gomery) in traps and seines. Reportedly, up to five hundred buffa-loes could be caught at one time.[63] Herbert Weaver cites examples of planters who regularly seined nearby streams, and one Louisi-ana planter fed catfish to his slaves twice a day.[64]

In season, shad were taken from the Atlantic-flowing streams of the South. From the James to the Altamaha these fish moved upstream and during their annual migration accumulated in dense schools where, given a constriction in the stream chan-nel, a dip net could conceivably yield dozens (or even hundreds) of fish in a night.[65] Shad fishing was common in Georgia rivers during season, especially below the fall zone. A coastal planter carefully recorded his slaves' fishing activities in the plantation journal.

> *January 12, 1847:* At C [herry] Hill Peter and Shadrach fish-
>   ing caught 25 shad.
> *January 16*   Peter caught 11 fish last night.

January 18   At C Hill caught 15 shad.
January 19   At C Hill caught only 6 shad.

The journal entries continue with the catch varying from six to thirty-five fish; later they were sold. Such entries were especially common during January and February.[66] In coastal North Carolina shad fishing was quite well developed with many planters gaining considerable income from fishing; some even issued regular fish rations to their slaves.[67]

In his work on southern fisheries, Charles Stevenson states that the shad moved as far as 400 miles upstream and were taken in large quantities to be consumed fresh and salted for later use.[68] This estimate on distance would have placed shad above the fall zone cities and well within the reach of many inland inhabitants, and there is evidence that they were caught far inland.[69] Their absence from streams flowing into the Gulf was notable, and apparently the fish were important enough to stimulate proposals for transplanting Ocmulgee shad into the Tallapoosa River.[70]

Some southerners built ponds and tried to raise fish. An ambitious South Carolinian recorded his efforts at fish-raising in his diary.

February 5, 1857.   Built a dam for my fish. I have about 60 suckers that I caught with the hook. I want to see if I can raise them.
February 17, 1857.   This week I have caught 32 suckers and put them in the bath.
May 27, 1857.   Yesterday I put 44 fish in my fishpond. I have seen no young fish yet.[71]

Though most fishing was undertaken as a means of supplying food, game fish also abounded. While ill one summer, Timothy Flint lived in a cabin near a stream in the Piney Woods where he "took more than two thousand trout myself, besides pickerel and other fish." His angling successes so moved him that, upon leaving, his feelings were set to verse.

> *From thy pellucid wave I've drawn the trout,*
> *In all his pride of mottled white and gold,*
> *And borne the cumbrous prize, triumphant home.*
> *And still, with each returning summer morn,*
> *Thou didst supply the inexhausted feast.*[72]

Not all anglers were so skilled; a disgruntled Alabaman complained about going to the river perchance to fish a little ourselves. . . . My luck was one eel—one small cat—one ditto perch—and a moderate sized turtle. If I keep my sense, I think this will close my fishing exploits for this season. —It doesn't pay.[73]

A widespread use of fish by both whites and slaves is not difficult to imagine. The frequent references to planters actually encouraging their slaves to fish or designating certain elder slaves as permanent fishermen, as well as the constant travelers' references to slaves fishing on their off time, point to the importance of fish as Negro food.[74] Furthermore, whites commonly fished for their own supplies, although it is not clear whether they had as much fish as they would have wished. Saltwater fish, as well as shellfish, moved into the inland South, but this may have been a means of supplying the commercial interior market with some preferred kinds of seafoods. There is some evidence that freshwater fish were commercially marketed, but probably not on a scale comparable to that encompassed by the saltwater varieties. Even when large quantities could be caught in the interior, it is probable that they were not fully utilized due to lack of marketing channels or means of preservation.[75]

The quantities of fresh fish consumed in the interior South cannot be determined with any precision. The areas well endowed with good streams could have depended to a great extent upon fish. However, this writer feels the dependence was probably less than was the case among coastal plantations and farms. While fish could be had daily on some landholdings, others were situated so far from large streams that frequent fishing was out of the question. The commercial market usually was dominated by the port cities and little fresh fish was marketed. However, the fondness for fish exhibited by today's southern Negroes and whites suggests that there must have been enough fish available to whet southern appetites, and that the liking for fried catfish and catfish stew is not a recently acquired habit, but one which dated from the antebellum period.

The use of marine food other than fish and shellfish was not impressive, yet mention should be made of some of the more commonly utilized animals. Occasionally snakes, alligators, frogs, turtles, and terrapins furnished meals for southerners. But, on the whole, southern people of both races have never been too fond of such foods, generally regarding them more as curiosities than anything else. There might have been some exceptions, for example, turtle and frog legs often found their way into the urban markets. Travelers noted that slaves often caught the diamond-backed terrapin to sell, and from some accounts, it appears the box terrapin and "cooter" were also eaten.[76] Turtle soup, fins, and steaks were common on hotel menus and, according to John Mackie, no Louisiana "plantation yard was perfect without a terrapin pen in it." [77] Charles Lyell noted turtle soup being served on a Mississippi steamer, and a Carolina planter listed "turtle soup" and "turtle steaks" as a part of a sumptuous meal served in Charleston.[78] However, these instances were exceptional and their importance to the regional food economy quite negligible. Negroes not only lacked a taste for such foods, they had as aversion to them that has become proverbial.

Gathered food

Southern settlers learned the wild food-producing plants rather early and established a dependence upon them that was something more than casual gathering. Several species of grape, the persimmon, the pecan, hickory nut, chestnut, and blackberry all came to be protected and nurtured to the point where they could be regarded as semidomesticates. Soon after settling a land-holding, most farmers and planters located such plants quickly and looked to them for at least a partial supply of fruits and nuts. Obviously, these plants seldom were intended to supply a large portion of the needed food; they were sought as a means of varying an otherwise monotonous diet and providing preserved sweets as well as nuts for the winter season when fresh food variety was unavailable. During the early years of settlement, they took the place of orchard products and, after the orchard was well under way, served to supplement the domestic produce and add variety. Occasionally, they were planted in orchards to become a part of the domestic plant life.

A substantial proportion of the nondomestic food was consumed raw. Forays to the muscadine or fox grape vines were made by youngsters and the major part of the yield was so consumed. However, prudent housewives usually were able to procure enough for the jams, jellies, and preserves needed for the next year. In good locations, such vines yielded quite well; according to Anne Royall they "grow in profusion on all the rivers. . . . Ten bushels at the least might be gathered from one tree [vine]." [79]

Blackberries might well have been the favorite for preserving, since they occurred throughout the area and yielded abundantly. A number of varieties were found, and since berry bushes actively colonize burned-over areas, old fields, and forest margins where they do not have to compete with trees, they probably increased in abundance as settlement progressed.

Persimmon trees were common throughout the area and the fruit was used frequently for food. Persimmons were eaten raw, made into puddings, and occasionally used for persimmon wine, locally called "beer." Those who made use of persimmons often did so on a large scale, but the fruit was not universally liked. J. S. Buckingham found it used to some extent in Georgia, but it most often was used as animal feed.[80] An interesting and important contribution may have been its attraction for opossums. The animals flock to the trees in fall and are easily caught, sometimes several at a single tree.

A number of other fruits and nuts could be considered part of the natural production which served as a base for gathering. Plums, a number of berries, nuts, and, of course, honey were gathered from time to time. When found in abundance, these items must have been fairly important as food. Even if they did not provide large quantities of food, as supplements to a drab diet and as sources for badly needed nutrients, gathered foods may have been more important than the possibly small volume might suggest.

In addition to fruits and nuts, a number of other plants were gathered to provide herbs, tea, and vegetables. Yellowroot, ginseng, and sassafras served as healing herbs as well as "tonics" to build up or clean out "the system." One plant, whose omission in any discussion of southern foods could be considered criminal, is the pokeweed (*Phytolacca americana*).[81] Common to most of eastern North America, this plant has served as a source of greens in the South for generations. Poke thrives in a variety of habitats, but it appears to be an active colonizer of burned-over woods similar to the blackberry. It commonly occurs around farm outbuildings, along fencerows, and in the forest margins. Its quantitative importance was somewhat limited, since it was edible only during spring when the young shoots were tender, but during this period it was avidly sought by Negroes and whites. Poke often was mixed with turnip greens, since many believed combining the two enhanced the flavor of each.

On the whole, one must conclude that nature was rather generous to the southerner. A host of wild foods were available to him in the form of game, fish, and gathered food. That he availed himself of such food there is no doubt; the extent to which he did so is less sure. One strongly suspects that the use of such foods has been underestimated in the past, but, at the same time, the potential food available was probably never fully utilized. The restrictive effects of slavery upon Negro movement and the prohibition of slaves owning guns (though some did obtain and use guns) surely resulted in less game being taken than was possible. Moreover, the lack of well-developed market channels for distributing seafood and fish probably resulted in fewer fish being consumed but, on the other hand, both these factors may have postponed the ultimate exhaustion of fish and game for a decade or two with the result that both game and fish were available for a longer period of time.

5 Pork
The South's first choice

The use of swine for food in the South is proverbial. Seldom is
food mentioned by travelers through the antebellum South, by
historians of the area, or by twentieth-century chroniclers of current events without some reference to pork. Its place in the nation's economy during the early nineteenth century certainly was
notable, but its importance in the domestic economy of the South
was overwhelming. Swine were an integral part of southern agriculture during the colonial period; they were indispensable to
the frontiersman; and in the antebellum subsistence economy the
pig became the supreme food animal. Cotton often paid for the
land, and corn provided the bulk of the food, but the southern
agriculturist looked upon the hog as one symbol of his success,
and pork was the food item he sought with more vigor than any
other. Game he often depended upon, beef he liked, and dairy
products were welcome. Yet when he "ran out," hog meat was the
item considered so important the he went into debt to buy it.

In fact, as one examines the writings of southern agriculturists, it is tempting to conclude that the hog was second only to
cash crops in the attention it received. If the "king" of the ante-
bellum southern economy was cotton, then the title of "queen"
must go to the pig. So highly was the animal esteemed that many
producers constantly wrote about hog raising and kept detailed

records of hog numbers and weights. One southern diarist, apparently ecstatic over the prospects of a good pork year made the following diary entry:

Pigs! Pigs! Pork! Pork! Pork!
The first litter of pigs came to light . . . about 14 days
ago . . . being born [in] the woods—of the Pig [Big] Sow—
She only brought 4 up. —the Lawson Sow gave birth last
Sunday night to ten (10) fine healthy pigs.[1]

Much of this feeling found its way into agricultural periodicals of the day and almost every issue contained advice, admonitions, and testimonials concerning hog raising and pork curing.[2]

The production of swine in the South was astounding. In total numbers, most southern states ranked among the highest in the nation throughout the antebellum period and were matched only by New York, Pennsylvania, and the corn belt states of the Old Northwest (table 3).

Tennessee and Kentucky were the most outstanding producers among the southern states, but North Carolina, Georgia, Alabama, and Mississippi all ranked quite high. Both Louisiana and South Carolina had fewer total numbers. Being settled somewhat more slowly than the other states, Arkansas showed only about four hundred thousand animals in 1840 but the number steadily increased through the following decades to over one million in 1860. Arkansas was an exception, too, in that it showed a substantial increase during the 1850–60 decade while most states were either static or showed decreases.

The area also compared quite well with other parts of the country in per capita numbers. For the entire nation, the number of swine per capita was 1.54 in 1840 and 1.23 in 1860. In 1840, only two states of the South, South Carolina and Louisiana, showed less than 1.54 hogs per capita in 1840, and in 1860 only Louisiana was below the figure for the entire nation. In per capita figures, the southern states also compared quite favorably with the corn-pork producing states of the Old Northwest (table 3). In 1840, both areas were roughly the same and, though ratios were lower for both regions in 1860, the southern states began to show significantly higher ratios than most states of the West. Both Kentucky and Tennessee ranked very high in all three census years. Of the western states only Indiana had a ratio higher than two hogs per capita in 1860.

3. Number of swine by states.

	1840		1850		1860	
	NUM-BER	PER CAPITA	NUM-BER	PER CAPITA	NUM-BER	PER CAPITA
The East						
Maine	117	0.23	55	0.09	55	0.09
New Hampshire	122	0.43	63	0.20	52	0.16
Vermont	204	0.70	66	0.21	53	0.17
Massachusetts	143	0.19	81	0.08	74	0.06
Rhode Island	31	0.28	20	0.05	17	0.10
Connecticut	132	0.43	76	0.21	75	0.16
New York	1,900	0.78	1,018	0.33	910	0.23
New Jersey	261	0.70	250	0.51	236	0.35
Pennsylvania	1,504	0.87	1,040	0.45	1,031	0.35
Delaware	74	0.95	56	0.61	48	0.43
Maryland	417	0.89	353	0.61	388	0.56
The South						
Virginia	1,992	1.61	1,830	1.29	1,600	1.00
North Carolina	1,650	2.19	1,813	2.09	1,883	1.90
South Carolina	879	1.48	1,066	1.59	966	1.37
Georgia	1,458	2.11	2,169	2.39	2,036	1.93
Florida	93	1.70	209	2.40	272	1.94
Alabama	1,424	2.41	1,905	2.47	1,748	1.81
Mississippi	1,001	2.67	1,583	2.61	1,533	1.94
Louisiana	323	0.92	597	1.15	635	0.90
Arkansas	393	4.03	837	3.99	1,172	2.69
Tennessee	2,927	3.53	3,105	3.10	2,347	2.12
Kentucky	2,311	2.96	2,891	2.94	2,331	2.02
Texas	. . .	. . .	692	3.26	1,372	2.27
The West						
Ohio	2,100	1.38	1,965	0.99	2,252	0.96
Indiana	1,624	2.37	2,264	2.29	3,099	2.29
Illinois	1,495	3.14	1,916	2.25	2,502	1.46
Michigan	296	1.39	206	0.52	372	0.50
Wisconsin	51	1.66	159	0.52	334	0.43
Iowa	105	2.43	323	1.68	935	1.39
Missouri	1,271	3.31	1,703	2.50	2,354	1.99
The U.S.	26,301	1.54	30,354	1.30	33,513	1.07

Source: *U.S. Censuses of 1840, 1850, and 1860*

This importance of swine in the South becomes even more impressive when one considers that, in contrast to the Old Northwest where there was a substantial export of swine products, almost the entire southern crop was consumed within the area. Nowhere in the nation at any time have swine ever reached the importance in regional dietary resources they did in the South during the three or four decades prior to the Civil War.

Data on swine numbers by county are available since 1840 and figures *10* and *11* indicate their distribution for the years 1840 and 1860. Both the cotton belt and the Hill South had the highest densities, but swine were by no means confined to these areas. No matter how remote the location, both planters and farmers depended heavily upon hogs. In general, the high number in the cotton belt reflected higher densities of human population but among hill farmers the per capita numbers were extremely high since they also produced swine for market.

Quality and treatment

While the large number of hogs can scarcely be disputed, there is some question about their quality and the treatment they received.[3] Improved swine were far from universal during the first half of the nineteenth century, and most evidence indicates that any improvements that were occurring in the East and the Old Northwest were slow in reaching the South.

The southern razorback hog certainly was not notable for his illustrious ancestry and, especially during the early period, he was almost universally maligned as being more like a greyhound than a pig. Until the late 1840s, common swine were an admixture of various strains and had degenerated to the point where the characteristics of the parent European breeds were no longer distinguishable. The practice of allowing, indeed encouraging, swine to forage for much of their food led to a "natural selection" that placed a premium on fleetness of foot, hardiness, wariness—in short—on the techniques of survival in the forest. Unfortunately, these attributes of the semiferal animals were not conducive to rapid gains in flesh.

Though some agriculturists began to evince interest in hog improvement during the forties and fifties, many carried on in the traditional neglect of pigs and, indeed, one can find these

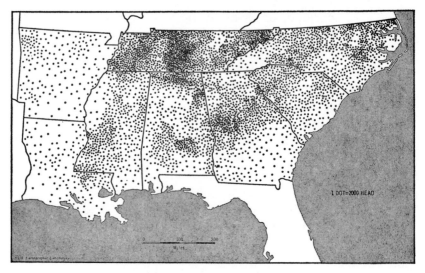

10. SWINE, 1840.

same razorbacks in parts of the piney woods even today. A visitor
to Alabama described such beasts very well when he commented:

> The southern hogs are a queer breed . . . with their sharp
> thin backs, long heads, and tall legs, looking so little like
> hogs . . . From the amount of liberty which is granted
> them, and their consequent habits of self-protection and
> self-dependence, they are very wild . . . perfectly owner-
> less, swift of foot, and strong withal.[4]

Upgrading of the quality of southern swine was encouraged
by many farmers and planters. In fact, there might have been
considerable demand for improved breeds. One writer stated that

> the demand for bacon and the high prices paid for this uni-
> versal article of slave-food, has caused almost a mania in
> hog raising throughout the South. The Berkshire [a breed of
> hogs] mania was nothing compared to the rage which now
> invests the cotton-lords, as to the introduction and posses-
> sion of the best and most profitable breeds of swine.[5]

Reflecting this trend, the agricultural journals of the day carried
many pleas for improvement, but the obstacles were severe.[6] The
very large numbers of hogs in the South would have required the
introduction of thousands of blooded animals to have achieved
upgrading comparable to that occurring in the Old Northwest at
the time. Many planters recognized the need for improved ani-

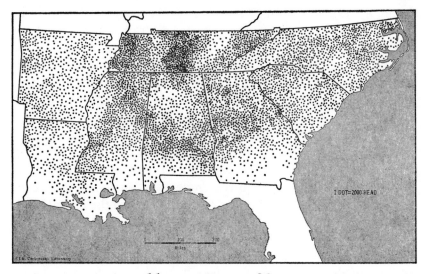

11. SWINE, 1860.

mals, but their advice to the prospective hog grower was aimed primarily at improving the system of husbandry rather than the breed itself.[7] This approach was unquestionably sound, since better husbandry would have increased the meat output of existing swine and prepared the way for more highly bred animals later.

The improvement of southern swine, while severely limited, to be sure, probably had greater effects than some critics have realized. There was a small but significant importation of improved boars during the twenty years before the war, and this slowly but steadily improved the general quality of southern hogs. Admittedly, improved animals might suffer somewhat under the poor treatment they received, but it is difficult to dismiss, as Genovese has done, the effects of the improved boar upon the quality of his progeny.[8] The importation of quality sires was a method used quite successfully in the case of both swine and cattle improvement in the Old Northwest. And, though the effects were more limited in the South, the overall quality of southern swine did improve, and it would be an oversimplification to equate the southern hog of 1860 with the typical range hog of the 1820s and 1830s (see below).

Related to the improvement of breeds and the production of meat hogs was the practice of spaying and castrating. Most growers regarded pregnant gilts (young females) as unsuitable for slaughter and spayed all female piglets not intended for breeding. Of the two sterilizing operations, castration was less dangerous since it did not require penetration of the abdominal cavity, yet the lack of fences and the practice of allowing feeder pigs to forage for mast in the forests where they mingled with the neighbor's swine or perhaps some feral stock made spaying necessary to protect one's feeder stock. John H. Moore states that Mississippi agriculturists castrated their males, but this writer feels that spaying the females was the preferred method of dealing with the feeder pigs.[9] In fact, many of the older inhabitants of southern Georgia today who remember the "no fence" days can recall such practices, and many can still perform the operation.[10] In the case of the brood sows, however, the grower faced a more difficult problem. Since he could not spay brood sows, he was forced to pen them until they were bred to his preferred boar; otherwise, they "took to the woods" to mate with some long-tusked, long-nosed paramour of the piney woods.

It has been pointed out that many agriculturists felt the answer to the South's hog problem lay not in breed improvement but in improving the system of hog raising. The abundance of nonagricultural land upon which hogs could be pastured plus the long experience of raising them under range conditions led most agriculturists to utilize the forests for hog pasture. During the early period, hogs were allowed to run loose in the woods to forage for acorns, roots, nuts, and a number of other wild foods. In fact, the value of land was affected by its ability to provide mast and woods forage. In describing an Alabama plantation to a prospective buyer one writer said, "It is all canebrake land very rich and Black there is a creek running through it, for those who wish to raise their own Pork, it is very advantageous." [11] This practice was feasible only where unimproved land was widely available, and it was altered as population densities increased and as available forage and mast declined. However, it did not disappear during the antebellum period but remained a substantial, though diminishing, part of swine raising throughout the century. The early system of almost complete dependence upon the forests for food was described by James Stuart.

> Hogs are very generally allowed to feed on the nuts in the woods . . . The climate is so mild during the winter . . . that they are allowed to roam about during the whole year,

feed on nuts, acorns, etc., which are very abundant in the woods of this country, and occasionally on fallen fruit.[12]

As a consequence of being allowed such freedom many hogs ran wild and had to be trapped or rounded up by dogs or, on occasion, became feral to be hunted like deer.[13]

Generally, though, there was some attempt to supplement range mast and forage with corn or other feed. Some farmers and planters thought it best to feed hogs small amounts at regular intervals. This served to keep them in better shape the year round and somewhat tame so that a fall "hog hunt" would be unnecessary. On one Alabama plantation "the hogs were fed at a regular hour every day: the most appropriate time was sunset. Resting at night, undisturbed, they were ready to be turned out in their range in the morning." [14] Others preferred to allow swine complete freedom during the spring and summer, but penned them in the fall for fattening. In a letter to a North Carolinian who owned a Loundes County, Mississippi plantation, the overseer described his plans for making pork.

I made a good corn crop and have a plenty of hogs to make pork for the plantation if I can get them up but they are scattered very bad at this time in consequence of the acorns which is [sic] plenty this year.[15]

The system of fall fattening often meant turning the hogs into the cornfields, where cowpeas had been planted, or into peanut fields so they could do their own harvesting. Sweet potato patches also were favorite spots, since hogs relished both the vines and small potatoes left after the tubers were harvested.[16]

As the area underwent an intensification of production and small agricultural units evolved into more complex systems, the available forage land was reduced substantially. With this intensification came a corresponding shift from woods grazing to more efficient systems of swine management. Moreover, increased population and a growing sense of "sectional patriotism" prompted planters and farmers to reevaluate their pork production systems in an attempt to achieve greater regional independence.[17] While this desire for self-sufficiency was not rewarded by complete independence from outside sources for meat, there were many farmers and planters who improved their systems of hog raising materially. In response to proddings by agricultural leaders for ideas on improved methods of swine culture, many planters and farmers voiced their feelings on the subject. Agricultural journals of the day were replete with advice, admonitions, and pleas proposing a myriad of innovations, most of which centered around producing pork as cheaply as possible. It was fairly well recognized that corn made excellent pork, yet most planters used corn for slave rations and for work animals, leaving limited quantities available for swine. Most planned to finish their hogs on corn, but preferred not to dole out corn to them all year. The result was a two or three stage operation in which corn was fed in the final stage.

On landholdings where woods forage and mast was available in sufficient quantities, swine were allowed to run loose for a part of the year where they grazed and picked up acorns, other nuts, and wild fruits such as persimmons and grapes. In late summer and fall, as fields were being harvested, the hogs were fed on sweet potato vines, allowed to run in the orchards, and turned into patches of small grain or peas. After the potato and corn harvest, these fields were open to swine. Many planters and farmers raised fields of peanuts upon which hogs grazed. In fact, there seems to have been an increasing dependence upon peas and peanuts toward the end of the antebellum period. Many established regular "routines" in order to keep hogs on good feed throughout the year. The more elaborate systems involved: 1] during winter, grazing on small grains; 2] in spring and summer, running on ranges where orchards were planted to provide fruit; 3] in June and July, turning the hogs into the oat fields; 4] in late summer, turning them into the pea, corn, and potato fields and 5] then into the fattening pens.[18] There was a variety of feed from which the hog grower could choose, and many took advantage of such a profusion.

The fattening process commonly was a matter of penning the feeder hogs and providing them with either ear or ground corn. Some growers insisted on cooking the feed and mixing other edibles with the corn; in other cases hogs were not fattened on corn but were left in the peanut or pea fields to gather the crop themselves.[19] Apparently, a coastal North Carolina planter used both systems as he recorded: "*Nov. 27, 1856* The Fattening Hogs, 70 in number in the Housefield—They seem to be improving—eating Peanuts chiefly—" Later: "*Jan. 3, 1857* The Fattening Hogs are eating about 9 bbls. corn per day." [20] As would be expected, this marked variation in the fattening process from one grower to another resulted in a corresponding variation in the size and quality of the "finished" hog.

The amount of such foods needed to fatten feeder hogs is not easy to determine, since the usual practice was to "hog off" many crops with no account taken of the quantity eaten. However, where corn was fed to penned hogs the amount could be measured and recorded and, though the practice was not universal, corn fattening probably was widely practiced. The hog-fattening system that evolved was similar to, but much less well developed than, that operating in the Ohio Valley. The amount of corn used by the western producers depended of course, on the size of the hog, his ability to put on weight when fed corn, and the time allowed for fattening. Most Ohio Valley growers used substantial amounts of corn, probably up to about ten or fifteen bushels per animal. According to Charles Cist, the Cincinnati system "packs fifteen bushels of corn into a pig and packs that pig into a barrel, and sends him over the mountains and over the ocean to feed mankind." [21] Southerners were hardly so lavish and were more apt to spend ten bushels or less per pig with perhaps three to five being the average.[22]

With somewhat less corn used in the fattening process and a poorer quality hog with which to work, it was inevitable that the typical southern hog would be substantially lighter than the commercial hog grown in the West. In the Cincinnati market commercial hogs were averaging close to two hundred pounds by 1840 and this figure may have increased a few pounds by 1860. This weight is cited frequently for hogs in the Ohio Valley, yet there is little evidence that such a figure would be representative throughout either the Old Northwest or the East. Presumably, hogs sold to abattoirs were well-fed specimens specifically destined for slaughter and were not necessarily representative of the entire swine population. Farm-slaughtered animals almost surely weighed less, though northern hogs certainly were not as light as those of the South.

Due to the widely different conditions under which they were produced, southern hogs' weights varied widely. Some growers reported killing huge hogs weighing 500 pounds or more, but usually these were animals that received special care. The typical southern hog was considerably smaller. Records of individual hog weights from a number of plantation and farm journals examined by this writer indicate an average of less than 150 pounds. Such records show extreme variation with carcass weights from 50 to 500 pounds being reported, the average for 11,212 animals being 146 pounds.[23] It seems reasonable, then to assume that most hogs of the South yielded somewhere between 100 and 180 pounds of meat with the average being somewhere around 130 to 150.

Annual pork production

As was the case with all livestock, the census reported only animal numbers, leaving us the problem of estimating the annual crop of animals and its meat yield. Such estimates must be made from what is known about animal numbers, litter sizes, and survival rates.

The possible annual increase of hogs is quite high. Considering that one boar could serve a number of sows and that each sow could have eight to twelve pigs perhaps twice each year, then the advantage of swine over other animals such as cattle is appealing. This high reproductive rate made them superior to cattle or sheep as meat producers, and extremely sensitive to changes in demand. In practice, though, potential increases never were matched by actual performance, and the swine grower had to accept a somewhat lower annual production figure.

Several factors tended to reduce the reproduction rate of southern sows, and most were related to the treatment they received. First, mast-fed hogs (those allowed to forage in the woods) were poorly nourished during a part of the year which increased the number of abortions, decreased the number of litters, cut down on litter size, and reduced the survival rate.[24] Second, pig mortality was fairly high among woods-grazed hogs due to a number of factors, including theft and drowning during floods. Occasionally, sows turned cannibal and ate their own young, but since a sow's worth was judged by the number of pigs she raised successfully, such beasts usually ended up in the slaughter pen the following fall. Finally, hog diseases took their toll.

The actual reproduction rate of the semiwild "land pike" will never be known accurately, but it is possible to get some idea of litter size and survival rates by examples extracted from the periodical literature and plantation documents (table 4).

4. Sow-pig ratios.[25]

EXAMPLE	BROOD SOWS	BOARS	PIGS	SHOATS AND FEEDERS
1 [a]	40	. . .	25	100
2 [b]	8	1	37	95
3	3	1	. . .	102
4	22	2	75	54
5	1	. . .	10	. . .
6	8	. . .	40	. . .
7 [c]	1	. . .	8	. . .
8	21	1	. . .	121
9 [d]	22	. . .	15	. . .
10	6	. . .	30	. . .
11	2	. . .	8	. . .
12 [e]	1	. . .	3	. . .
13	20	1	85	89
14	4	. . .	31	. . .
15	2	. . .	14	. . .

[a] Forty sows had 98 "fine" pigs from Jan. 1 to May 14.
[b] Numbers 2, 3, and 4 represent the same landholding but different years.
[c] Sow farrowed nine but raised eight.
[d] Numbers 9, 10, 11, and 12 represent the same landholding.
[e] A wild sow.

On occasion, litters of nine or ten were raised, but such numbers were not the rule. To be sure, such litters were farrowed but seldom were they able to survive even on the better managed landholdings. Litters of four to seven at birth were more common and even then one suspects that the birth rate for range sows might have been lower. When all reasonable factors are considered, an annual production of three or four pigs per sow is perhaps a realistic figure for the area as a whole. On better plantations and on the presumably better managed farms in the hill country, the figures undoubtedly were higher, while in the piney woods they might have been even lower.[26]

If these general postulates are accepted as reasonably accurate, then one can assume each brood sow brought at least three pigs to maturity each year. However, since southern producers did not always slaughter year-old swine but let them grow two *or* three years, the pigs were held over the next year or even the third year. Therefore, two or three generations of hogs may have been present at the same time, with the "feeder generation" going to the slaughter pen while a new generation was being added.

1st year: 1 sow + 3 pigs = 4
2nd year: 1 sow + 3 pigs + 3 shoats = 7
3rd year: 1 sow + 3 pigs + 3 shoats + 3 feeders =
            10 subtract 3 for slaughter = 7

Therefore, under the system outlined above, seven swine were needed in order to produce three for slaughter. This would have produced an annual output of 43 percent. If the system is shortened to two years, the estimated output jumps to over 70 percent.[27]

Pork consumption

Though the actual amount of pork consumed in the South is not known in detail, a strong dependence upon pork by the great bulk of southern people is well established. Rations issued to slaves had become quite standardized by 1840 or so, making estimates of the slave intake relatively simple and fairly accurate. Most cotton planters issued pork to slaves, and while the ration varied among masters, an allowance of two to five pounds per hand each week was considered adequate. A few masters may have allowed more but most thought the three-and-one-half pound ration enough and this is the figure often given as the "standard." [28]

This ration, of course, was for a working adult and was reduced for children and the aged; even field hands had their ration cut during the nonwork season.[29] In some cases it could have been lower in late summer and fall since many planters "allowanced" their meat very carefully in order to avoid purchasing meat.

In addition to the variation in rations among age groups and seasons there were regional differences depending upon the type of landholding and the availability of alternative foods. The standard three-and-one-half-pound ration was much more common in the cotton belt than along the rice coast where a more vegetarian diet was the rule. Moreover, a coastal location encouraged many planters to use seafood as a replacement for both beef and pork. For example, some planters in coastal North Carolina engaged in commercial fishing and issued fish periodically as slave rations.[30] Conversely, on Louisiana sugar plantations the meat ration might have been somewhat higher.[31] Within the cotton belt, however, the average intake was not over three and one half pounds, and when one considers the number of planters who deviated from this during the nonwork season, and the number of adults who were rated as "half-hands" or were superannuated, the average may have been three pounds or less.[32] Moreover, the tendency toward lighter meat rations in the rice area may have reduced the average even further. Taking all factors into account it seems to place the average annual intake for slaves in the South at approximately one hundred and fifty pounds, or about three pounds per week.

Estimation of pork consumption by whites is more difficult than that by Negroes. There are few detailed records of white consumption and, due to the greater dependence upon beef, mutton, poultry, and game there was considerable variation among the population. The average annual consumption of meat in the nation probably was more than 150 pounds during the antebellum period. If we assume the southern white's consumption of meat to have been comparable to the national average and that whites consumed more beef, mutton, and poultry than Negroes then the white intake of pork was little, if any, more than that of the Negro. Studies of farm families in North Carolina, Georgia, and Texas during the 1920s revealed a meat consumption of 138 pounds of pork and lard and 12 pounds of beef per adult.[33] It well might have been that more beef was consumed during the Ante-Bellum period in which case the consumption of pork was less. Even so, it seems reasonable to estimate white pork consumption to have been roughly comparable to that of the Negro. The differences in quality of diet between the two groups was largely the result of higher consumption of other meats by the white population.

While the effectiveness of the southern agriculturist's attempt to provide pork sufficient for his own consumption will never be understood fully, some measure of his success can be demonstrated by comparing production with estimates of the

amount consumed. Using the data on meat production postulated
previously, ratios of pork production to pork consumption can be
calculated for each areal unit for which census data are available.[34] Presumably, where high ratios prevailed local production
was sufficient to supply the demand; conversely, counties showing low ratios were deficient in pork.

The areal distribution of these ratios provide a general picture of the effectiveness of the southern pork producing effort
and, while the absolute figures might be open to question, the
spatial distribution of low or high ratio areas probably represents
conditions as they existed in the *1840–60* period. Figures *12, 13,*
and *14* represent swine numbers per consuming unit. The counties showing less than 2.2 swine per unit presumably represent-
ing pork deficit areas, were grouped into six or seven major areas.
As would be expected, the number of counties showing such deficits varied between census years, but the overall pattern remains
essentially the same. These areas are:

1] The lowland counties along the Mississippi River in western Mississippi.
2] Southern Louisiana and the Gulf coasts of Alabama and
   Mississippi.
3] Parts of central Alabama.
4] Northern Alabama along the Tennessee River Valley.
5] The Eastern Piedmont of Georgia and upstate South
   Carolina.
6] The "rice coast" counties along the Atlantic in Georgia
   and the Carolinas.
7] Central North Carolina.

In general, the remaining counties had ratios higher than 2.2.[35]

Reasons behind the deficits outlined above appear to have
been related either to the ready availability of pork from external
sources, competition from intensive cotton production, or the
presence of a sizable urban population consuming large quantities of pork. The deficit counties in western Mississippi resulted
from their proximity to the Mississippi River which acted as a
transportation artery. Many planters operating on the Mississippi
floodplain were located on or near navigable streams in which
case pork was easily (and relatively cheaply) procured. Both
Natchez and Vicksburg acted as ports for such goods and each

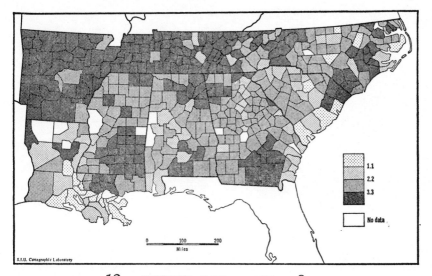

12. SWINE PER UNIT, 1840.

supplied its own hinterland, but the most important external source was the reexport trade upriver from New Orleans. Factors in New Orleans actively sought such markets and often circumvented merchants in the interior by selling directly to the planter. A third, though relatively unknown, source during the early years was the trade carried on by bargemen along the river. Rivermen and farmers commonly moved goods down the Mississippi stopping at private landings to deal in a number of items. Undoubtedly, some of this was pork.

Louisiana showed the lowest per capita numbers of hogs of any southern state and, as would be expected, was the largest market for commercial pork. Almost all southern and eastern Louisiana counties were deficient with some reporting only a few hundred hogs (figs. *10* and *11*). Moreover, these "sugar counties" had relatively high populations resulting in a heavy demand for meat. New Orleans, with a population exceeding one hundred thousand at mid-century, consumed huge quantities. Moreover, its function as a major world port and terminus for the Mississippi steamboat trade made it a large market for pork used as ships' provisions.

Farther east, along the Gulf coasts of southern Alabama and Mississippi, a few counties also showed sizable pork deficits. With a population of nearly thirty thousand in 1850 and over forty

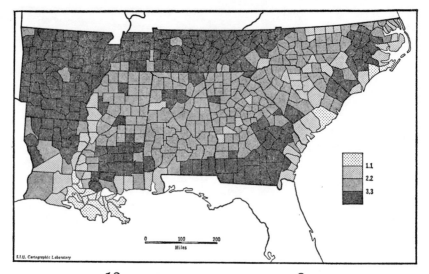

11
22
33

13. SWINE PER UNIT, 1850.

thousand in 1860 Mobile County needed more meat than the
surrounding area could supply. With coastwise transportation
facilities well developed, western provisions moved from New Orleans into Mobile relatively easily. Mobile also acted as an entrepôt for the counties in interior Alabama. The concentration upon
cotton in the Black Belt was especially intense and the consequent
lack of attention to pork production led to deficits in some counties. Landholdings located on or near streams tributary to Mobile
had easy access to pork that moved upriver while those in the
Tennessee Valley or the northern black belt relied to some extent
on supplies coming overland out of Tennessee.

The Tennessee route also supplied pork for the deficit counties in the eastern Piedmont of Georgia and upstate South and
North Carolina. It is difficult to pinpoint reasons underlying these
low ratios. One of the first areas in the Deep South to become settled, it should have been in a good position to supply its own
needs. It well may have been that Tennessee pork was cheap
enough to encourage planters and farmers to buy rather than
raise their meat. In any event, there is little doubt that the area
was somewhat deficient in pork, since the movement of animals
out of Tennessee and Kentucky is well substantiated.[36]

Counties along the coasts of Georgia and the Carolinas also
showed relatively low production ratios. Apparently, such a loca-

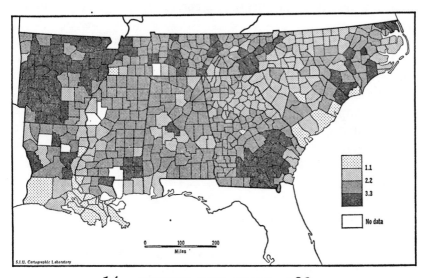

14. SWINE PER UNIT, 1860.

tion encouraged planters to depend upon purchased meat. Furthermore, the urban population of the port cities placed a strain on local supplies. On the other hand, it is possible that the total requirements of the rice area have been overestimated and that the relatively low production figures reflect a lower demand for pork due to different food preferences.

Inland North Carolina is a paradox. Some counties were quite high in pork production, yet a surprisingly large number were below the figure postulated as being minimum for self-sufficiency. Apparently, North Carolina planters were similar to those of inland Georgia and South Carolina in their dependence upon the hill states.

On the whole, the greater part of the area had production ratios higher than the 2.2 figure postulated as the number needed to produce ample pork. These data, of course, do not prove that all the high-ratio counties were self-sufficient in meat during the period nor do they prove that deficient counties imported meat, but they do indicate that pork production in relation to population was extremely variable and that in the major part of the South, hog numbers were relatively high. Even in those areas falling below the 2.2 level, the number of animals was often large and a substantial proportion of the pork was probably home-produced, yet for a variety of reasons the amount was not enough to supply local needs.

While the reasons underlying the low ratios varied from one deficit area to another, there was one recurring factor common to them—the availability of the alternative sources of meat. In every case where local pork production was inadequate there was a ready supply from outside the area. Whether this tendency to neglect hog raising reflected an inability of the plantation-slave system to compete effectively with other producers or a deliberate choice on the part of the planter to concentrate on other crops is not clear, but the relation between pork deficits and the availability of commercial meat is unmistakable.

Aside from the areal variation exhibited by the maps, comparison of the three census years reveals a striking increase in the number of deficit counties from 1840 to 1860 and a corresponding decrease in the number of counties having very high ratios (over 3.3). There are several possible explanations for this change. First, it is likely that southern pork production was not keeping pace with the expanding population. This explanation is supported by numerous comments by travelers into the area and by the pleas for more pork production by correspondents to southern agricultural journals. Admittedly, the rising tide of southern nationalism with its push for regional independence may have induced such writers to overstate the case, but one finds it difficult to ignore their comments completely. Assuming this deficit to have been on the increase, it is not clear whether the entire amount was made up by imported meat or not. Imports into New Orleans increased during the period, but it is possible that the amount of meat moving into the area did not increase as rapidly as did the pork deficit. If such was the case, then pork consumption might have declined during the period. This seems quite likely since most landholdings were in a better position to produce adequate supplies of fruits and vegetables after they had been in operation for several years. A likely possibility is that there was an upgrading in the quality and treatment of southern hogs with a consequent increase in the meat output per animal. There is no question about the decline in per capita numbers during the period, but this was not confined to the South. A similar decline occurred on a national scale as well. Presumably, it reflected better hog breeding and better care, resulting in a higher quality hog by the late antebellum period. However, a regional comparison of per capita numbers indicates that the decline was not uniform. The national figure declined at relatively similar rates in both intercensal periods but the South and West differed markedly. Ratios in the West showed a higher decline from 1840 to 1850 than from 1850 to 1860. The South, on the other hand, showed no decline during the first decade, but dropped some 22 percent from 1850 to 1860 (table 5).

5. Per capita swine numbers by regions.

| | PER CAPITA NUMBERS | | | PERCENT CHANGE | |
	1840	1850	1860	1840–50	1850–60
Old Northwest	1.90	1.44	1.24	−24.2	−13.9
South	2.35	2.35	1.82	0	−22.5
U.S.	1.54	1.31	1.07	−14.9	−18.3

Source: *U.S. Censuses of 1840, 1850, and 1860*

Undoubtedly, these figures reflect an increase in pork output per animal, but the effects occurred earlier in the West than in the South. Apparently, this process of hog improvement was well underway during the 1840s as the ratios in the West declined sharply during the 1840–50 period. A similar decline in the South during the fifties may also reflect the same process, though somewhat belated.[37]

On the whole, the South managed to provide pork for itself reasonably well. That some areas within the South did not produce enough meat for local needs is unquestioned. Yet, the extreme areal variability of the pork-producing system coupled with important dietary differences from place to place make loose generalizations about self-sufficiency quite dangerous. Moreover, the existence of sizable urban populations that had to be fed and the important markets in the ports for ships provisions suggests that western pork was not all consumed by the "overcommercialized" planter and his chattels. Finally, when we consider the huge surpluses produced in the hill states of Tennessee and Kentucky, then the traditional interpretations of southern dependence upon the Old Northwest are further undermined. Pork certainly was the primary meat for southern stomachs, yet, the source of such meat varied widely depending upon location within the area, and most of it was produced within the South.

6 Beefsteaks and buttermilk

The student of the antebellum South, whose task it is to study, interpret, and present the character of the area, faces some challenging tasks. Not the least among them is the assessment of the importance of cattle in the economy of the area. Many have wrestled with the problem, and while various answers have been suggested, the question remains essentially unanswered. Agricultural data for the three census years prior to the Civil War show that large numbers of animals existed throughout the entire South, but paradoxically, much of the nineteenth-century literature suggests a shortage of work animals and livestock products in some areas.[1] Considering this apparent contradiction between a surfeit of animals and a shortage of animal products, a number of questions present themselves. Where were the large numbers of cattle? How effective were they in supplying southern subsistence needs? What role did they play in the region's economy?

The existence of a grazing economy in the South Atlantic states during the late eighteenth century is fairly well recognized and needs little elaboration.[2] Cattle were grazed over much of the Carolinas and Georgia and were especially numerous on the wiregrass pastures of the pine forests and swamp prairies of the coasts. Moreover, this early woods-ranching had its counterparts in the Spanish lands of Florida and French Louisiana.[3]

With the opening of land in the interior South to white settlers and its accompanying expansion of settlement came an increase in cattle numbers. Spreading from the core grazing areas were numbers of cattlemen who moved onto the newly opened land with their herds. In addition, thousands of animals moved into the area as property of the farmers and planters taking up new land. Most migrating settlers took a few animals with them as they moved, and many continued to import stock from the hill states even after they were well settled.[4] This spread of cattle from the Atlantic seaboard states, the French and Spanish grazing areas, and the hill country into the remaining parts of the South continued through the eighteenth century and, indeed, well into the second quarter of the nineteenth century. Another factor in the spread of cattle, though a minor one, was the Indian. The "civilized tribes" in the South were quick to adopt white customs, and it is likely that Indian owned cattle were numerous. Many of these ran wild and became completely feral, merging into the existing forest fauna to be hunted and shot like game by the earliest white settlers.[5] Apparently, the conditions were similar to that of the Atlantic states during the eighteenth century. Stories of "wild cattle" were common in writings during the colonial period; for example, Peter Kalm was told of "wild cows which exist in Carolina, and other provinces to the south."[6]

This spread of cattle, both domestic and feral, continued during the first decades of the nineteenth century until cattle were well established in all parts of the South. So complete was the spread of cattle that they were noted by observers in all parts of the area. Travelers' accounts and other contemporary reports almost invariably comment (often with surprise) upon the large numbers of cattle encountered. Furthermore, these reports extend from the very early period up to the Civil War and include most of the Gulf South from the Carolinas to Texas including Florida.[7] Cattle were especially numerous in relation to population in the southern portions of the Gulf South and were the basis for a fairly large-scale herding economy. Huge herds were seen by travelers in Georgia, Florida, Alabama, Mississippi, and Louisiana, and there are reports of single herders owning hundreds or even thousands of cattle.[8]

The first census data on livestock numbers, though less reliable than one might wish, are available for 1840, and they tend to substantiate the nonstatistical reports of large numbers of cattle. In total numbers cattle in southern states compared quite favorably with those of other parts of the nation, and in per capita figures the area was outstanding. All southern states were among the nation's leaders in cattle per capita in 1840 and, while the per capita figures declined in the next two decades, they ranked quite high relative to the eastern states up until the Civil War (table 6). Dot maps, based on the censuses of 1840 and 1860, indicate a

6. *Number of cattle by states.*

	1840		1850		1860	
	NUM- BER	PER CAPITA	NUM- BER	PER CAPITA	NUM- BER	PER CAPITA
The East						
Maine	327	0.8	343	0.6	377	0.6
New Hampshire	276	1.2	268	0.8	264	0.8
Vermont	384	1.6	349	1.1	370	1.2
Massachusetts	283	0.5	260	0.3	280	0.2
Rhode Island	37	0.4	36	0.2	39	0.2
Connecticut	239	0.9	213	0.6	242	0.5
New York	1,911	1.0	1,878	0.6	1,973	0.5
New Jersey	220	0.7	211	0.4	239	0.4
Pennsylvania	1,173	0.9	1,154	0.5	1,419	0.5
Delaware	54	0.9	53	0.6	58	0.5
Maryland	226	0.6	220	0.4	253	0.4
The South						
Virginia	1,024	1.1	1,076	0.8	1,044	0.7
North Carolina	617	1.1	694	0.8	694	0.7
South Carolina	563	1.3	778	1.2	507	0.7
Georgia	884	1.7	1,098	1.2	1,006	1.0
Florida	118	2.7	261	3.0	388	2.8
Alabama	668	1.5	728	0.9	773	0.8
Mississippi	623	2.2	734	1.2	730	0.9
Louisiana	381	1.3	575	1.1	517	0.7
Arkansas	189	2.6	293	1.4	568	1.3
Tennessee	823	1.3	751	0.7	765	0.7
Kentucky	787	1.3	753	0.8	836	0.7
Texas	. . .	. . .	330	1.5	3,536	5.9
The West						
Ohio	1,218	1.0	1,359	0.7	1,635	0.7
Illinois	626	1.7	912	1.1	1,584	0.9
Indiana	620	1.2	715	0.7	1,069	0.8
Michigan	185	1.1	274	0.7	480	0.6
Wisconsin	30	2.2	183	0.6	522	0.7
Iowa	38	1.1	137	0.7	540	0.8
Missouri	434	1.5	792	1.2	1,169	1.0
The U.S.	14,972	1.1	17,779	0.8	25,616	0.8

Source: *U.S. Censuses of 1840, 1850, and 1860.*

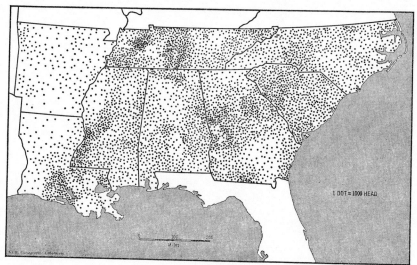

15. CATTLE, 1840.

rather wide distribution of cattle with surprisingly little variation
from one area to another within the South (figs. *15* and *16*).
Apparently, they were common in the hill country, the more
densely populated plantation and farm areas and the relatively
empty piney woods of the southern coastal plain. Moreover, they
were found on all types and sizes of landholdings within these
areas and were owned by most agriculturists.

With such a wide geographical distribution there must have
been considerable variation in the quality of the animals, the
treatment they received, and the use to which they were put.
Since most American cattle were quadruple purpose, their utilization depended upon specific local needs. In the case of the crop-
oriented planter and farmer a strong emphasis was on draft use.
Where row crops were not outstanding, draft use was minimal,
but cattle were needed also for hides, meat, milk, and butter. In
some cases there was a strong dependence upon the herd for subsistence, and where the traditional agricultural systems were absent full-time cattle herders were found.

The southern herder

As an agricultural occupant of the South, the herder is easy
to overlook since he was not especially numerous, he occupied
areas of relatively low population density, and often was an

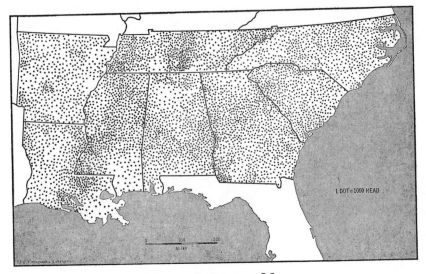

16. CATTLE, 1860.

ephemeral element in the landscape. Most important of all, he left no records from which one could glimpse the kind of life he led and the details of his profession. Despite this the herder was observed by a few travelers and, on occasion, has been the subject of writers who reminisced about the "old days." Further evidence of his existence has been presented in the detailed studies of census manuscripts by persons such as Herbert Weaver and Frank Owsley.[9] Out of these bits and pieces a picture has emerged of a group of semiagriculturists whose major efforts ostensibly were devoted to herding but whose sustenance was derived from small-scale subsistence cropping and hunting, as well as cattle raising.

Inheriting a system of woods grazing from the Carolinas, herdsmen spread their cattle across the Gulf South in the first decades of the nineteenth century. During the early period the herders were well established along the Gulf Coast. Timothy Flint found them in both Florida and Louisiana and describes them as

a peculiar race of "petits Paysans" . . . engaged in raising cattle. . . . Some have two thousand cattle; and the swamps afford ample winter range, while the pine woods furnish grass in the summer.[10]

John Claiborne described a similar group he encountered while traveling through southern Mississippi.[11] No doubt their counterparts existed wherever grazing and open land were to be found.

They occupied large portions of southern Georgia during the very early period, perhaps as much as half the state. Later their domain was reduced by the expansion of cotton production to the point where the herder essentially was confined to the pine forests of the southern third or fourth of the state.[12] Even there, herding was reduced somewhat by the encroachment of cotton into the extreme southwest. The herder either was pushed out by the farmer and the planter or, more likely, joined their ranks. In discussing former occupations of early settlers, many writers of the postwar period referred to the "old-timers" as being cattlemen. Apparently they were cattle herders during the early years and shifted to crops later.[13] George Smith describes the relation between herder and planter in southwestern Georgia.

> The larger part of its scattered inhabitants were engaged in stock raising. Their cattle ranges covered large areas of the wire-grass lands, though now and then in some fertile hammocks, there were the prosperous cotton planters.[14]

This belt of grazing lands upon which the herder was best able to resist encroachment extended west from Georgia to include substantial portions of southern Alabama, western Florida, southern Mississippi, much of Louisiana and Texas. The "petits Paysans" referred to by Flint, must have represented the French herders in Louisiana, but their American counterparts occupied a large part of Mississippi, Arkansas, and Alabama.[15] William Sparks referred to those of the Pearl River as refugees from Carolina and Georgia who sought out the sparsely populated pine woods.

> Here they reared immense herds of cattle, which subsisted exclusively upon the coarse grass and reeds which grew abundantly among the tall, long-leafed pine, and along the small creeks and branches.[16]

Numerous other observations tend to support his description.[17]

It would be a mistake to take the term "herder" too literally or precisely. Very likely most men so described were part-time croppers as well. The cattle, usually foraging freely in the open woodland, needed little attention. Periods of roundup, branding, and droving were busy ones, but they were short leaving plenty of free time for other activities. These included hunting, fishing, and raising food crops for both subsistence and occasional sale or barter.[18] For example, John Claiborne found the inhabitants of

Greene County in Mississippi enjoying a lucrative trade with Mobile in such items as butter, cheese, honey, and eggs.[19] Timothy Flint described the people near Pensacola as "devoted to raising cattle, hunting, and drinking whiskey." [20] This dependence upon game declined as settlement densities increased, but as late as mid century in many areas game, such as deer, were slaughtered in large numbers for food.[21]

The operations of these herders varied to some extent from one area to another as conditions might have demanded. Yet, most practiced an open range system allowing their cattle to run loose through the forests and clearings to pick up enough grazing to live, reproduce, and sometimes to put on enough weight to be considered "beef."

During the early years, herders utilized the public domain and had no claim to the land. After substantial portions of the area went into private hands, herders either were forced out or became squatters on land taken up but not yet settled. It is likely that many became owners of small tracts using adjacent unsettled lands to pasture stock. Such a practice is suggested by the tendency of early herders to become farmers as their range either diminished in size from encroachment by agriculturists or deteriorated from overgrazing. It is probable that those living in remote areas were seminomadic and had no title to the land, while others operating nearer the settled areas acquired small tracts, presumably to establish an operating base.[22]

Except for roundups and branding, the open range system necessitated little labor. Apparently, the "salt licks" so frequently found in the northern Appalachians were not very common in the Deep South, and "salting" was one of the operations performed periodically.[23] Some herders "minded" their herds, but it is not likely that the larger herders could possibly have given much attention to several hundred head.

The major task of the herder was the "roundup" which was similar to those that became so well known half a century later on the High Plains. Differing perhaps in scale from the later plains' roundups and made more difficult by the forests and poorly drained stream courses, the roundup came to be the usual procedure throughout the entire area for herding forest-grown cattle. Most herders used small, fast ponies for minding and rounding up cattle and often employed dogs as well.[24] Apparently there was a regular spring roundup for counting and branding the young animals and additional roundups later as the older cattle were readied for market. Both frequently were cooperative ventures involving several herders and their families.[25]

Since they moved on occasion, the headquarters of the herders were not very substantial, perhaps a log cabin or a lean-to for the more ephemeral operations. Around the hut were grouped a shed for the horses and milk cows, corrals for cutting, branding, and marking and, nearby, a clearing for cultivation. If long distances were involved in the herding operation, "line shacks" made of bark were used for overnight occupancy.[26] Since dairy products were needed, not all cattle were allowed to run loose. Usually, the herder kept a few lactating animals penned after the spring roundup for milk and butter. However, considering the quality and treatment of the woods-grown cows, it is unlikely that dairy production was more than enough to supply minimum needs. A few quarts of milk per day was a likely yield from each cow.

It is difficult to be sure of the numbers of cattle involved in these operations.[27] Travelers into the area reported many herds of "several hundred," while others reported "thousands." In southern Georgia, Emily Burke reported that "It is common for one man to own one thousand or fifteen hundred cattle." [28] In Southern Alabama and Mississippi, too, large herds must have been common.[29] Probably, the largest herds were in the prairies of Louisiana and the grassy wastes of Florida where herds of thirty to forty thousand cattle were reported. We read of single owners branding five thousand calves at a time. Such figures seem almost incredible, yet there must have been "vacheries" that were very large.[30] Surely such extremely large operations were exceptional, but herds of several hundred or even a thousand or more head must have been common. The outer Coastal Plain with its large expanses of unimproved land and the relatively sparse population was an inviting area for the large-scale herder. Moreover, the relatively low quality of the stock meant low value per head, thus encouraging the herder to concentrate on volume.[31]

The existence of the southern herder can scarcely be questioned, but it is difficult to assess his role in the economic community. The numerous contemporary accounts of cattlemen and their relative isolation lead one to question whether this relationship was one of direct subsistence upon them for food or whether it was a commercial one in which animals were marketed outside the region. There is little doubt about the herder depending to some extent on his cattle for milk, butter, and meat, but on the whole, this dependence appears to have been less than one might expect. Often there was a scarcity of milk due to the simple fact that owners did not bother penning the cows. Occasionally, cattle wore bells and were rounded up at night for milking, but most of the time the animals were too wild to be so handled. Unpenned cattle were apt to be miles away from the corrals much of the time, except for occasional trips to the "salt stands." A common traveler's complaint was that fresh milk was hard to obtain. While traveling through the South with a child, Captain Basil Hall recorded that

> for several days at a time we could not get a drop of milk, even for the child; and though we saw hundreds of cows, they were all let loose in the woods, and not tied up for domestic purposes till a later season. [Later, at another place in the forest, they were] . . . brought a glass of milk, warm from the cow, for the child.[32]

At times the cattle were so wild they became virtually feral and were hunted and shot like deer whenever beef was needed. In this respect herding was, at times, more like hunting than farming.[33]

The commercial aspect of the herders' operation, however, obviated such drastic action as shooting, since the animals had to be transported out of the area on the hoof. This necessitated a late summer or fall roundup, cutting out the most desirable animals, and droving to market. Important markets for cattle in the South were the major towns and cities, but their significance is difficult to demonstrate. Each port city probably acted as a focus for the cattle trade of its own hinterland. Cattle from Georgia and the Carolinas were driven to Charleston and Savannah, while Alabama producers depended upon Mobile. Mississippi herders could have moved cattle to either Mobile or New Orleans. Some were sold in Baton Rouge or other upriver ports ultimately to be marketed in New Orleans.[34] Towns such as Pensacola were smaller outlets for such beef, and significant numbers of cattle must have been marketed in the growing interior towns.[35]

The movement of cattle into the port cities can be documented reasonably well, yet determining the use to which these animals were put seems to be much more of a problem. During the early period, presumably, such cattle were exported to the West Indies. Almost certainly some were consumed in the urban areas themselves which, by 1850, were becoming fair-sized cities.

New Orleans, especially, was in a position to consume large quantities of such beef. A third possibility was that the cattle were slaughtered in these coastal centers and then the leather and meat shipped back into the cotton belt and sold to planters in the interior through the better-organized market channels connecting the factor and the planter. All three alternatives quite likely were applicable at one time or another, but it is difficult to document any one as being especially important as a large-scale consumer of beef.

The West Indies, an important market for foodstuffs produced in the United States, was supplied largely from ports in the United States throughout the colonial period and during the early nineteenth century. Other Latin American countries as well as Europe also were markets for American meat throughout the entire period. New Orleans undoubtedly played an important role in supplying such markets, but it is questionable whether much of the beef leaving the port of New Orleans was of southern origin. Presumably Louisiana cattle were marketed in New Orleans, but the supply was augmented by shipments from upstream, making it difficult to estimate the role of southern cattle in the export trade.

Exports from Mobile, on the other hand, represented output only from Alabama and southeastern Mississippi, but exports of animal products from Mobile were small and irregular. Existing data for Mobile and other Gulf and South Atlantic ports are not detailed as those for New Orleans, but the scanty record strongly suggests a falling off of animal-product exports after the 1850s. Moreover, even during the early period, the commodities were tallow, hides, and horns rather than beef and their total quantity quite small (table 7).

7. Exports of cattle products from Mobile.[36]

	1847	1849	1850	1855	1858
Hides (bales)	331	458	14	. . .	. . .
Hides (loose)	8,527	6,872	1,500	22,366	. . .
Horns	6,300	4,000	4,500	. . .	. . .
Tallow (barrels)	217	. . .	185	. . .	. . .
Tallow (casks)	85	214	104	. . .	. . .
Tallow (hhds)	3	. . .	. . .	. . .	. . .
Tallow (lbs.)	. . .	. . .	. . .	8,800	87,000

While this negative evidence does not "prove" the absence of a significant West Indian trade in cattle or beef, it suggests that such a market was limited and must have decreased during the antebellum period. Such an interpretation is buttressed by the reports of processed beef being imported *into* Mobile after the mid-1850s (table 8).

8. Beef imports into Mobile.[37]

	1855	1856	1857	1858	1859
Beef imported (barrels)	1,154	1,057	1,225	1,837	2,988

On the other hand, the export of tallow, hides, bone, and horn do indicate some utilization of the numerous cattle known to have existed in Mobile's hinterland. The question is, what happened to the beef produced by the annual slaughter of the ten to twenty thousand or so animals from which these exported products came? Possibly the animals were slaughtered in the up-country with the by-products moving downriver to Mobile. More likely, however, was the existence of a small slaughtering industry in Mobile itself which catered to the urban market and ships plying the port as well as the possible, though undocumented, reshipment of beef upriver.[38]

In addition to the major ports of New Orleans and Mobile, other ports had small exports of animal products. Charleston, Appalachicola, Savannah, and Darien all shipped small quantities of beef, tallow, and hides occasionally.[39]

The farmer and planter

The herder was a notable figure in certain parts of the area, but most southern cattle were in the hands of other agriculturists. The plantation usually has been regarded as engaged primarily in the production of field crops with little regard for livestock. This preoccupation with field crops is undeniable, but almost all planters kept cattle; many exerted special effort to manage them properly; and some achieved a fairly high standard in both the quality and treatment of cattle.[40] Unlike the herder, the planter's use of stock was fourfold. He utilized them not only for meat, leather, and milk, but being engaged in crop cultivation, he needed oxen as well. For this reason most plantations boasted large herds of cattle, many more, in fact, than the limited use of them for beef would lead one to expect. Data in census manuscripts indicate that cattle were not restricted to any particular size holdings, but were common to all agriculturists. Ralph Flanders, after examining a number of probate records and private accounts relating to agriculture in Georgia, concluded that "practically every planter and farmer" owned a variety of stock.[41] James Sellers, in his study of Alabama, also found in records of individual holdings that many plantations had an impressive inventory of livestock with cattle usually listed as being almost as numerous as swine.[42]

As one studies plantation documents and census manuscripts it is tempting to regard the planter as being *more* diversified than the small farmer operating in the cotton belt, especially with respect to cattle. Furthermore, there is some evidence to indicate that planter-kept cattle were of higher quality and that their treatment was somewhat better than on the smaller holdings and certainly better than on the herding operations.[43] This seems, on the face of it, to be in direct contrast to what is known about the "diversified" farmer and the "specialist" planter, yet when one considers that the planter was much more literate and better read than the farmer, the advantages he had in purchasing and importing blooded stock, and the relative abundance of slave elders and children who could care for stock, it is not unbelievable that the plantation could have developed and maintained higher standards in livestock care and breeding than the southern small holder. To be sure, the care and breeding of southern cattle on plantations left much to be desired, yet conditions on some southern farms or on the herding operations were often much worse. Moreover, there is ample reason to see the farmer located in the cotton areas as being less like the "diversified" hill farmer in parts of Tennessee and northern Georgia than the planter in the cotton belt. In his detailed study of antebellum agriculture in Mississippi, John H. Moore concluded that cotton belt farmers differed from planters only in size of landholding and labor force. They were interested primarily in the commercial production of cotton and cherished no ideals about diversified agriculture. In this sense, such holdings were small "cotton plantations" with few or no slaves and were quite distinct from the hill farmer of the South.[44]

While the number of cattle on individual handholdings varied from one to another and from year to year, the total numbers were quite high. On a typical plantation with one hundred slaves, the cattle might vary from fifty to two hundred or more with most of them listed as "other" cattle. Both census manuscripts and plantation records indicate a surprisingly large number of milking cows, perhaps one fourth to one third of the total cattle. Oxen were less numerous than milk cows. Furthermore, they declined in relative importance as mules were recognized as being better suited for draft work under plantation conditions.[45]

The census of 1840 gives us little help in studying cattle since it has only one category, "neat cattle," but in 1850 and 1860 the census lists three categories: milk cows, oxen, and "other" cattle. Ostensibly, this was intended to distinguish between cattle bred for milking, for draft, and for beef. In practice, however, these appellations are not particularly revealing, since the animal most common in the South was basically the "native" cow of eighteenth-century America, or the "Spanish" from the southwest, plus a variable amount of Devon or Durham blood introduced somewhere along the line. With this sort of nondescript ancestry, one would scarcely expect the cattle to be outstanding as either dairy or beef cattle. Most were simply "cattle" and were labeled "oxen," "beef," or "milk" depending upon their function at a given time.[46] Some producers attempted to import improved cattle and it is likely that a gradual improvement in bloodlines took place. In most cases upgrading was accomplished by the purchase of an improved bull, in which case there was diffusion through the native stock in the surrounding area. It was common for one operator to keep a bull for service for his neighbors' cattle, and such a practice could have had notable effects on the poorer native stock.[47] Some attempted to raise purebreds. For example, an Alabama diarist proudly entered the results of his efforts at cattle breeding.

> My English cow Victoria had a heifer calf yesterday. This calf is by the English bull Prince of Wales, consequently full blood. [Later he noted] Sue came up this morning with a heifer calf—this is a half-breed English.[48]

Like the herders, most planters utilized the forests for cattle forage whenever possible. In this respect plantation cattle and herder-owned cattle were scarcely distinguishable. Many planters simply marked their animals and turned them loose in the woods to forage for themselves.[49] An example of this kind of treatment comes from the labored pen of a Mississippi plantation overseer who reported that his "cattle is scattle about sow I doant know much about them. Tha have not all bin at home at one time since I have bin hear." [50] However, most planters were situated in the cotton belt which lay, for the most part, outside the piney woods to which the herder had retreated. In the more densely populated cotton belt, the planter had closer neighbors and often was restricted to grazing cattle on his own land. Under these conditions he developed a rather crude management system under which cattle were allowed to run loose when natural forage was at its best but were given care during winter or when forest grazing was especially poor. A Mississippi correspondent to the Patent Office reported in 1850: "Cattle are little or no trouble: they raise themselves. We seldom feed them, and it is only the cows and oxen we ever feed, and these only in the winter months." [51] In Jackson County, Alabama, a similar situation existed: "We have no system of raising stock here, of any sort; and never count the cost, as the cattle live half the time on Uncle Sam's pasture." [52] While this system of depending heavily upon the forest for grazing must have been quite common during the first few decades of the century, toward the latter part of the antebellum period cattle raising became more centered on the plantation. There is good evidence that range forage was declining due to overgrazing; consequently, planters and farmers were being forced to alter their system so as to provide better cattle feed.[53] By the 1850s many had begun to supplement their cattle's foraging with winter feed, or perhaps they turned them into the corn and pea fields after harvest. In a letter to his overseer one planter gave instructions to "turn cows . . . into that field and then commence milking the cows to make fall butter." [54] Milk cows and oxen usually were fed an allowance of fodder (corn blades) regularly, while other cattle probably received some during the winter months. A Georgia agriculturist described the treatment of cattle in his area.

Cattle and sheep are left to shift for themselves in the woods, except two or three months of winter, when they receive a daily allowance of corn shocks or other course fodder. In the summer they become fat on the native grasses of the forest, and milk cows, after June, when our wheat, oats and other winter crops are harvested yield an abundance of milk and butter from the crop of crabgrass pastures of these fields. . . . During the winter months milk cows are fed on pumpkins, sweet potatoes, cornmeal, cut-straw, etc.[55]

In some cases cattle were penned during winter in order to make manure and then released in spring.[56]

As was the case with hogs, the more knowledgeable planters as well as other writers in the agricultural journals of the day were agitating constantly for better practices.[57] The better planters attempted to improve their stock and many had slaves designated to act as stock minders who watched the animals while they grazed, rounded them up and drove them back to the plantation at night, and salted and fed them regularly.[58]

While planter-owned cattle were common in much of the South, they also were kept by the more numerous small farmers. Within the plantation area, the treatment and use of cattle probably varied little from the small holder to the larger planter. As mentioned earlier, the operations of the larger farmers and small planters were quite similar and could be considered either farms or plantations depending upon the criteria used to define the groups. Of greater importance than landholding size or the kind of labor employed was the location of the landholding and the kinds of markets accessible to the operator. Operators outside the cotton belt had a more diversified output; thus they were in a good position to grow more corn, small grains and hay. Consequently, the production of cattle products was higher in these areas. Such farmers were numerous on the periphery of the cash-crop areas, and were especially common in the Hill South where they constituted a majority of the agriculturists.

On these smaller farms the quality and treatment of livestock varied depending upon the individual operator and the use for which the animals were intended. In the Hill South where there was a stronger dependence upon cattle for subsistence than elsewhere, the animals probably received reasonably good care. The production of small grains and forage crops was relatively more important and this probably resulted in better food and treatment for the animals. But, despite this there is a surprising dearth of evidence to support any widespread commercial exploitation of cattle in the Hill South. Tennessee and Kentucky were outstanding producers of both cattle and hogs, and both were marketed in the Deep South and the Northeast. But, such commercial production was notably absent in the hill sections of the Deep South states. There were, to be sure, cattle-raising farmers in the Southern Appalachians, but it appears that such operators were most common in the ridge and valley region of East Tennessee or on the high meadows and "balds" of North Carolina. Their distribution in northern Alabama and Georgia must have been spotty. Northern Mississippi was rather late in being settled, but there seems little reason to assume any significant differences from the areas to the east.[59]

The absence of commercially marketed cattle and cattle products from the hill country seems unquestionable, yet the reasons are obscure. Tennessee growers had no trouble selling their cattle and hogs. They simply herded them through the mountains and off to market. Just why farmers in northern Georgia and the Carolina hills failed to do likewise seems a puzzle. Most likely such an industry failed to materialize simply because the limited forest forage prohibited extensive grazing operations, and there were not enough farm-produced cattle to market. The lack of an environmental base for widespread grazing must have been a strong factor. Unlike the pine forests where an understory of fairly rich grasses existed, the large-crowned deciduous forest trees tended to shade out the grasses, and the existing herbaceous growth was insufficient for operations involving large numbers of animals. Mast for hogs was abundant, and there is evidence that a sizable surplus of hogs was produced. However, cattle production must have been limited to a few animals sold to Tennessee drovers who passed through herding their own animals to market.[60] Most of the references to exports from the hill country include corn and hogs but little or no cattle or cattle products, except for small amounts of dairy products, but the extent of this trade must have been limited.[61] Another factor may have been that Tennessee growers could move cattle up the Appalachian valleys into Virginia and the Northeast quite easily, while Georgia and Alabama growers were oriented to the Deep South. Considering the relative markets it is likely that the Northeast was a better market, a fact which placed the Tennessee producers in a better competitive position.

The lack of a commercial cattle industry in the Hill South

did not preclude a rather strong dependence upon cattle to supply local needs. There appears to have been a relatively intense (for the South at least) utilization of the existing animals for both beef and dairy products. While the number of cattle per capita generally was lower than in those areas farther south, butter production was higher. At the same time there was a higher output of butter per milk cow. It appears, therefore, that the utilization of cattle in the hill country was limited to local needs, and that the small amounts that were sold went to supply the local market.[62]

Cattle on farms in the hill country may have fared better than elsewhere, but this is not easily demonstrable. The small farmers kept cattle, but only a few head to supply family needs and no more.

As was the case with hogs, we have no data on animal production, since the census merely lists numbers of animals and not annual meat production. Consequently, conversion from numbers given at ten year intervals into annual production figures presents considerable difficulty and is fraught with imprecision.[63] Where southern cattle are concerned, the problem is further obscured by the lack of specific knowledge about the animals. Since beef was less important than pork in the southern diet, there are fewer references to cattle size, weights, and meat yield. Consequently, any estimates must be considered approximate and should not be taken too literally.

Under most conditions, cows calve once a year. Under adverse conditions, however, disease and poor nutrition might lead to low conception rates and increased abortion in which case the figure might possibly decrease to once every two years.[64] Such a low calving frequency seldom occurred over large areas; therefore, it is likely that the rate for southern cattle was somewhat higher. Calf loss was a problem, too, but considering the mild winters losses may not have been quite as high as those of the areas further north. In the Carolina cowpens of the early years, it was estimated that the number of calves surviving until branding time would be about 60 percent of the brood cow herd.[65] Considering the rather poor treatment given southern cattle during the period and the likelihood of later losses, 50 percent appears to be a reasonable figure to accept as the annual yield. However, all cattle were not brood cows, nor were they destined to be. The numbers given in the censuses included all animals one year old or older including all animals not yet marketed or slaughtered. Since it was common to slaughter or market three- or four-year olds, the census figures must have represented brood cows, yearlings, two-year olds, and in fact, all cattle except oxen which were enumerated separately. If it is possible, then, to construct a hypothetical herd, the breakdown by groups might be: first year—one hundred cows and fifty yearlings; second year—one hundred cows, fifty yearlings, and fifty two-year olds; third year—one hundred cows, fifty yearlings, fifty two-year olds, and fifty three-year olds; fourth year—one hundred cows, fifty yearlings, fifty two-year olds, fifty three-year olds, and fifty marketable cattle. Thus, a herd of two hundred and fifty cattle was needed to produce fifty for sale or slaughter. This yield of one-fifth seems quite low when one considered that many cattle were slaughtered or sold earlier than four years and that the older heifers were calving long before their fourth year. Too, the censuses reported only cattle one year old and older, leaving a generation of calves unreported. But, no allowance has been made for oxen or brood cow replacement so the writer has chosen a conservative estimate.

Though the size of the animals produced is difficult to determine, most reports describe them as smaller than the best kept animals of the North and West. Live weights probably ranged from 500 to 700 pounds with dressed weights being about one-half. Occasionally animals weighed more (perhaps retired oxen), but the usual carcass yield must have been about 300 pounds of meat.[66]

Though southerners did little to upgrade the quality of their cattle, the large numbers of animals in the area were capable of supplying huge quantities of meat. Admittedly, it was far from "prime" beef but it was no worse than much of the nation's beef. A lot has been written about the poor quality of southern stock and, compared to the fat cattle slaughtered in the eastern markets, there is no question about their general inferiority. But, it is grossly unfair to compare southern woods-grazed animals with the pampered English beeves being imported into the Northeast at the time. These improved animals were by no means universal in the Northeast or Old Northwest even as late as 1860. Moreover, the trans-Mississippi West began producing range-fed stock which were descendants of the scrawny Spanish cattle, certainly no better than the southern animals. Even after the Civil War, Texas cattle moved into the midwestern markets indicating that American tastes for beef had not become so sophisticated that the tough, stringy trail beeves were scorned.

It is likely that most of the southern supply of beef was locally produced. Moreover, the modest demand for beef in comparison to pork suggest that southern needs were supplied largely from within the region. It is true that some animals were driven into the South, but their numbers were small relative to the indigenous cattle. Furthermore, these "drove" cattle came from the Hill South which represented an intraregional rather than an interregional trade.

The amount of beef consumed in the South is extremely difficult to estimate. Being relied upon less often than pork, few people bothered to keep records of beef weights and beef rations. Estimates of national per capita annual meat consumption during the period from 1830 to 1880 place the average at around 175 pounds.[67] If we assume southern meat consumption to have been comparable to the national average and that the southern intake of pork was around 150 pounds, then the beef and mutton intake would have amounted to some 25 or 30 pounds.[68] Estimates of meat consumption by Georgia and South Carolina correspondents to the Patent Office placed the average annual meat consumption fairly high but indicate a pork/beef ratio of roughly three to one.[69] This ratio was surely unrealistic for the slave population but perhaps represented white consumption fairly accurately. Many planters and farmers slaughtered at least one beef each year, in which case each adult might have eaten 40 to 50 or more pounds of beef. But, the substantially lower consumption by the slave families depressed the average intake considerably, possibly to as low as 25 to 30 pounds. Even so, this is still twice the beef consumption reported in parts of the South during the 1920s.[70]

Slave beef consumption certainly was substantially less than that of whites. The plantation practice of killing several beeves each year for the slave families was common but not universal. In most cases it amounted to one or more killed at intervals to provide relief from the monotony of pork or to make up deficits whenever pork ran out. Only on rice plantations was beef a regular issue and there seldom was it a daily or even weekly ration. When beef was issued in lieu of pork, the allowance was apt to be increased, but on coastal plantations where a regular pork ration was not universal, the beef carcass was simply divided among the families with little regard for ration size.[71] On plantations where beef was issued regularly, the slaves might have had as much beef as many whites, perhaps 30 or 40 pounds per year. But, the large number of slaves who tasted beef only occasionally or not at all depressed the average considerably. Considering the entire area, it is unlikely that many slaves consumed much over ten pounds annually.

Comparing probable beef consumption with production it is apparent that most counties had ratios above that postulated as minimum to meet local needs (figs. *17, 18,* and *19*).[72] The distribution of these ratios reflect the high numbers of cattle known to have existed in the pine forests. The deficient counties were scattred, but there were four areas showing consistent groupings of deficient counties. These were:

1] A very few counties along the coastal fringe and Mississippi river counties containing sizable urban places.
2] The Alabama black belt.
3] The Tennessee River Valley of Alabama.
4] The Piedmont of Georgia.

Conclusions concerning the importation of beef to fill out the deficits in these areas are more difficult than was the case with pork. It is known that quantities of beef moved into the port cities from the East and the Midwest, yet it is doubtful if this importation was sufficient to compensate for the entire deficit. It is more probable that the deficit counties simply consumed less beef than the average postulated here. This was entirely possible since beef was an ancillary meat and could be done without. Pork, on the other hand, was a dietary staple and when supplies ran short purchases were necessary. Furthermore, the maps may not account for all southern beef since milk cows and oxen were not included in determining the ratios. Presumably, retired oxen and cows also could have contributed to the beef supply.

Another segment of the cattle industry that deserves consideration is dairy production. Data are available for only two dairy products, butter and cheese, and if conclusions can be drawn from such data, the southern output was far below that of the rest of the nation. Using butter production as an index, virtually all

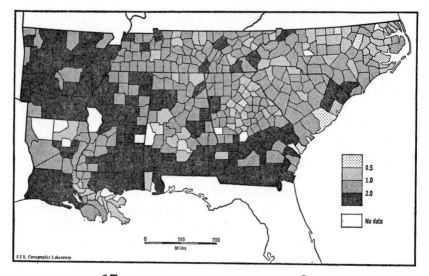

17. CATTLE PER UNIT, 1840.

northern and western states exceeded the per capita production in
the South, which was ten pounds or less in both 1850 and 1860.
Compared to the embryonic states of Vermont, New York, and
Ohio butter production in the southern states' output was pitiful
(table 9). Southern-made cheese was virtually nonexistent.

Further evidence of the poor southern dairy industry is revealed by computing butter output per milk cow. The ratios for
southern states are far below those of all other states in both census years. We can conclude either that the southern milk cows
were poor producers or that southerners reported to the census
large numbers of female cattle as "milk cows" regardless of their
breeding. This supports our earlier assertion that southern milk
cows were simply "lactating females."

The reason for this poor showing lay in the quality of the
animals, the poor care they received, and perhaps more than anything, the fact that little effort was expended to increase milk and
butter production. On plantations there were attempts to produce
milk and butter for the planter's family, but in few cases were the
slaves fed dairy products. On smaller holdings the production per
person undoubtedly was higher but very rarely did farmers exert
a concerted effort to produce commercially.[73] In examining census manuscripts for Georgia this writer noted that the most commonly occurring notation in the column reserved for butter pro-

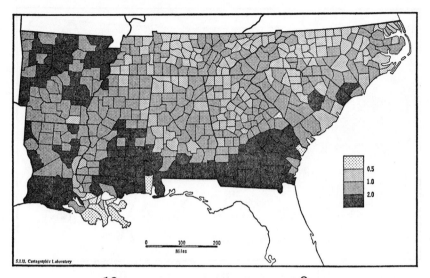

18. CATTLE PER UNIT, 1850.

duction was "50 lbs." or "100 lbs." Very likely, this reflects the
producers estimates; when asked by the census taker "how much
butter did you produce last year?" he replied, "about a pound a
week," or "about two pounds a week."

One of the most important detriments to the development of
a respectable cattle industry in the South was the dearth of improved pasture, hay, and other forage crops. The neglect of these
crops and the practice of encouraging stock to forage for themselves on unimproved land raises questions about the adequacy of
such forage and the production of animal products possible under
such conditions. While little quantitative data exist to facilitate an
evaluation of southern stock treatment, it seems worthwhile to
examine the available documentary evidence in light of what is
known today about natural forage and the nutritive qualities of
the domestic forage and feed used.

The natural vegetation of the area has been discussed previously, and in that section it was noted that grazing conditions
varied markedly. Perhaps the best was that of the pine forests of
the Coastal Plain and the oak-pine forest of the central parts of
the area. The pine forests offered grazing for more stock over a
longer time period than the oak-pine forests both because they
were slower to be affected by the encroachment of the cotton
growers and because the shorter winters permitted a longer graz-

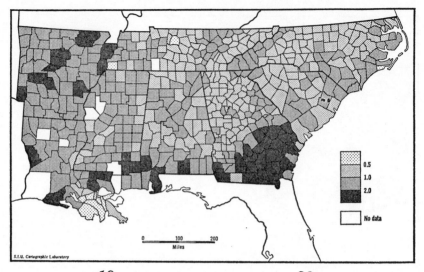

0.5
1.0
2.0

No data

0   100   200
Miles

S.I.U. Cartographic Laboratory

19. CATTLE PER UNIT, 1860.

ing season. In fact, most of the land area of the entire pine forests
was not cleared until after the Civil War; large parts (most, in
fact) of the piney woods have never been fully utilized for crop
cultivation down to the present day.

There is no way of determining accurately the quality of
grazing offered by southern forests during the antebellum period.
However, a few studies have been made in the twentieth century
from which some generalizations might be drawn and applied to
the earlier period. A study of the Georgia Coastal Plain in the early
1940s illustrates the grazing possibilities and limitations of the
Georgia pine forests. A total of five distinct grazing habitats were
recognized, each offering grazing in certain seasons. The natural
grasses had a fairly good seasonal balance with various species
offering grazing during a large part of the year. The best summer
grasses were the bluestems and panic grasses, while winter grazing was offered by Curtiss dropseed. Spring grazing was primarily
upon Pineland three-awn. Broadleaved herbs and browse plants
offered some winter grazing but usually were not the preferred
forage. Apparently, forest grazing offered ample and fairly nutritious food during eight or nine months of the year, but was deficient in both quantity and nutrients during the winter. If not
overgrazed, it could carry animals through the winter, but lactating or gestating cows needed supplemental feed.[74] It is likely that

animals had slightly better winter grazing during the antebellum period than indicated in the Georgia study since there were large canebrakes upon which they fed. Though not found to any large extent in the pine or mixed forest areas today, such brakes were common during the early nineteenth century and may have helped materially to winter the animals.[75]

The amount of forest land needed to sustain cattle depended upon a number of variables and, although accurate determination is impossible, it does seem feasible to estimate roughly the carrying capacity of the southern grazing lands. H. H. Biswell found that pine forests could support about one cow for every five acres in summer, but during winter animals required as much as fifteen.[76] Whether the deciduous forests offered the same grazing is open to question. One suspects they were poorer than the pine forests, but may have been adequate if grazing pressure was not severe. They were grazed widely in the hill states and the Old Northwest during the early period.

If we assume that fifteen acres of forest land could support one animal, then there is no question but that ample forage existed in most of the area. Except for the most densely populated areas, the ratio of unimproved land to cattle equaled or exceeded fifteen acres per animal. If we consider the entire area the figure was much higher; for example, at mid-century the eight states contained more than two hundred million acres of unimproved land, which amounted to over forty acres per head of cattle.[77] Admittedly, the value of such a gross comparison of area to cattle is extremely limited since there were so many variables involved. Many cattle were not located in the areas offering the best grazing, much of the grazing land could not support an animal on fifteen acres, and the figure does not take into account the competition from swine, sheep, and wildlife. But, for that matter, it assumes no supplemental feed was given, a fact that was not true in the more settled areas. Furthermore, in much of the area, cattle densities were so low that we could double the fifteen-acre estimate and still have ample range to handle existing cattle.

It would be a mistake to leave the impression that forest grazing was comparable to improved pasture, but it is equally fallacious to dismiss the wild forage as unfit for animal feed and the range-fed cattle as worthless. True, many animals fared poorly, especially in winter where canebrakes had been overgrazed or where the annual burnings had been stopped, but summer grazing of the forest and light winter grazing with supplemental feed could and did produce the major part of the cattle needs of the area. The forests certainly were not ideal grazing by any means, but as a cattle-producing medium they provided animals at low cost with little effort.

Natural forage sometimes was supplemented by additions of grain or other concentrates as well as cured fodder and hay. The extent of such feeding practices depended upon the natural forage available, the amount of supplemental feed produced by the operator, and the personal decisions of the individual concerning the care he wished his animals to receive. Where natural grazing was good, most cattle owners were tempted to rely more upon such forage with a corresponding neglect of domestic feeds. Most operators recognized, though, that work animals and lactating cows needed supplemental feeding. Moreover, toward the end of the antebellum period many were beginning to realize the advantages of improved pastures and other domestic feeds in stock raising. Although such pastures and tame hay were never very important during the antebellum period, most farmers and planters began to search for substitutes. Peavine hay, crabgrass hay, green corn, and corn fodder, all were used in an attempt to discover a suitable replacement for the hay crops used elsewhere in the country.

There seems little doubt about "fodder" (corn blades) being the chief domestic hay in much of the South. It offered a cheap roughage, easily harvested without implements by slave labor, and it came straight from the cornfield with no extra effort such as seeding, cultivating or mowing. Collecting or "pulling" such fodder was a simple task and could be performed with virtually no training or skill. It involved stripping the blades from each stalk, tying the blades of several stalks into a bundle, and then attaching the bundle onto a cornstalk to cure in the sun. There was some argument about the effects of "fodder pulling" upon corn yields, but most operators waited quite late in the year before pulling and regarded the loss in grain yields as negligible.[78]

The amount of fodder harvested annually from southern cornfields is not really known. Census schedules had a column for recording hay production, but most enumerators interpreted this not to include corn-blade fodder. Consequently, hay production appeared quite low. M. W. Philips noted this around 1850 and concluded that Mississippi probably produced around 100,000 tons of fodder and peavine hay each year. A Georgia agriculturist estimated that cornfields would yield about 1,800 pounds of fodder for each 100 bushels of corn.[79] In Alabama, fodder yield was estimated at 1,000 pounds of fodder per 100 bushels of corn.[80] Philips, an outstanding agriculturist and certainly not typical of the entire South, claims to have saved over a ton per hand.[81]

There is no question about the common use of fodder. Dairies and plantation daybooks constantly refer to "fodder pulling" during much of the season.[82] One planter regarded fodder important enough to keep a "fodder book" recording dates, number of wagon loads, and weights.[83] In other cases it entered into the local trade. For example, two Georgia planters kept accurate records on their corn and fodder trade. On his Georgia plantation Mr. Lamar recorded a transaction that must have been typical. "Let Dr. Moses L. Barrow have 900 bundles fodder making 3240 lbs at 75 cts . . . $24.30."[84] Apparently, some planters valued fodder so much they paid their own slaves to harvest it.[85]

The most revealing evidence this writer has yet found concerning fodder production comes from the census manuscripts. While examining Schedule 4 of the 1850 census for Greene County, Georgia, the writer discovered that the census enumerator had written in "fodder" at the top of the column reserved for hay and had entered data on fodder production. A sampling of fifty-one agriculturists in the county revealed that only three failed to produce at least a ton of fodder and that most produced several tons. Comparing fodder production to corn production, most agriculturists produced about half a ton per hundred bushels of corn. Some produced only a few hundred pounds while others pulled as much as a ton per hundred bushels of corn; the average for the group was almost twelve hundred pounds. While there is no way of demonstrating that Green County was representative of the South, or even Georgia, the existence of such data strongly suggests that corn-blade fodder has been grossly underestimated and that the southern production probably was quite large. If, for example, we assume that corn growers pulled fodder at the rate of one thousand pounds per one hundred bushels of corn then the output for the states of South Carolina, Georgia, Alabama, and Mississippi would have amounted to almost half a million tons.

Another way in which such fodder has been underestimated is in its nutritive qualities. There appears to be some confusion about just what the term meant. As was stated before, most southerners stripped the blades off the stalk and fed only the blades. This practice eliminated the bulky, pithy, unappetizing, and nutritiously poor stalk. While such roughage does not offer the nutrients of concentrates such as corn or cottonseed meal, it is not nearly as sterile as is generally believed and might compare favorably with all but the best cured hay. Southerners did occasionally shock their corn or cut the "tops" of the stalks, but the preferred method was stripping the blades.[86] The practice was very common as late as the 1940s and, indeed, may be found in some locations even today.

Another nutritious feed crop that increased in importance during the antebellum period was peavine hay. As has been indicated, peas were planted in the corn to be grazed by both cattle and hogs and, toward the end of the period, peas were being sown for hay.[87] Other forages which served from time to time were crabgrass hay, green corn sown for hay, oat straw, corn shucks, and unthreshed oats.[88]

More concentrated feeds, such as corn, oats, cotton seed, and occasionally pumpkins or turnips were given to work animals and milkers. Of these feeds, corn, oats, and cottonseed were perhaps most used with corn and oats being preferred for work animals while cottonseed was fed to milkers. Cottonseed should not be overlooked as a digestible feed or nutrient-rich fertilizer. In the postbellum years oil mills in the South poured out millions of tons of cottonseed meal which served as the winter mainstay of southern milkers. The protein content is very high and small quantities materially improve the condition and yield of milk cows. While many farmers and planters threw cottonseed away during the very early years of the nineteenth century, it is doubtful that they continued to do so for long, and the seed was relied upon increasingly during the prewar period as feed and fertilizer.[89]

There is little question about the general inferiority of southern cattle as compared to those of many areas in the Northeast and Old Northwest. In both beef and dairy production the South lagged. There is evidence of a fairly substantial production that was sufficient to provide for family use on the smaller landholdings and for the use of white families, at least, on plantations, but there was little surplus production of dairy products. When the slave population is considered the area actually was quite deficient. In fact, cattle production seems to have been almost exclusively a home-oriented function and, as such, seldom produced a sizeable surplus for market. The port cities imported much of their cheese and butter and a portion of their beef, while the interior towns depended upon a few "coffee cows" kept in small pastures or lots for dairy products and nearby farmers for occasional supplies of beef.[90]

The reasons for the underdevelopment of the southern cattle industry are many. A primary one was the competition from cotton and other cash crops. The labor required for an efficient dairy industry would have interfered severely with cotton, sugar or rice growing. Another factor was the presence of the slave who never really was a large consumer of beef or dairy products, and few attempts were made to provide for his needs. Perhaps most basic was the absence of a well-developed commercial livestock market. Given an incentive to produce either beef or dairy products for market both the farmer and the planter would have exerted much more effort to acquire good animals and provide them with the proper care. The southerner was tempted by the mild winters and large expanses of unimproved land which provided fairly good forage—an environment that could produce fair livestock with little care—to depend too heavily upon such resources resulting in a relatively poor cattle industry.

7 The occasional diversion

The traditional interpretation of the American farmstead is not unlike the theme of the children's song, "Old MacDonald's Farm." With "quacks," "gobbles," and "moos" everywhere, it supposedly contained animals sufficient to provide a variety of food for the needs of the farm family. Accordingly, diet in rural America has reflected this proliferation. From this menagerie a host of products have emerged to give us a number of succulent meat dishes. Thus, we have turkey for Thanksgiving, goose for Christmas and, of course, chicken on Sunday. The typical antebellum southern operation may not have lived up to the "self-sufficient" ideal, but most kept a variety of fowls for eggs and meat and many also raised sheep and goats for their flesh.

The importance of such animals to the overall southern meat diet is open to question. One reason for this blank in our economic and alimentary picture of southern life is the overwhelming importance of pork which obscures the role of other meats. Another is the lack of data on the production of the minor animals. The agricultural censuses reported only sheep, leaving to us the task of speculating on the importance of the other animals such as goats and poultry.

The South was by no means committed to growing sheep on a large scale or, for that matter, was any part of the nation. There was a substantial need for wool, and sheep were kept for that purpose, but few American farmers ever looked upon sheep as a major food animal. On the other hand, they were by no means absent. Many farmers encouraged sheep husbandry and, during the colonial period, they were kept on many American farms. Of course, wool production was the major object of sheep growing during the early period and, after the mechanization of wool spinning and weaving, a sizable commercial market developed. After that, considerable attention was devoted to sheep husbandry and improvement, and some areas underwent a "sheep craze," as the industry was seen as an important agricultural activity to replace traditional crop agriculture.

While this increased interest in wool growing and sheep improvement is worth tracing in itself, the primary emphasis for the moment is the use of sheep for food. Neither mutton nor lamb ever became a dietary mainstay of any large group of Americans prior to the Civil War, and southerners were no exception. However, the preference for pork and beef throughout the country and the particular emphasis placed upon pork in the South has tended to emphasize American preferences to the point where mutton and lamb have been overlooked as minor foods. Moreover, this preference for pork and beef probably stemmed from the greater availability of swine and cattle rather than any dislike of mutton. Knowing the propensity of the Englishman for sheep flesh, one wonders why (or if) English colonists lost their tastes for lamb and mutton so quickly.[1]

Sheep growing was primarily a northern occupation, the leading areas being New England, New York, and Ohio. Tennessee, Virginia, and Kentucky were the most significant producers among the southern states; the Deep South states relatively unimportant. The warm southern climate lessened the need for heavy clothing and this fact, along with the competition for land and labor from cotton, tended to retard the development of sheep husbandry. Many farmers and planters kept sheep, and there was a substantial production of wool. Yet, the output was intended for home use with comparatively little going into the commercial market.

Even though the area was unimpressive in its sheep production during the antebellum period, it was not the poorest area in the country. The area showed 3,220,033 sheep in 1840 and 4,-111,977 in 1860. This amounted to about .64 animals per capita in 1840 and .84 in 1860 or approximately 58 sheep for every 100 head of cattle in 1840 and 64 per 100 head in 1860. Swine outnumbered sheep about 4 to 1 in both 1840 and 1860. The per capita figures compare quite well with the southern New England states but are well below those of the sheep-growing states such as Ohio and New York. Sheep were quite numerous in some areas, especially in Kentucky and Tennessee, and a large proportion of the farmers and planters kept them (figs. 20 and 21).[2]

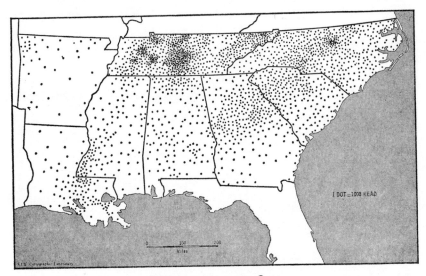

20. SHEEP, 1840.

Sheep husbandry differed little from cattle raising in that
the animals usually were allowed to roam in the forests with little
or no care. The native sheep subsisted quite well on the rough
grazing, but often suffered from the depredations of the few
wolves, bears, and mountain lions left in the remote areas.

Even where human settlement was dense enough to dis-
courage the larger predators, semiferal and domestic dogs took
their toll, often roaming the woods in packs causing considerable
losses. One Georgia agriculturist wrote to the *Southern Cultivator*
complaining bitterly: "my favorite stock is sheep [but], I have
been killed out three times by the infernal dogs. I'll bet fifty dollars there are five dogs to one sheep, in some parts of Georgia." [3]
In addition to such depredations, sheep also suffered somewhat
from internal parasites, although forest-grazed animals may have
fared better than those kept in pens.[4]

Most of the animals found in the South were "natives" with
no special strains being outstanding. Some of the sheep in Mississippi and Alabama had a French origin, but most were common
sheep moved west and south from the Carolinas, and the Hill
South. The Merino craze that infected other parts of the country
spilled into the southern agricultural periodicals with the hills and
mountains being viewed enthusiastically by some as ideal sheep
country, but few purebreds actually were imported.[5] Mutton
sheep were introduced by well known planters, and there was

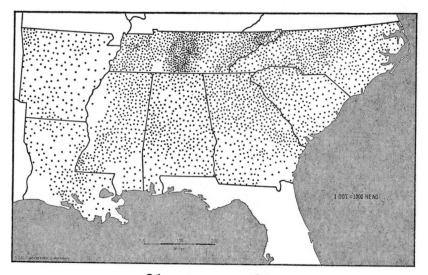

21. SHEEP, 1860.

some spread of the improved blood into the natives. Such introductions were scattered, however, and the total impact upon the
large numbers of natives must have been limited.[6]

The goat may have been used to some extent in the South,
but the absence of quantitative data casts even more doubt upon
the numbers and use of goats than was the case with sheep. Goats
sometimes were kept for their milk and, on occasion, they were
eaten; but it appears that goat meat was a relatively rare dish.
Occasionally, one finds references to goats being kept and sug-
gestions that goat meat be used more often, yet it is the writer's
opinion that its use was infrequent and can be virtually ignored
as an important dietary item. The use of many wild animals for
food, such as squirrel, rabbit, even possum, was more common.

Unfortunately, no worthwhile statistics exist on the production and use of poultry in the nation before the Civil War.[7] The
widespread use of poultry in the South today and the regional
"love" for "southern fried chicken," "chicken and dumplins," and
other succulent poultry dishes suggest a long history of fowl en-
joyment, yet one can only guess at their frequency on the table
and importance relative to other meats. References to poultry by
travelers in the antebellum South are frequent, and other sources
confirm the fact that fowl were numerous and were important
sources of food. On the other hand, such meat was seldom a staple

but was used for special occasions. In this sense it served in much the same manner as mutton, though much more frequently.

Poultry lent itself quite well to antebellum farm conditions, and every prudent housewife took advantage of this fact by keeping an assortment for family use. Not all kept every kind of fowl, but the variety on most operations was impressive. Research into plantation documents gives us some hint of their importance. For example, the following inventory was made on a South Carolina rice plantation in 1851.[8]

17	gobblers	7	roosters
18	turkey hens	50	hens
19	English ducks	10	young chickens
25	young ducks	2	old geese
1	old Muscovy duck	6	goslings
34	Guinea fowls	3	pea cocks
		4	pea hens

Records from Beaver Creek plantation in Virginia contain detailed lists of poultry and poultry killed and sold from 1833 until well into the 1840s. For example, on November 26, 1840 the records list:

Geese	68
"Chickens besides friable ones"	68
puddle ducks	37
muscovy ducks	37
Turkeys	21
Guinea fowls	6

This is followed by a series of entries where specified numbers were killed. Apparently, they were well used on this particular landholding.[9]

Poultry offered several advantages over the larger animals; they could be kept on a minimum of feed (chickens can pick up enough food in cow and mule droppings to subsist fairly well), had a high reproductive potential, offered eggs as well as meat, and could be killed on short notice with little worry about spoilage. Every young girl learned to "wring a chicken neck" long before she was ready for marriage, and with very little preparation the bird could be readied for the table.

Poultry raising, however, was not without its hazards. Much

of the area was relatively thinly settled up to the time of the Civil War, thus a variety of small predators such as foxes, skunks, weasels, and hawks abounded. The depredations of these animals caused the farmer or planter to keep a loaded shotgun handy, and the hatred for hawks engendered by their raids on domestic poultry has become proverbial.[10]

The common dunghill or barnyard fowl was the most numerous of the southern poultry and was the bird that supplied most of the meat and eggs. They were of no special breed, having acquired their unique characteristics from a long evolution during which the premium was placed on survival. For this reason, such birds could fly as well as quail or grouse, forage for sustenance among the stables or in the forest, and hide their nests skillfully from both human and animal predators. Most chickens roosted at night some twenty to fifty feet above the ground to avoid falling prey to foxes and, on the whole, were experts at survival in an era when protection provided by humans was minimal.

The science of egg production in the South is relatively new, and one would hardly expect especially heavy producers among southern hens during the nineteenth century. Admittedly, egg production was receiving attention elsewhere in the nation, notably New England, but attempts to improve southern stock were limited. Some birds were introduced from Europe, but fowl importation was probably limited to "show birds" with little serious attention given to egg production.[11] Today, hen breeding has reached the point where an annual production of two hundred, three hundred, or even more eggs per hen can be expected out of good stock, but such "machines" are products of the twentieth century and were unknown a century ago. Nineteenth-century farm hens never approached such production figures, more often laying only for a few weeks or months during spring and summer. In the wild state, most gallinaceous birds lay a clutch of from six to fifteen eggs and then proceed to incubate them. Domestic hens have the same tendency and, if left alone, will "set" as soon as enough eggs are accumulated. Southern housewives often thwarted the hen by stealing eggs, usually one at a time as they were laid, thus extending the laying period and increasing the number of eggs produced. However, this was possible only if adequate houses or pens were provided. If left unpenned, the wary hens sought hedgerows, haystacks, and other hiding places

for their nests. If the treasure was found before the hen began
to incubate, it usually yielded a "hatful" or an "apronful" of eggs
for table use. If not, then the eggs were left to hatch. Often the
hen was able to "fool" everyone until the chicks hatched, then
she surprised the plantation or farmyard by emerging triumphant
from the bushes with her brood. Since hens usually lay in the
morning, a common method of chicken care was to pen the birds
until the eggs were laid and then release them around noon to
pick up food. Under such circumstances, it was possible to "set"
a few hens in order to insure progeny for meat or to maintain or
increase the flock while "robbing" the remaining hens to obtain
eggs for consumption. Even so, a year-round supply of eggs was
hard to maintain, as few hens laid for more than a few months
at a time.

The difference which might have existed between poultry
kept on large and small holdings do not appear to be as marked
as was the case with other livestock. It appears that most agriculturists kept poultry, though in the case of the plantations,
many of the birds belonged to the slaves. On some plantations
the white population depended almost entirely upon the slave for
poultry meat and eggs.[12] The more careful planters, however, had
their own poultry and often charged the overseer with the re-
sponsibility of caring for them or instructed certain slaves to
handle the task.[13] It was common for a planter to receive poultry
and eggs from his plantation even though he resided off the premises. One planter requested that such products be sent regularly
to his town house, while another visited the plantation and took
poultry with him to his urban residence.[14] Judging from the frequent references, large numbers of plantation poultry must have
been the rule.[15] In Mississippi, one writer aptly described the
abundance of plantation fowl: "on evenings all the trees of the
plantations are covered with chickens and turkeys." [16]

The facts about commercial poultry production are largely
unknown. Organized channels for marketing either birds or eggs
on a commercial scale have not been discovered by this writer,
but the known practice of local stores taking poultry and eggs in
urban markets, and the observations of travelers concerning sales
by slaves, point to the existence of an unorganized but significant
trade in poultry products. The smaller holders in particular were
drawn to poultry as a means of providing cash, and they fre-

quently traded poultry and eggs at the local store.[17] These products trickled into stores and small interior towns to be consumed or shipped to market in the port cities.[18] As previously mentioned there is good reason to believe a substantial portion of the commercial trade in poultry and poultry products in the plantation area was carried on by slaves and is discussed further in the section on slave livestock.

Ducks and geese were less common than chickens. Such birds had the added attraction of offering down for pillows and mattresses, but were inferior to chickens in providing eggs. Geese were favorites since their down was the most prized, and their loud squawking warned of approaching danger. Both the geese and their eggs could be eaten, but it was not common to consume eggs since geese usually lay only enough for a clutch and each egg was considered valuable in that it represented a possible ten or twelve pound feast in the fall or winter.[19] Ducks were quite common also and presumably were kept for the same reasons as geese.[20]

Both ducks and geese were more susceptible to predators than other poultry. Being somewhat more clumsy than other poultry on land and not possessing the habit of roosting in trees, they were vulnerable to ground predators such as foxes. Moreover, the females usually took their broods straight to the ponds and creeks upon hatching, and the young were easy prey for alligators and the vicious snapping turtles.

Turkeys were more common on southern landholdings than either geese or ducks. The birds adapted very well to woods forage, could fly almost as well as wild turkeys, and were large enough to be an important meat item to place on the table. Given any sort of protection at all, turkeys could survive and reproduce quite well under the frontierlike conditions in most areas. Consequently, turkey was one of the more common meats found in the South. Judging from the frequent references, it was as important as chicken.[21] On the Capell plantation, for example, turkeys often were reported in the yearly inventories and in some years compared quite favorably to chickens in importance.[22]

Guineas were common in the South and were looked upon with great favor by farmer and planter. Their raucous screeching could be heard for a mile, and they acted as the self-appointed warning system for the entire farm yard. Guineas were extremely wary and thus were good at surviving under limited care, but they were not regarded highly for food. Their eggs were seldom found and when the fowls were consumed for food, they were small and tough. Pigeons, pheasants, peafowls, and other exotics also were found occasionally, but their importance for food was negligible.[23]

A substantial though unknown quantity of the southern poultry production was carried on by slaves. The value of such a practice was recognized by most planters, but the occasional abuse of the privilege by stealing corn to use for pig or poultry feed or sneaking away after curfew to sell or trade surplus eggs or poultry led some planters to revoke the privilege and forbid any slave-owned livestock. However, few went so far and many came to tolerate the practice even though they may have been less than enthusiastic.[24]

Apparently, the keeping of poultry was encouraged much more often than pig raising. After examining the many reports of visitors to plantations, it is easy to visualize the slave quarters as being overrun with a number of raucous chickens scurrying around picking up bits of food. They required little or no care and provided an occasional relief from the usual slave ration. Moreover, they produced eggs which could be eaten, sold, or bartered. Quite often (it is impossible to say how often), both the poultry and eggs were sold rather than eaten. In many cases such sales of both poultry and eggs went to the master or housewife rather than at the local store. In one case, Olmsted found that eggs became "a circulating medium on the plantation." Apparently the planter family had no other means of supplying its need for poultry and eggs.[25] Whether this represents the usual situation is not clear, but it certainly was not uncommon. On occasion, slaves were forbidden to sell their poultry products at nearby stores, but this must not have been the rule.[26]

On the whole, it is questionable whether the livestock kept by slaves were very important in supplying food for the slaves. There is some doubt about the practice being an accepted custom, and the effectiveness of such animals for slave food was lessened materially by the tendency of the slaves to barter or sell such products. It should be noted, however, that the sale or barter of such items did not remove them from the overall supply of food in the area. Even when lost as a supplement to the Negro diets such items usually remained within the region to be consumed either by the plantation families or by urban dwellers nearby.

8 Corn pone and light bread

One of the most distinctive features of antebellum southern agriculture was the emphasis on crop production. The strong concentration on cash crops such as tobacco, cotton, rice and sugar is well known, but this preoccupation with field crops as opposed to livestock extended to the subsistence production as well. Most of the basic plants and animals common to American farms were found on farms and plantations of the South, but the importance of livestock relative to crops was much less than on American farms in general. Moreover, planters and farmers within the cotton belt favored clean-cultivated row crops over small grains. Furthermore, since livestock production was not an important commercial industry, there was a marked dearth of hay, forage crops, and improved pasture.

Corn

Introduced into American relatively early during the seventeenth century, the common European cereals were found on most farms during the antebellum period. However, the chief cereal of United States farmers was a New World domesticate, corn. Adopted quite early by English colonists in both New England and Virginia, in time it came to be one of the most important crops of farmers from New England to Georgia. Furthermore, it was especially well suited to frontier conditions and was retained as an important food for both man and his domestic animals as settlement moved west. By the time of the Civil War, corn was produced in every major agricultural region east of the Great Plains and, in most areas, was one of the two or three most important crops grown.

By the end of the eighteenth century, the use of corn as hu-

man food had begun to decline in some parts of the country, but
this was more than balanced by the growing demand for it as an
animal feed. During the first decades of the nineteenth century,
the northeastern states depended little upon corn for food, while
the West, with more typical frontier characteristics, used it both
for food and animal feed. But, by mid-century the West, too, was
turning to other grains for bread, leaving more and more corn
available for animal feed. In contrast, southerners retained the
eating habits of seventeenth- and eighteenth-century America by
clinging to corn for food throughout the nineteenth century and,
indeed, well into the twentieth.

Corn was well suited to conditions in most of the South and
was, beyond question, the most widely grown crop in the area.[1]
From the mountain valleys to the coast and from Virginia to
Texas, it was grown on all sizes of landholdings and under a
variety of conditions. Virtually every farmer produced corn for
family use the year round and for stock during the heavy work
season and winter. The planter (most having small to medium-
sized operations) and his family had the same eating habits as
the farmer and, in addition, had a larger labor force to be supplied. Thus, he planted corn in proportion to his needs.

The importance of corn to each landholder varied with the
location of his operation and his major crop emphasis. In some
areas corn was slighted in favor of cotton or other food crops,
while in others it was the dominant crop. U. B. Phillips felt that
corn at least equaled cotton in acreage and, during the early years,
exceeded it by about one third.[2] This may represent a reasonable
estimate for parts of the South but planters in southern Georgia,
Alabama, and Mississippi may have relied more on sweet potatoes
and other crops with corn acreage reduced accordingly. Conversely, operators located in the hill country and parts of the
Carolinas grew *much* more corn. In fact, the ratio of corn to cotton varied considerably from one area to another within the
South. Plantations located within the major cotton-producing
areas showed much lower ratios than those on the periphery of the
region.[3] Moreover, small holdings within the cotton belt concentrated on cotton almost as markedly as did the planters. The census manuscripts indicate that landholding size was much less
significant than location in determining corn/cotton ratios. For
example, a sample of agriculturists in Baldwin County, Georgia

(located 20 or 30 miles northeast of Macon; Milledgeville is the county seat) who produced both corn and cotton in 1850 revealed that only 8 percent planted more acres to corn than cotton, and among the remaining producers the ratios of corn to cotton acreage from about 0.6:1 to about 0.3:1. On the other hand, a similar sample from Jackson County, Georgia (northwest of Athens, on the fringe of the cotton belt) showed all holdings planting more land in corn than cotton with the corn/cotton ratios ranging from about 2:1 up to 10:1 or more.[4] This lack of spatial correspondence between the two crops is revealed strikingly by comparing the maps of cotton and corn production (figs. 2, 3, 22, and 23). Corn most certainly was grown in the cotton belt but the heaviest producing areas were in the hill country, far removed from the core of cotton production.

Corn received much poorer care than cotton, but being hardier it generally did fairly well. In many cases, corn was pushed onto the poorer lands and, since it competed for labor with cotton, was slighted during much of its growth. Both cotton and corn required labor at about the same time during the growing season, and corn lost out when a choice had to be made concerning the allocation of labor. It could be planted somewhat earlier than cotton, perhaps in early April or even March, and when so planted often yielded quite well, maturing before the dehydrating mid-summer temperatures and common short droughts of late summer could do their damage. Such early seeding, however, was all too frequently not the case. The feverish preparation for the coming cotton crop often prohibited such concern for corn, resulting in its being planted well after the cottonseeds were safely in.

In competition with other cash crops such as rice or sugarcane, corn fared no better. Under the prevailing slave labor system with its emphasis on hand methods, both rice and cane were labor intensive and little time remained for other crops. Fortunately, both the rice- and sugar-producing areas were located either along the Mississippi or near seacoasts so that corn was easily and cheaply procured from elsewhere. Too, many rice planters used cracked rice as the staple cereal thus reducing the need for corn. Handicapped by the relatively poor implements used on most southern farms and plantations and committed to a cash crop economy, the grower saw his corn crop for what it

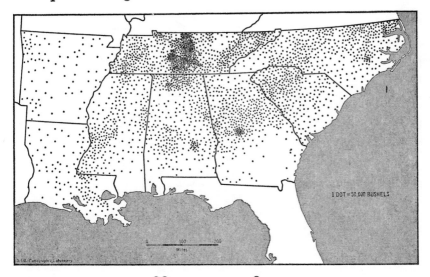

1 DOT = 50,000 BUSHELS

0   100   200
Miles

22.   CORN, 1840.

was – an ancillary crop – gave it a "lick and a promise" and barring
misfortune made, in the words of one diarist, "enough corn to last
me." [5] During most years, he was saved by the ability of corn to do
fairly well on a minimum of care.

The shovel plow, the common horse-drawn implement in the
South, was used to break the corn ground and lay off rows to be
planted. Not always available, it often was replaced by that prime
artifact of southern civilization, the heavy iron hoe, which served
as a breaking as well as a cultivating tool. Planting was done with
the hoe and, in more cases than not, the entire cultivating process
saw no other implement. Depending upon the time planted and
labor available, corn was worked once, perhaps twice, or occasionally three times. In late July or early August, it received its last
cultivation or was "laid by." Sometimes when labor was in short
supply or when excessive rains put cotton "in the grass," all available labor was devoted to the cash crop and the corn was not
worked at all.

In much of the cotton belt, agriculturists commonly planted
field peas or beans among the cornstalks.[6] This intertillage provided vegetables for table use and also served as forage into which
livestock were turned in autumn after the ripe ears had been harvested. Whatever diminution of yield such a practice may have
caused allegedly was offset by the production of peas and forage

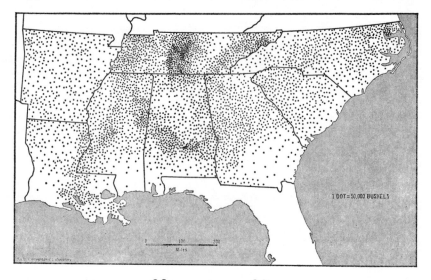

23. CORN, 1860.

and the beneficial effects to the land of such legumes. We have already noted one other use for the already overworked cornfield, the stripping of the corn blades for fodder. This was practiced commonly throughout the South, and fodder often provided the major part of the roughage for work animals used on farms and plantations.[7]

Though certainly less demanding than cotton, rice, or sugarcane, corn required considerable time and labor during harvest. In areas with fairly low late summer and fall precipitation, it was not necessary to haul corn in until after cotton harvest, but most operators thought it advantageous to get it in, away from fall rains and hungry predators.

All things considered, corn did fairly well in the South—not nearly so well as in the heart of the Midwest—but well enough to supply most of the wants of the area. Yields were fairly low, probably less than half of those of Ohio or Illinois, yet high enough to justify its growth. Southern corn was handicapped by a number of factors. In addition to those already mentioned, e.g., methods of cultivation and competition from cash crops, it also suffered from a lack of commercial markets. Since it was virtually ubiquitous, corn was cheap and had little market value. Most producers planned to grow enough for home use but with no organized market for an export trade in grain there was little incentive to produce a surplus. Consequently, trade in corn was only a local enterprise. Bad years often created strong local demands and when shortages occurred, prices were quite high. Many producers took advantage of this fact by selling to neighbors when corn prices were inflated. For example, a Mississippi plantation overseer reported to his employer: "I have put up plenty of pork and will have enough corn to serve the place and I think I will sell some in the spring for I think it will be worth $1.00 per bushel." [8] This was especially true in the newly settled areas, where newcomers commonly bought or borrowed corn from neighbors until a good crop was made. In the case of planters who moved west with a large labor force to settle a new plantation, the quantities involved could have been substantial. Additional markets were in the urban places, since they needed corn for both food and animal feed. In some areas, the corn trade reached impressive proportions and both planters and farmers actively sought markets for corn. This was especially true in the Hill South or North Carolina where the lack of emphasis on cotton, rice, or sugar permitted more attention to corn production.[9] Despite these exceptions, the southern corn trade did not compare with the trade in other cash crops such as cotton and, except for years with widespread crop failure, did not extend over large areas or involve substantial amounts of corn. Usually, when one farmer or planter had corn everybody had corn.

The amount of corn produced in the South in relation to both human and livestock population was huge and it compared quite favorably with other sections of the country. Except for Florida, Louisiana, and South Carolina, all states had a per capita production above the national average in 1840, 1850, and 1860. Most southern states far outstripped the eastern states in corn production and were surpassed only by the Midwest's corn belt. The border states of Tennessee, Kentucky, and Arkansas ranked with the best producers of the Old Northwest. From a regional standpoint at least, there is little doubt that the southern states produced their share of the nation's corn (table 10). Within the South, the distribution of corn production roughly paralleled the distribution of population but was by no means coincident with the cotton belt. Tennessee was by far the heaviest producer with the Nashville Basin being the most important single area. Areas of low production were: Arkansas, Louisiana, the Cumberland

10.   Corn production by states in number of bushels.

	1840 *		1850		1860	
	BUSHELS	PER CAPITA	BUSHELS	PER CAPITA	BUSHELS	PER CAPIT
The East						
Maine	951	1.9	1,750	3.0	1,546	2.5
New Hampshire	1,163	4.1	1,574	4.9	1,415	4.3
Vermont	1,120	3.8	2,032	6.5	1,525	4.8
Massachusetts	1,809	2.5	2,345	2.4	2,157	1.8
Rhode Island	450	4.1	539	3.7	461	2.6
Connecticut	1,500	4.8	1,935	5.2	2,060	4.5
New York	10,972	4.5	17,858	5.8	20,061	5.2
New Jersey	4,362	11.5	8,760	18.0	9,723	14.5
Pennsylvania	14,240	8.3	19,835	8.6	28,197	9.7
Delaware	2,099	26.9	3,146	34.4	3,892	34.8
Maryland	8,233	17.5	10,750	18.4	13,445	19.6
The South						
Virginia	34,578	27.9	35,254	24.8	38,320	24.6
North Carolina	23,894	31.7	27,941	32.2	30,079	30.3
South Carolina	14,723	24.8	16,271	24.3	15,066	21.4
Georgia	20,905	30.2	30,080	33.2	30,776	29.1
Florida	899	16.5	1,997	22.8	2,834	20.2
Alabama	20,947	35.5	28,754	37.3	33,226	34.5
Mississippi	13,161	35.0	22,447	37.0	29,058	36.7
Louisiana	5,953	16.9	10,266	19.8	16,854	23.8
Arkansas	4,847	49.7	8,894	42.4	17,824	41.0
Tennessee	44,986	54.3	52,276	52.1	52,090	46.9
Kentucky	39,847	51.1	58,673	59.7	64,044	55.4
Texas	. . .	. . .	6,029	28.4	16,501	27.3
The West						
Ohio	33,668	22.2	59,079	29.8	73,543	31.4
Indiana	28,156	41.1	52,964	53.6	71,589	53.0
Illinois	22,634	47.5	57,647	67.7	115,175	67.3
Michigan	2,277	10.7	5,641	14.2	12,445	16.6
Wisconsin	379	12.3	1,989	6.5	7,517	9.7
Iowa	1,406	32.6	8,657	45.0	42,411	62.8
Missouri	17,333	45.2	36,215	53.1	72,892	61.7
The U.S.	377,532	22.1	592,071	25.5	838,793	26.9

Source: *U.S. Censuses of 1840, 1850, and 186*

* The years 1840, 1850, and 1860 refer to specific census years when, in fact, the crop da
actually represents the previous year's crop.

Plateau, western North Carolina and the outer coastal plains of the Carolinas, Georgia, Alabama, Mississippi. Florida was the least significant corn producer, though her per-capita production was close to the national average. While southern corn growers did not match the yields of their counterparts in the Old Northwest, the total production of corn came closer to fulfilling the region's needs than was the case with any food crop. This was true despite the heavy demands of both slaves and farm animals.

The demand for corn in the South was substantial. Because it was used as a cereal by both whites and Negroes and as a feed for hogs and work stock, huge quantities were required annually. In areas where slaves made up a large proportion of the population, they undoubtedly were the major corn consumers. The huge body of information on slave care and food rations presents us with a fairly clear picture of the slave cereal diet and makes estimates on slave corn intake fairly accurate. The usual slave ration was a peck of corn or meal per full hand each week and, if followed, this allowance would have amounted to fifty-two pecks or about thirteen bushels per adult each year. References to this amount are so common that there appears to have been little deviation.[10] Occasionally, one and one half pecks were issued but seldom less than one except in the case of children. Frequently, masters allowed as much meal as the worker needed without regard for any set ration.[11]

Southern whites undoubtedly had access to a wider variety of cereal foods than the slave, thus the greater availability of other grain such as wheat may have reduced the intake of corn. Therefore, white consumption of corn probably was less than that of the Negro, but the difference was small. In order to simplify computations an average consumption of thirteen bushels of corn per year for both Negroes and whites will be assumed in this study.

However, to this human use must be added the amount consumed by animals, which varied considerably depending on the availability of other feeds such as oats and the treatment accorded the animals. It was common practice to feed corn to horses and mules but, toward the end of the antebellum period, oats were used increasingly as a substitute. For example, one planter used corn for stock on his Virginia plantation, but after moving to Alabama and starting anew, relied more on oats for animal feed

in order to have corn enough for his slaves.[12] Hogs received corn
during the fattening period but seldom saw corn at any other time
of the year.[13] U. B. Phillips reported an Alabama planter using
four bushels for fattening each hog while other estimates vary up
to eight bushels. A writer to *DeBow's Review* estimated the annual
animal intake of corn in the 1850s at:

horses	5 bushels per head [14]			
cattle	1	"	"	"
sheep	¼	"	"	"
swine	5	"	"	"

Feeling the intake of both sheep and cattle to have been insignificant, the writer has modified these figures somewhat and
has chosen four bushels as the average consumption for swine
and seven and one half bushels for horses and mules. In computing the relation between corn production and consumption, the
following formula is employed:

$$C = \frac{\text{CORN PRODUCTION (bu)}}{(13 \times Z) + (4 \times S) + (7.5 \times H)}$$

Z = number of human consuming units
S = number of swine
H = number of horses and mules

The answer (C) represents a figure which, if more than 1.000,
indicates that corn production (within an areal unit) exceeded
the estimated needs and, if less than 1.000, that corn production
was below the level postulated as necessary for self-sufficiency.

Plotted on outline maps for the entire South, the distribution
of these figures indicate in a general way the level of subsistence
achieved by various areas with the South. Counties with ratios
less than unity were located primarily in the southern portion of
the area with the most consistent groupings being near the Gulf
and Atlantic coasts (figs. 24, 25, and 26). In one or more census
years, scattered counties in the interior were below unity, and by
1860 many of the interior counties were showing deficits as a result of the growing inland cities such as Augusta and Columbus.
The two largest contiguous areas of corn deficits occurred in
coastal Carolina and Georgia and the Gulf coast of Alabama and
Mississippi. Here again, the presence of sizable urban areas along
the coasts with their higher population densities and need for
stock feed greatly affected the county averages.[15]

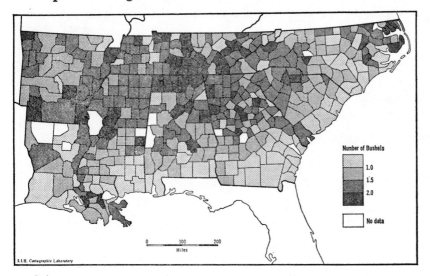

24. CORN PRODUCTION-CONSUMPTION RATIOS, 1840.

Another reason for the low production ratios near the coasts was that these counties lay between the relatively densely settled rice coast and cotton belt and were essentially nonagricultural resulting in very low corn production. The huge herds of livestock reported and the extremely low proportion of improved land lead one to conclude that grazing was the principal occupation and that crop cultivation was a minor activity.

Considering the hypothetical corn deficits in the coastal counties the question of how it was remedied must be raised. One solution was to import corn via ship, and there is evidence that some corn moved into the port cities from outside the region. In addition, many planters turned to alternative foods. Where rice could be grown, rice was consumed in large quantities by whites, and often the cracked rice (grains broken in the milling process) and the poorer grades were fed to slaves.

Counties located inland from the commercial rice-growing area attempted to cultivate small fields of rice for home use, but there the sweet potato was preferred as a replacement for corn in the diet.[16]

If we assume that the production-consumption figure of 1.000 represented an adequate level of production then most counties in the South succeeded in meeting local corn needs. The

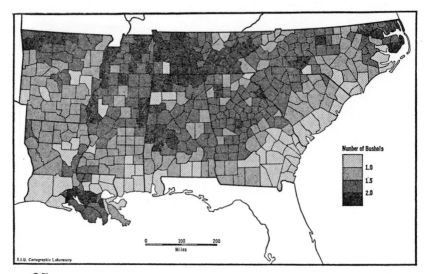

25. CORN PRODUCTION-CONSUMPTION RATIOS, 1850.

exceptions were the coastal counties noted previously, but in their case a reasonable argument can be made for a stronger dependence upon rice and sweet potatoes. Where large urban populations created substantial deficiencies corn was brought in but the total amount was small relative to southern production. Furthermore, a number of counties such as those of the Tennessee Valley and much of the black belt of Alabama, far exceeded this minimum and produced more than twice the amount postulated as necessary for self-sufficiency (figs. 24, 25, and 26).

Small grains

Unlike corn, small grain production was far from universal in the South nor was it important when compared to corn. Some small grains, notably wheat and oats, were grown widely, and in the Hill South and parts of North Carolina were produced commercially. Rice, too, was a commercial crop but its production was confined to a small belt near the coast of the Carolinas and Georgia. Even with these local concentrations the place of small grains in the region's dietary economy was decidedly secondary to the main cereal crop, corn.

The major small grain used for human food was wheat and,

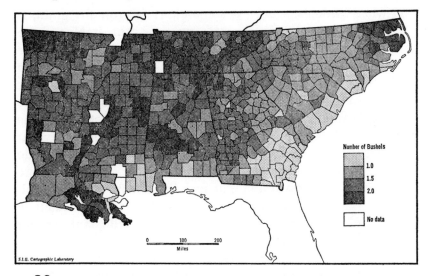

Number of Bushels

1.0

1.5

2.0

No data

0   100   200
Miles

S.I.U. Cartographic Laboratory

26.   CORN PRODUCTION-CONSUMPTION RATIOS,
1860.

when available, it was consumed eagerly. Southern wheat production was not enough to meet the region's needs, and some grain
was imported each year. However, even if we add the amount of
extraregional wheat to that produced locally, it is still doubtful
that southern wheat consumption was anywhere near as high as
that of northerners or westerners. The slave intake was negligible.

The most important factors limiting wheat growing in the
pre–Civil War South are not absolutely clear. The so-called "natural" environment was not quite as favorable for wheat as in other
areas in the country. The relatively high precipitation and warm
temperatures encouraged disease, while the mild winter often
permitted rapid growth during November and December with the
result that later winter "cold snaps" sometimes did considerable
damage to the growing grain. Too, in some areas heavy summer
showers caused lodging and delayed the harvest. Perhaps more
important than climate was the adverse effects of poorly drained
alluvial soils among rivers, especially near the coasts. Wheat
simply did not yield well on such soils since it had a tendency to
grow immense stalks and little grain. Despite these conditions,
though, one finds it difficult to accept environmental conditions
as the only or even the primary cause for the limited production of
wheat. Wheat is (and was) widely grown in most of the South,

and where producers exerted some effort to grow the grain, it yielded fairly well. Yields, of course, were not comparable to those on the best soils of the Old Northwest, but for that matter, neither were southern corn yields and corn was the "chosen" cereal crop of the South. One suspects, then, that the low production of wheat in much of the South reflected as much a conscious choice on the part of farmers and planters as the detrimental effects of the physical environment. It is true that physical limitations to wheat growing were strong factors along the marshy Gulf and Atlantic coasts and in the poorly drained Mississippi floodplain, yet there is little reason for assuming that such limitations extended to all of the South or even to all the cotton belt. Most farmers and many planters of the inland South grew wheat in small quantities, but few planted large acreages.

The problem of determining just why farmers in a given area chose not to grow a certain crop is often a difficult one. In the case of the inland South, it appears that the prime factors inhibiting wheat production had to do with the decided preference shown for corn or cotton. Assuming there were two reasons for growing wheat, e.g., home consumption and commercial market, it appears that corn partially replaced wheat as the cereal crop while cotton replaced it as the money crop. The South's preference for corn may have stemmed not from any recognition of corn as a superior food but simply from its wider availability and lower production cost. These factors most likely led to its early adoption as the ideal cereal for slaves and may have been decisive in its being preferred by many whites. The details of this preference for corn has been discussed elsewhere and, for the moment, it is sufficient to say that corn did replace wheat as a food item and this undoubtedly resulted in less wheat being grown than would otherwise have been the case.

The production of wheat for the commercial market depended to a great extent upon the existence of a market and an organized system for supplying it. Although a local market for wheat may have existed, it was small and often erratic. As for the means of supplying this market, trade channels were either absent or poorly developed in much of the area before the Civil War. The dietary preference already mentioned effectively reduced the regional demand for wheat and at the same time so discouraged the planting, sale, and movement of wheat that extraregional markets, often large and requiring well-organized transportation systems, were out of reach of the small-scale producer. Moreover, wheat is semiperishable and requires somewhat better care in both storage and transit than does cotton which can be left in the weather for some time before excessive spoilage occurs. There is little reason to believe that wheat could not have been sold profitably in extraregional markets if the facilities for moving wheat off the farms into the port cities and onto ships had existed. In his study of South Carolina during the same period, Alfred Smith felt the same factors inhibited the expansion of commercial corn-growing in that state.[17] It is worth noting that Charleston began to receive small but steady quantities of wheat from inland Georgia and South Carolina as soon as the Carolina Railroad reached into the up-country, but by that time cotton was well entrenched as the cash crop and large-scale wheat growing was out of the question.[18]

Perhaps, the most important factor in the lack of large-scale wheat production in the cotton belt was the competition from cotton. Whether grown by farmer or planter, cotton brought in more money than grain, consequently, wheat was pushed out. Faced with diverting labor from the cotton fields to handle a large wheat harvest, most farmers chose to concentrate on the cotton. Rare was the slave who operated the cradle or reaper, and rarer still was the one who was taken out of the cotton patch to follow the harvest. Theoretically, at least, the labor needed for wheat growing did not greatly conflict with the cotton season, but in practice cotton harvesting often extended well into the winter so that there was little time for plowing and planting wheat. Additional conflict occurred in early summer when the labor needed for wheat harvest also was needed for cultivating cotton. A South Carolina correspondent stated the position of wheat in the economy very well when he replied to a Patent Office inquiry:

> I must be allowed to say one thing, though, in favor of us poor Southern farmers, on the subject of growing wheat. Our lot is cast in a cotton region, and no man can be a successful wheat cultivator and cotton planter at the same time: They interfere materially with each other from beginning to end. Wheat is not cultivated for a crop, but a little is put in for family use; and cotton, cotton, cotton won't give us time to do that very well.[19]

Evidence tending to support such a view is the relative distributions of the two crops (figs. 2, 3, 27, and 28). Some wheat was
produced in the cotton-growing counties but the highest production was in North Carolina and Tennessee, away from the core
of the cotton belt. It was here, too, that the most significant wheat
surpluses were produced.

It would be misleading to present too dismal a picture for
wheat in the South. Actually, wheat was widely grown, though
not in large quantities. The agricultural schedules of the census
manuscripts in both 1850 and 1860 recorded a small but significant production in most counties within the South, especially inland counties. Moreover, other evidence supports this view and
suggests that many agriculturists seldom failed to plant a small
crop for family use.[20] The point is that wheat production was relatively small-scale though widespread industry in the South. In
that respect, it was more of a "garden vegetable" than a field crop
in much of the area. For example, a sample drawn from the agricultural schedules of Campbell County, Georgia, in 1850 shows
that about two-thirds of the operators produced wheat but with an
average production of only twenty-three bushels. This would probably have amounted to about two acres planted to wheat, indicating it was seldom more than a "family food" crop.

Southern wheat was almost exclusively winter grown. Planting was done in November or December with the harvest in the
following summer. Like most southern crops during the antebellum period, wheat land received a minimum of soil preparation
after which the seed was scattered and covered with a harrow.
Harvesting was done with a cradle and then the seed was either
flailed or trodden out. These rather primitive methods tended to
restrict the amount of wheat grown, but at the same time there
was little incentive to mechanize, since most planters and farmers grew small quantities they could not justify the use of the
relatively expensive harvesting and seeding equipment that was
becoming available.[21]

Compared with the remainder of the nation the South (excluding Virginia and Maryland) was not outstanding as a wheat
producing region. In total production most southern states surpassed the New England states, but were greatly overshadowed by
Pennsylvania, New York and states of the Old Northwest. In per
capita production, too, the South lagged, though the major east-

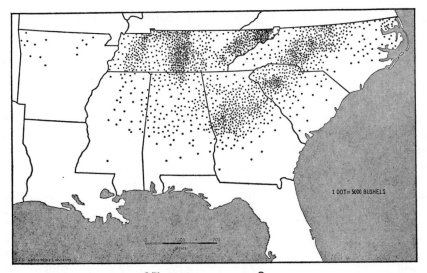

27. WHEAT, 1840.

ern producers, New York and Pennsylvania, had populations large
enough by 1860 to drive the per capita figure below the national
average. Though not included in this study, both Maryland and
Virginia were strong producers. Of the subject states, North Carolina and Tennessee were the highest producers but northern Georgia also grew sizable quantities. Both Mississippi and Alabama
were very poor wheat producers, and in Florida and Louisiana,
wheat production was negligible (table 11).

Wheat consumption in the area is extremely difficult to determine with precision. Unlike pork, where huge quantities were
imported to fill in deficits, the consumption of wheat depended
largely upon the amount locally produced with wheat being imported only in certain areas, such as the coastal cities and plantations, parts of the Alabama black belt, and the river counties of
Mississippi and Louisiana. A good deal of wheat and flour was
imported into the port cities and some trickled into the interior
to be purchased by the more affluent whites but, more often than
not, where wheat was not produced locally, it simply was absent
from the diet.

A major factor contributing to the low southern consumption was the competition from corn. Most white southerners liked
corn bread; in fact, many preferred it to wheat bread. Consequently, it was the dominant bread throughout the region. Fur-

11. Wheat production by states in number of bushels.

	1840		1850		1860	
	BUSHELS	PER CAPITA	BUSHELS	PER CAPITA	BUSHELS	PER CAPITA
The East						
Maine	848	1.7	296	0.5	234	0.4
New Hampshire	422	1.5	186	0.6	239	0.7
Vermont	496	1.7	536	1.7	437	1.4
Massachusetts	158	0.2	31	. . .	120	0.1
Rhode Island	3	. . .	. . .	. . .	1	. . .
Connecticut	87	0.3	42	0.1	52	0.1
New York	12,286	5.1	13,121	4.2	8,681	2.2
New Jersey	774	2.1	1,601	3.3	1,763	2.6
Pennsylvania	13,213	7.7	15,368	6.6	13,042	4.5
Delaware	315	4.0	483	5.3	913	8.1
Maryland	3,346	7.1	4,495	7.7	6,103	8.9
The South						
Virginia	10,110	8.2	11,213	7.9	13,131	8.2
North Carolina	1,961	2.6	2,130	2.5	4,744	4.8
South Carolina	968	1.6	1,066	1.6	1,286	1.8
Georgia	1,802	2.6	1,089	1.2	2,545	2.4
Florida	. . .	. . .	1	. . .	3	. . .
Alabama	828	1.4	294	0.4	1,218	1.3
Mississippi	197	0.5	138	0.2	588	0.7
Louisiana	. . .	. . .	. . .	. . .	32	. . .
Arkansas	106	1.1	200	1.0	958	2.2
Tennessee	4,570	5.5	1,619	1.6	5,459	4.9
Kentucky	4,803	6.2	2,143	2.2	7,395	6.4
Texas	. . .	. . .	42	0.2	1,478	2.4
The West						
Ohio	16,572	10.9	14,487	7.3	15,119	6.5
Indiana	4,049	5.9	6,214	6.3	16,848	12.5
Illinois	3,335	7.0	9,415	11.1	23,837	13.9
Michigan	2,157	10.2	4,926	12.4	8,336	11.1
Wisconsin	212	6.9	4,286	14.0	15,657	20.2
Iowa	155	3.6	1,531	8.0	8,449	12.5
Missouri	1,037	2.7	2,982	4.4	4,228	3.6
The U.S.	84,832	5.0	100,486	4.3	173,105	5.5

Source: *U.S. Censuses of 1840, 1850 and 1860*

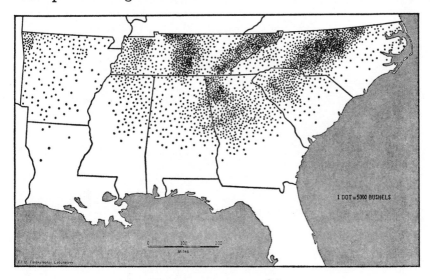

28. WHEAT, 1860.

thermore, the high proportion of slaves in the area, who consumed little or no wheat bread, depressed the overall average consumption even further.

Per capita wheat consumption in the United States during the antebellum period has been estimated at around four bushels.[22] Undoubtedly, southern consumption was well under the national average, just how far below is open to question. This writer doubts that the white consumption was over half the national average, and when the slave population is added, the figure well might have been one bushel per capita or less.

Using intervals of one, two, and four bushels per capita, the production of wheat in the South is shown on figures 29, 30, and 31. An important point to keep in mind is that the maps indicate per capita production only and do not attempt a comparison of wheat production and wheat consumption as was the case with both pork and corn. They do indicate some measure of self-sufficiency but only by implication. For example, one presumes that a county having a per capita production figure of four bushels would consume more flour and be less likely to run short than one having less than two bushels.

The areas most consistently showing high per capita ratios were Tennessee and the Carolina and Georgia Piedmonts. This wheat belt extended westward to include parts of northern Ala-

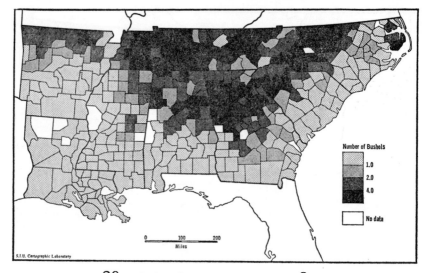

Number of Bushels

1.0

2.0

4.0

No data

0   100   200
Miles

S.I.U. Cartographic Laboratory

29.   WHEAT PER UNIT, 1840.

bama, but the core was in the Hill South. Toward the coasts, wheat production declined fairly rapidly and, except where imported flour moved into the port cities and upriver, consumption probably suffered a similar decline. The increase in the number of counties showing high ratios from 1850 to 1860 appears to reflect a strong renaissance in wheat growing throughout the Hill South. Apparently, the pleas for higher wheat production by the advocates of agricultural reform must have had some effect. This increase in wheat production shown in the 1860 figures must have meant more than simply a "good wheat year," since increasing quantities of wheat moved coastward and both Charleston and Savannah became wheat exporting ports in the late 1850s.[23]

Wheat and corn always have been the major cereals for most American farmers. Other grains were grown and some have achieved prominence in limited areas, but on the whole, agriculturists have remained loyal to wheat and corn. Rye, barley, and buckwheat were grown only as minor crops. Their total production was insignificant in most of the South, and there is little evidence to suggest they were grown for human food. Not only was the total production insignificant, but the agricultural schedules of the census show that few operations bothered with them (or else few bothered reporting them). Oats was much more common

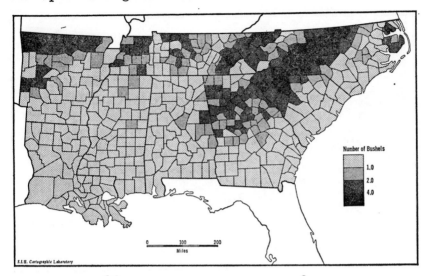

30. WHEAT PER UNIT, 1850.

than the others, but it was used primarily as a feed grain for work
stock and for winter grazing. Oats undoubtedly increased in importance during the antebellum period and, though seldom a food
crop itself, was used so widely as a grain supplement for draft
animals that the amount of corn available for other uses was increased materially.[24]

The production of rice was substantial. In fact, it was one of
the South's leading cash crops, but its distribution was spotty.
Rice was *very* important in certain restricted areas but virtually
absent throughout the remainder of the South. A few counties
along the coasts of Georgia and South Carolina produced the bulk
of the rice grown in the entire country and, for the most part, this
production was intended for cash sale. Within the rice area considerable quantities of rice were consumed by both whites and
blacks. Often the "cracked" or low grade rice was issued to slaves
in lieu of corn, but the best rice was sold since it would bring a
higher price than an equal amount of corn.[25] Although the bulk
of the South's rice was produced in a few counties, there were
many operators farther inland who grew rice on a small scale,
presumably for food only. Often a farmer or planter had a plot of
an acre or two located near a small inland stream which could
be used for irrigation.[26]

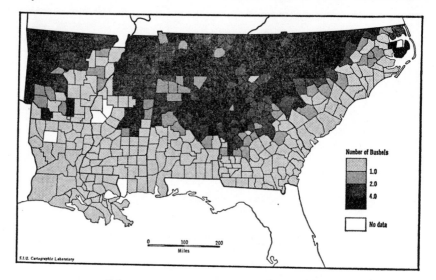

31. WHEAT PER UNIT, 1860.

Rice was reported in the census from 1840 on and figure 32 reveals the production and distribution in 1860. Although the inland rice production is worth noting, in total quantity it was eclipsed by the plantation production near the coasts.

Although our knowledge concerning the southern consumption of minor cereals such as wheat is not as complete as this writer wishes, generalizations about the relative importance of each of the cereals in the economic and dietary pictures of the South are obvious. Corn was the unchallenged favorite among cereal grains, and in total production outranked all others. For example, in almost all counties the ratios of corn to wheat were eight or ten to one and, except for some counties in the Hill South, usually were much higher. Corn was almost the only cereal issued to slaves; it was also the major cereal of whites; and, in addition, was fed to both work animals and hogs.

Wheat was consumed over a wide area, but its role in the diet was a minor one. It was grown in the Hill South in substantial quantities but elsewhere was more of a garden crop than a major field cereal. Wheat flour was seldom issued to slaves, and most chattels rarely tasted wheat bread.

Rice was the only other cereal of any importance on southern tables, but it was grown over such a limited area that its use was

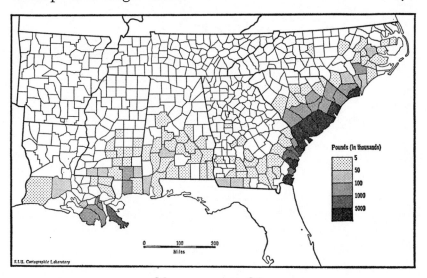

32. RICE, 1860.

by no means universal. All things considered, it must be concluded that the South was "corn country." No other grain came even close to it in popularity or importance.

9 Rounding out the fare

As elsewhere in the country, the garden and orchard were important segments of the southern food supply industry. Both small holders and planters had substantial acreages set aside to supply their fruit and vegetable needs; slaves often tended their own plots; and even urban dwellers cultivated small gardens that supplied "in-season" plants for table use. Throughout the South these plots, ranging in size from a few hundred square feet up to thirty or forty acres, produced cabbages, beans, peas, okra, turnips, potatoes, melons, peaches, scuppernongs, grapes, apples, and other vegetables and fruits for a host of hungry mouths, and though production statistics are lacking, the total quantity must have been enormous. The common generalization is that the yeoman farmers in the inland South were the better food producers, and it is likely that their gardens and orchards were similar to those of farmers elsewhere in the nation. But, the large slaveholder had special problems in providing for the needs of his labor force. Some planted huge acreage and many kept their plots quite well, but most found it difficult to keep a large slave force well supplied with a variety of fruits and vegetables. This section deals with the role of gardens and orchards in the food supply system of the South, and discusses some of the fruits and vegetables involved.

The garden

Southerners had a distinct advantage when it came to producing vegetables. With a growing season approaching three hundred days for most of the area, it was possible for gardens to produce continuously from March to November. The early spring was a real advantage, and southern gardens were always well ahead of those farther north. In writing to her parents in New York, a young North Carolina bride marveled at the early season.

In our garden we have peas, radishes, beets, cabbages and corn up. Plum trees are out of blossom, the peach blossom giving place to fruit and leaves. Crab apple trees are in blossom and others soon will be.[1]

Furthermore, hardy vegetables such as cabbage and turnips commonly were grown during winter, while garden peas and white potatoes were planted for spring harvest. Early planting of other vegetables in February was common, but the major part of the garden was planted in March or early April. A second planting could be made in May or June, and diligent gardeners often planted a third. In fact, many producers maintained huge gardens consisting of continuous plantings of a number of items. Beans, radishes, turnips, butter beans, and sweet corn were planted every few weeks to ensure a good supply of fresh produce. Others, such as okra and summer squash, were favorites that produced all summer long if tended properly and harvested regularly.

A number of vegetables were grown in southern gardens. This was especially true of the more knowledgeable and ambitious planters and farmers who had elaborate gardens in which every conceivable vegetable was represented. On one plantation the list of garden vegetables was so long it resembled a seed catalogue.[2] There were, however, some crops which became regional favorites and they were the plants most widely grown. These included white and sweet potatoes, cowpeas (as opposed to "green" or "garden" or "English" peas), turnips, squash, several kinds of greens, green corn, beans, watermelon, canteloupe, okra, collards, cabbages, green peas, onions, and pumpkins. "Roastin' ears" were a staple though it is likely that much of the green corn consumed in the South came straight from the cornfield rather than as sweet corn from the garden. The tomato, a favorite of twentieth-century southerners, was used very little as a vegetable during antebellum times. It was regarded primarily as an ornament and was more often found among flowers than in the vegetable garden.

The typical garden plot of a rural white family probably varied in size from a quarter acre up to one or two acres. In many cases, though, its size was quite misleading since most southerners planted a number of garden plants as field crops.[3] The garden plot itself contained beans, green peas, squash, collards, okra, cabbage, and a few other vegetables, but many plants were used in such quantities that they could be called field crops. This was especially true where a large labor force was involved. Obviously, fifty to one hundred slaves required acres and acres of vegetable crops.

The most important of these "field vegetables" was the sweet potato. One of the few vegetables that truly can be regarded as southern, it did well in most of the South except the hill and mountain country to the north and, even there, was grown to some extent. Yielding quite heavily with little attention, the sweet potato often replaced corn in the slaves' rations during part of the year. In fact, its high yields, ease of cultivation, and excellent nutritive qualities make one wonder why it was not used even more widely. Being a tropical plant, the sweet potato does best where temperatures remain fairly high. It grew very well throughout the cotton belt and was relied upon increasingly during the antebellum period for food. This was especially true in the southern portions of the Carolinas, Georgia, Alabama, Louisiana, and Mississippi where it partially replaced corn in the diet. A common practice was to plant both corn and sweet potatoes. The potatoes were fed to the slaves first in lieu of corn. After the potato supply was exhausted, planters then fed the corn. Undoubtedly, this was a prudent practice since corn kept better than sweet potatoes. A South Carolina planter recorded his experience in 1836: "Finished eating potatoes 10th March—great rotting from being dug after several frost[s] and put up in rain." [4] Another planter recorded: "Gave out the 1st allowance of *corn* at Old-Fort—Potatoes all used—" (The date was January 13.) Apparently, the potato crop did not always last until January, for the previous year's supply was even shorter; on September 15, he wrote:

> The root potatoes [as opposed to slips] at Wiltown [a plantation] turned out so badly that they [the slaves] will have to finish eating them in a few days and it will be necessary to send up corn. . . . The like has never occurred to us before. . . . [Later, on Sept. 27, he sent] . . . to Wiltown 30 bushels of corn.[5]

Being sensitive to low temperatures, sweet potatoes required special care during winter to keep them from rotting and ensure the next year's "seed" crop against frost. The plant produces seed only in the extreme southern part of the country, therefore the most common means of propagation was by vegetative reproduction. This was accomplished either by allowing the tuber itself to sprout or by cutting branches off the potato vines and rooting them. In addition to the huge quantities stored for food, most operators "banked" a special bank of potatoes through the winter as a seed crop for the next year.[6] A few weeks prior to planting time, these "seed" potatoes were imbedded in a compost in order to encourage sprouting. The sprouts (called "slips" or "draws") were then transplanted into the fields. In planting large acreages, it was difficult to obtain enough slips from the original beds; therefore, southerners took advantage of the potato's excellent rooting qualities by cutting small branches of the older vines and using these cuttings for planting stock. By using this method of propagation, a small early spring planting could be expanded as time and labor permitted. In some cases, this process could be extended well into the summer, and most producers who needed provisions for a large slave force devoted any spare labor to expanding the potato patch.[7] In a letter of instructions one planter expressed what must have been a common goal when he ordered his overseer to "plant as much slip ground as you can possibly get time to plant."[8]

The potatoes started yielding on a small scale by mid-summer. The usual method for early harvest was to dig into the hills and extract a few tubers for immediate use without disturbing the plant. In this way, the plant continued its growth and produced potatoes throughout the summer and into the early fall. The main harvest usually took place in the early fall or after the first frost had killed the vines. The rows were plowed up and the potatoes hauled in from the fields to be "banked" for winter. This method of food preservation, so widespread in America at the time, was used for turnips as well.

The production of sweet potatoes was most heavily concentrated in the southern two-thirds of the area (fig. 33). The potato could be grown farther north, even in the Old Northwest, but its susceptibility to frost and the method of propagation which necessitated "banking" the seed stock and the use of cuttings to multiply the plants limited its use where the growing season was too short.

While the sweet potato made its niche in the southern portions of the South where milder temperatures and longer growing seasons prevailed, the white or "Irish" potato remained a relatively minor garden crop. But in the northern parts of the South

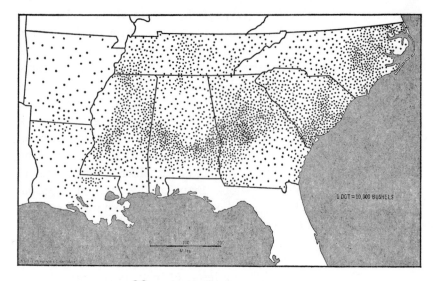

33. SWEET POTATOES.

it became a major garden vegetable (fig. *34*). To be sure, it was grown farther south, even into Florida, yet its preference for cooler temperatures led to its being more common in the interior of the South, especially the northern hill lands. Where the white potato did extend into the Gulf Coast area, it did so as a winter or spring crop. In this respect it often was a complementary crop to the sweet potato. As a Georgia correspondent put it:

> The common or Irish Potato can only be raised successfully as a spring crop. We plant in February and have them . . . by the first of May. . . . After June or July, the sweet potato takes their place on our tables.[9]

The culture of the white potato was similar to that of "yam." [10] Propagation was accomplished by planting bits of the seed potato and allowing them to sprout. However, there was no slip multiplication process such as was the case with the sweet potato. Preservation was a problem with both potatoes. The white potato was harvested in late spring and early summer and seldom could be kept until the next year as either food or seed potatoes. The high summer temperatures and humidity encouraged sprouting; thus, most white potato production was on a relatively small scale for table use during the season. Seed potatoes were for sale during planting season and many producers purchased their seed stock each year.[11]

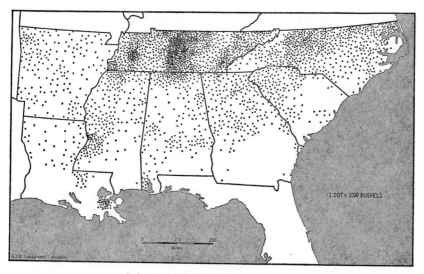

34. WHITE POTATOES.

Another crop grown in quantities large enough to be called a field crop was cowpeas. The production of peas in the South during the antebellum period has not been fully appreciated. Grown on almost all landholding and under different conditions, the pea developed into one of the most important food crops of the South.[12] Usually planted as a field crop, it was useful both for food or animal feed. The most common planting method was to drop the peas in the corn rows to be covered as the corn was "laid by" (given its final cultivation).[13] The peavines then matured while the corn was ripening and the plant was utilized in a number of ways. An early gathering could be made while the peas were green, yielding shelled seed and "snaps" (the entire pods broken into pieces); later the dried peas could be harvested, in which case they were already preserved for winter use. Finally, after gathering enough for household use, both the peas and peavines served to fatten stock. A Georgia planter reported:

> We plant peas in all our corn crop. . . . Of a good season, they will yield some six or eight bushels per acre, in addition to the corn, and serve to fatten our stock after we have gathered the corn, and what peas we want. . . . The most of our bacon is fattened in our pea fields.[14]

Such yields must have represented only the amount gathered, since it was common to leave a substantial portion in the fields for grazing.[15] Some farmers and planters felt that peas were harmful to stock and refused to feed them. Others, after experimenting for a while, found them to be quite palatable.[16] In addition to their value as food items, peas were recognized for their soil-building value. Although the process of nitrogen fixation was not clearly understood, most agriculturists knew that crops did better when they followed peas in a rotation program.

The production of peas reported in the area was substantial, and there is reason to believe that it was much higher than census data shows. The practice of sowing peas among cornstalks and harvesting only a portion of the crop have led to their being under-estimated by the agriculturist and the census enumerator. Benjamin Wailes noted in the 1850s that the Mississippi pea crop of 1849 was far in excess of that enumerated in the census.

> One million of bushels is reported as the production of 1849; but, when it is remembered that a very large portion of the crop is consumed by stock in the field—that being culti-vated . . . mainly for the amelioration of the land, the pe-riod for gathering coming on also in the press of the cotton-picking season; and that consequently, a large proportion of planters save little more than is necessary for seed, it will at once be perceived that the quantity stated in the census re-turns . . . is very greatly below that actually raised.[17]

In his detailed study of census manuscripts Herbert Weaver noted that the census enumerators in Mississippi often ignored the column reserved for peas and beans.[18]

Rivaling or even surpassing cowpeas as a food crop was the turnip. Made famous by the comic strip, "Li'l Abner," it is one of the crops most frequently identified with the South. Although data on production are lacking, the turnip almost surely rivaled the sweet potato in importance and, in some areas, may have been relied on even more. Turnips were sown with a minimum of preparation and could be seeded at any time. The best roots were produced on fall- or winter-grown plants, but by sowing every few months a farmer could keep a steady supply of "greens" or "salet" for table use throughout the year. Turnips were "broad-cast" by hand and covered lightly with a rake, harrow, or crude tree branch drawn by a mule. Once planted, they required no further care and produced leaves sufficient for greens in a very short time. This trait made them a favorite of the new settler; consequently, the turnip usually was the first food item grown on a newly opened landholding in the South, corn notwithstanding.[19]

In Canada and northern Europe, turnips were used commonly for animal feed and there are instances where they were so used in the South, but it is doubtful that such a practice was very common.[20]

Other field-grown food crops were both sugar and sorghum cane, pumpkins, cantaloupes, and watermelons. Pumpkins were usually interplanted with corn to be consumed or marketed in fall, but watermelons and cantaloupes were grown in their own fields. Every landholding had its "patch," and from July until frost the succulent fruits nourished both whites and Negroes. Especially delicious when cooled in spring water, the melons were invariably offered to visitors, and the Sunday afternoon "melon cutting" was a common social custom.[21]

Both garden- and field-grown vegetables unquestionably were important in the southern diet. Unfortunately, quantitative data on the production and consumption of most vegetables are either fragmentary or nonexistent. A few crops, such as peas and potatoes, were enumerated in the decennial censuses, but one strongly suspects that other foods, such as the garden vegetables, might have been equally important in the food economy even though they are missing from the census records. Moreover, one is strongly tempted to regard the twentieth-century South's penchant for turnips and greens, peas, beans, melons, summer squash, and okra as indicative of earlier food choices. One can only guess, however, at their importance in the two or three decades before the Civil War. Undoubtedly their use was common and, judging from present-day attitudes, such foods made up a substantial proportion of the diet. They served to vary the monotonous "hog and hominy" so common in the frontier South; they added vital nutrients to an otherwise substandard fare; finally, they provided necessary food during seasons when the basic foods were in short supply.

Orchard crops

During the late antebellum period most American farmers developed a strong interest in horticulture. Throughout the country farmers were trying all sorts of fruit and nut trees; agricultural journals devoted large sections to horticulture; and many books were appearing on the subject.[22] The South certainly was not immune to this fever; in fact, the area appeared to have excellent prospects for orchard products. Believing the mild climate to be ideal for horticulture, writers in southern periodicals often rhapsodized about orchard crops to the point where one would almost have visualized a latter-day Garden of Eden. Travelers through the South, too, were struck by the mild climate and its possibilities for fruit culture.[23] Naturally, they were more intrigued by the tropical fruits not found in northern areas, but many also commented on the more common fruits such as apples, pears, peaches, plums, and vine fruits which were found over the entire region. For example, Timothy Flint noted that all northern fruits except the apple did well as far south as the Gulf Coast.[24]

In practice, however, orchard crops did not attain the importance in the southern agricultural economy that was expected by some enthusiasts. The interest so evident in the periodical material of the day was not necessarily manifested in well-managed and productive orchards. The more literate and affluent planters as well as many large farmers attempted to plant and maintain sizable orchards, and many were avid experimenters who kept the nurseries in business by their desire to obtain and evaluate new strains. The landholdings of such persons reflected their knowledge and concern about horticulture and were the showplaces of their respected areas. One such holding was that of M. W. Philips of Mississippi which probably represented the ultimate in addiction to fruit culture. His plantation boasted an almost incredible orchard.

> Between seventy and eighty acres were devoted to his orchards, gardens and groves. An apple and peach orchard embraced about fifteen acres; a peach orchard twenty-two acres; a pear and peach orchard, twenty-five acres. . . . It is said that his pear orchard contained as many as sixty varieties of pear trees.[25]

More common, however, were the less imposing, often poorly tended orchards of the disinterested operators. Perhaps, the more usual picture of most plantations and farms was that of a more limited plot of from one to five acres upon which peaches, apples and a few pears were planted. Adjacent to the orchard or garden were probably one or more scuppernong or other grape vines. The peach was the favorite fruit in most of the South and was prized as food either fresh, dried, or preserved.[26] If sufficient quantities were produced, the surplus was fermented to wine and distilled into brandy. Many farmers fed them to hogs, as they were considered very nutritious, and often were encouraged to plant orchards to serve specifically for animal feed.[27] Apples were grown as far south as the Gulf Coast but did better to the north, closer to the mountains, where they became more common than peaches. In some areas, apples were abundant enough to enter the intraregional trade, with the northern areas supplying fruit to the towns and plantations farther south.[28] Other fruits such as pears, plums, figs, citrus fruits, and vines were grown but were relatively minor compared to peaches and apples. The typical southern agriculturist seldom bothered to maintain the numerous varieties of vines and trees available; he simply concentrated on the few he knew best.

On the whole, orchards and vineyards in the South were not outstanding, at least not when considered in relation to the areas of commercial production elsewhere. Travelers often commented on orchards and fruit growers, occasionally quite favorably, yet the efforts must have been relatively unimpressive.[29] Solon Robinson, often sympathetic in his remarks about the South, delivered a rather severe indictment against southern fruit producers when he said: "Suitable as all this country is to produce fine fruit, there is a criminal neglect, upon the part of the planters, that they do not plant orchards sufficient to feed themselves and all their people [slaves]." [30] Andrew Soule, in discussing orchards and orchard production in the South, concluded that a great deal of progress had been made prior to the Civil War in the development of the fruit industry, but that it was primarily in the realm of experimentation and represented the framework upon which postbellum orchard developments would be based. By and large, he felt the South was in a rather poor position in comparison with other areas.[31]

After studying documents relating to antebellum southern agriculture in detail, (and having grown up in Georgia) it is difficult for this writer to disagree with Soule's conclusions insofar as they relate to commercial orchard production, yet one suspects a rather large local production of orchard crops not intended for the commercial market. As such, it well might have gone relatively unnoticed by the traveler. Southerners always have had some rather peculiar habits concerning the planting of vines and trees, preferring not to have formal orchards but rather a loose agglomeration of plants scattered about the farmstead. The better-organized planters who wished to provide fruit for all the labor force generally kept their orchards intact to cut down clandestine depredations by hungry slaves. However, the smaller planters and farmers had trees scattered all over; some peach trees in the hog lot, a few apple trees in the mule pasture, plum trees by the barn, pear trees in the garden—each nook and corner had its own tree with each being a shrine for the children during fruit season. Southerners loved vine fruits (an affection that still persists), not so much the imported grapes as scuppernongs or muscadines grown, not in rows normally used for grape vineyards, but on "arbors" often covering several hundred square feet. On the whole, the rather fragmented orchards so commonly found throughout the South must have been relatively unimpressive to the traveler, yet those trees and vines played an important role in supplying food.

Slave provision patches

The slave garden plot certainly was widespread in the South. Frederick Law Olmstead, the best known of the travelers through the South, noted their existence frequently and is perhaps the source for many later references to such patches.[32] Other contemporaries also observed these provision patches, and the frequency of their comments is a strong argument for assuming the widespread existence of such plots.[33] Apparently, many planters felt it was to their advantage to encourage gardens, as they contributed materially to the diet of the slaves. Although such gardens were quite common throughout the area, there is reason to believe the practice was most common among the rice coast plantations. L. C. Gray felt that this might have been due to the prevalence in the coastal area of the task system which provided the slave with free time he could utilize in cultivating the garden.[34]

The crops grown in these provision patches probably reflected the special likes of the slave or perhaps the plants he knew best. Vegetables were the items usually found in the plots, with potatoes, peas, beans, turnips, and greens being the favorites. Corn was the cereal usually grown. On occasion, tobacco may have been tried.[35]

The importance of such plots as food producers depended

upon the size of the plot and the proportion of produce sold. Estimates of plot sizes range up to about two acres.[36] Although some
plots may have been as large as two acres, the average must have
been less. One planter allotted an acre to each male slave, while
Olmsted reported half an acre per family on a Georgia rice plantation.[37] Considering the physical arrangement of some of the
plantations the writer has had occasion to observe, it seems that
one acre or less would be the more common size. Cabins arranged
50 feet or so apart would allow room for about half an acre behind
each cabin, providing the garden plots did not extend more than
100 or 125 feet back from the cabin. Of course it is possible that
additional plots were granted some distance from the slave quarters, but most planters were more apt to plant a common garden
than grant such dispersed plots.

It seems likely that a patch from half an acre to an acre in
size would, if well tended, keep a family in vegetables throughout
the season. Perhaps the larger families could have used more
space, but it must be remembered that the plots normally were
not intended to be the major food supplier, but rather to supplement the basic allowance. The rations issued by the master often
included sweet potatoes, peas, turnips, and sometimes other vegetables, in which case the garden plots would have been more than
adequate to fill out the remaining needs.[38] However, some evidence suggests that many planters were lax in providing regular
vegetable rations when the slave was working his own patch. All
too frequently, the planter or overseer issued cornmeal and meat
only, letting the hands worry about making all the vegetables.[39]

Of greater importance to the overall question of slave garden
output was the practice of selling, rather than consuming, the produce coming from these patches. The effects of these sales are not
measurable, yet the frequent reference to slaves selling produce
merits consideration. Where urban areas were nearby, slaves occasionally were allowed to go into town to market their output. A
traveler in the rice plantation area remarked:

> On the country side was heard the song of the Negroes as
> they rowed their boats up the river on their return from the
> city, whither they had taken their small wares—eggs, fowls,
> and vegetables—for sale, as they do two or three times a
> week.[40]

Where urban markets were not convenient, the goods were traded
to itinerant peddlers or, more often, sold to the master.[41] Olmsted,

while on board a boat bound for Mobile, noted that Negroes came
on board the craft at each landing to sell goods to the cook.[42] On
the whole, there is little doubt but that a substantial proportion
was sold either on the premises or traded at nearby markets.[43]

Related to the practice of allowing slaves to sell produce
from their gardens was the granting of plots specifically for the
production of cash crops. There is no way of distinguishing between the two types of plots. The cash crop plot probably grew out
of a growing realization among slave owners that their chattels
worked and behaved better when given some incentive. The
slaves' desire for some "luxury" goods beyond what they were issued was evident from the very early years of slavery. In order to
provide these amenities, many planters allowed plots of land
upon which the slave could grow cash crops to be sold or bartered
to bring in the goods most slaves fancied. On occasion, planters
allowed "rows of corn" rather than a patch in order to give the
workers a little income.[44] The practice might well have evolved in
an attempt to prevent stealing, since planters found that the Negroes would steal livestock and machinery and trade them to peddlers at night in order to obtain desired goods.[45] On the other
hand, the cash crop plots themselves tended to fall into disfavor
primarily because they encouraged a different sort of stealing,
that is, pilfering from the master's crop in order to augment their
own yields. Apparently, the temptation to pilfer was quite strong,
and when slaves were allowed to grow corn or cotton it was easy
to add a little of the master's crops with their own. This, together
with the slaves' tendency to exhaust themselves on their own
crops rather than the master's, led to sharp criticism of the system.

> It was, at one period, much the custom of planters to give
> each hand a small piece of land, to cultivate on their own
> account, if they chose to do so; but this system has not been
> found to result well. It gives an excuse for trading, and en-
> courages a traffic on their own account, and presents a
> temptation and opportunity, during the process of gathering,
> for an unscrupulous fellow to mix a little of his master's pro-
> duce with his own.[46]

Other reasons for the dissatisfaction with the system was stated
by a correspondent to the *Southern Cultivator*.

> Most persons allow their Negroes to cultivate a small crop
> of their own. For a number of reasons this plan is a bad one.

It is next to impossible to keep them from working their crops on Sabbaths. They labor on nights when they should be at rest . . . they will pilfer to add to what corn or cotton they may have made.[47]

Such attitudes toward the granting of cash-crop plots may have extended to the garden plots as well, since there was a strong temptation to convert even the garden edibles into more desirable luxury items.

Another variable in this evaluation of the slave garden patches was the care such plots received. It is quite possible that some slaves learned quite a bit about gardening and were success-ful in their own plots, but it is questionable whether the typical slave was competent in crop raising on his own. Of course, he could learn from the master or overseer, but this transfer of knowledge must have been limited. Moreover, the slave was scarcely in a position to expend much labor on his plots, since he often was required to work from "sun to sun" six days a week. Only where the task system was employed did he have time off from his regular duties to work his own provision plot. Contem-porary observers reported that the slave gardens were poorly tended, and one suspects that they received poorer treatment than the fields of the master.[48]

Conclusions regarding the output and importance of slave provision patches are quite shaky. It is probable that most plant-ers in the South granted at least small garden plots of perhaps half an acre to an acre in size and that these plots were substantial producers of food crops. Their effectiveness as food producers was lessened somewhat by poor management practices and lack of skill on the part of the slave. Moreover, their importance in the slave's food supply was diminished further by the slave's own practices of selling or bartering the produce rather than consum-ing it. Of course this food often remained on the premises or was later consumed in the urban areas thereby contributing to the lo-cal food supply even though it might have been lost to the slave.

10 Making up the shortage

In the preceding chapters, the areal variation in the production and consumption of foodstuffs in the South was emphasized. In that discussion, some areas were cited as having had a relatively low production of one or more food commodities. Presumably, this resulted either in a lower consumption of such foods or a movement of foodstuffs into the area to satisfy the need. It is with the latter alternative that this section deals.

The sources for foodstuffs involved in the southern food trade were varied. In some cases, there was a local movement of surplus items from farm to town or even from one landholding to another. In others there was a movement of food from adjacent regions within the South such as the trade connecting Alabama and Tennessee or the Carolinas and Tennessee. Still other sources were extraregional such as the Old Northwest, the West Indies, or Europe.

Intraregional trade

A notable characteristic of southern economic development was the comparatively slow urban growth, and hence few well-developed interior market channels. Also the nature of the plantation-slave system and the extraordinary emphasis placed upon cotton inhibited the development of facilities for trade in other commodities. The system was highly specialized and controlled by the cotton merchants and was designed to move the principal cash crop out of the area.

Despite the lack of a well-organized marketing system, there was a small but significant local sale or exchange of goods throughout the South. Evidence of this commerce is rather spotty, but there are enough references to such a trade to substantiate its existence. For example, the minor towns in the cotton belt functioned as local markets for nearby farmers who brought produce to trade for merchandise. In addition, the country store acted as a collecting point for produce which was resold to nearby agriculturists in short supply. In his detailed study of the southern country store, Lewis Atherton found that most storekeepers accepted a wide variety of goods in trade and were compelled to dispose of such items either through the wholesaler to pay off debts or by resale to local consumers across the counter. In some cases, storekeepers loaded goods on a wagon and peddled through the country in order to dispose of accumulated produce.[1] If the store were located in a small town with a substantial nonagricultural population, the merchant had an easier market for the goods he had accumulated, and the small cities offered an even better and more concentrated market. The larger cities, of course, had access to goods from outside the region, but it is quite possible that most of the provisions handled in the country and small town stores were of southern origin and much was produced locally (excepting, of course, items such as salt, coffee, tea, and other exotic foods). Olmsted noted small farmers moving produce into the towns for sale or barter and, in his opinion, most of the southern towns were "mainly supplied by the poor country people."[2] These people brought meat, grain, poultry, eggs, butter, vegetables, and fruit into town for trade or sale. In cases where the country stores and towns could not absorb this produce, it moved out into the port cities via the wholesale houses. It is more likely, though, that the greater portion of the food produced locally was consumed in the towns or on plantations nearby.

The importance of this local trade is difficult to estimate. Certainly it was essential to the small holders who marketed the goods, and it well may have made up a substantial proportion of the foodstuff trade of the merchant. Our best evidence on this trade comes from a number of extant store accounts which show a surprisingly large over-the-counter trade in many foodstuffs.[3] A variety of items were handled by the small-scale retailers, but for most consumers the food sales were quite repetitious.[4] For example, one North Carolina ledger revealed steady sales of pork.[5]

July 15, 1854   *John Gilbert 13 lbs. bacon $1.30*
July 26   "   *Charles Savy 21 lbs. bacon $2.10*
July 27   "   *Edward Coffey 22 lbs. bacon $2.20*
July 28   "   *John Gilbert (by wife) 50 lbs. bacon $5.00*

Another North Carolina store devoted entire ledgers to the meat trade and the individual accounts indicated that many persons were regular customers. One man spent $47.17 ¾ on meat at 4 to 8 cents per pound from May 9 to August 19, 1837 with no single purchase amounting to more than $5.00. In addition to pork, he also bought beef, mutton, and lamb.[6] Pork undoubtedly was the main southern meat, but beef and mutton were sold frequently, and in some cases it is clear that the animals were killed and sold very quickly. For example, a man in Mecklenburg County, North Carolina, kept detailed records of both slaughter and sales. On one occasion, there were twelve successive ledger entries for the sale of beef, the smallest being 13 pounds and the largest 102.[7] In addition to meat, the major cereals and a host of other items appear on an individual's account. In order to give the reader some notion of the nature and frequency of store purchases, a partial account of one customer named James Dorin is given.[8]

November	22, 1853	1½	bu.	corn
	29, 1853	10	lbs.	bacon
December	6, 1853	1½	bu.	corn
	9, 1853	47	lbs.	beef
	14, 1853	32	lbs.	"broken meat"
	20, 1853	2	bu.	corn
	23, 1853	31	lbs.	flour (and cash)
January	5, 1854	2	bu.	corn
	13, 1854	32	lbs.	pork
	17, 1854	2	bu.	corn
	26, 1854	29¾	lbs.	pork
	31, 1854	2	bu.	corn
February	10, 1854	29½	lbs.	pork
	11, 1854	2	bu.	corn
	23, 1854	2	bu.	corn
	24, 1854	28	lbs.	bacon
March	7, 1854	2	bu.	corn
	9, 1854	33¼	lbs.	bacon
		8	lbs.	salt
		½	bu.	I. potatoes
	17, 1854	2	bu.	corn
	24, 1854	37¾	lbs.	bacon
	30, 1854	2	bu.	corn

April	10, 1854	23¼	lbs.	bacon
	11, 1854	2	bu.	corn
	14, 1854	18	lbs.	flour
	27, 1854	2	bu.	corn
		25	lbs.	bacon

If this ledger represents his only food source, then Mr. Dorin and his family used 157 pounds of bacon, 91 pounds of pork, and 79 pounds of beef during the period. Other foods totaled 25 bushels of corn, 49 pounds of flour, and half a bushel of white potatoes; an impressive list of purchased food, though not unreasonable if we assume it to have gone to an entire family. There were other accounts, too: small dabs sold at infrequent intervals, often on credit—a few pounds of meat, half a bushel of meal or grits, coffee, salt—apparently the random purchases of farmers who rarely made trips to the store. In some cases, ledger entries for a single individual were separated by a period of four to six months. In others, weekly or biweekly purchases were made. The examples run into the hundreds, and the variations are legion. If we can visualize dozens of similar accounts in each of the hundreds of stores from Virginia to Texas, then the foodstuffs needed to sustain such a trade must have been huge.[9] To be sure, not all the food items were locally produced, but neither were they all imports. A portion of the pork may have been imported, especially in the marginal producing areas outlined earlier. Some hogs undoubtedly were drove animals slaughtered and cured by the retailer. Beef was surely slaughtered locally, though it may have traveled from the Hill South on the hoof.

Undoubtedly, both North and South Carolina utilized "drove" beef, but this writer feels that the numbers were small and their importance to the total meat supply quite insignificant. For example, one store account lists periodic sales of small quantities of beef, but the entries are punctuated with notes on periodic slaughterings. Usually, the person making the entry identified the animal (such as the "Fletcher heifer," the "Wells heifer," or the "Ferguson bull") so specifically that a local origin is almost certain.[10] Most likely, the locally produced foods were more common where small farmers prevailed.

In those areas dominated by intensive cotton growing the factor was an important food retailer and the emphasis was on quantity buying. Here the sales were quite different, and very

likely local products were less significant. The account of William
M. Otey with Mr. J. M. Devlin of Yazoo City is an example. Otey
lived in Meridianville, Alabama, but the account is for a Yazoo
County plantation. Compare his account with that of James
Dorin.[11]

1852

March 15, 1852	75	lbs.	coffee
	125	lbs.	sugar
	2	bbl.	molasses
	1	bbl.	flour
	1	bbl.	I. potatoes
April 14	1	sk.	salt
	1	gal.	whiskey
June 11	3	bbls.	Mess Pork
July 5	6	bbls.	Mess Pork
Aug. 7	1	sk.	salt
	2	gals.	whiskey
Sept. 8	1	bbl.	molasses
22	1	gal.	whiskey
Oct. 30	1	sack	salt
Dec. 20	3	gals.	whiskey

1856–1857

Dec. 12, 1856	1	bbl.	sugar
	1	bag	coffee
	1	sk.	salt
23	2	gals.	whiskey
Jan. 3, 1857	2	sks.	salt
31	1	bbl.	flour
	1	bbl.	I. potatoes
	1	sk.	salt
April 2, 1857	4	bbls.	pork
	1	bbl.	molasses
May 12	2	sks.	salt
June 17	1	gal.	whiskey
	1	loaf	sugar
	15	lbs.	rice

Aug.	21	2	bbls.	pork
		1	sk.	salt
Oct.	30	1	sk.	salt
Nov.	25	1	bbl.	pork
		3	sks.	salt
Dec.	25	3	sks.	salt

Note that the term "Mess Pork" (June 11, July 5) is virtual proof that he was dealing in western rather than locally produced pork. Note, too, that he bought no pork until late summer when he had "run out" of his own meat. Undoubtedly, this kind of account was much more common in the plantation areas, especially those areas in a position to deal easily with factors in the port cities.

Not all the local food trade was carried on by stores. In many cases itinerant merchants roamed about the countryside trading with small farmers and slaves. In fact, a North Carolinian used peddling as a means of selling his own crops and animals. After producing enough to make a journey worthwhile, he would set out from home on selling trips lasting several days or weeks, driving cattle and sheep or pulling wagons loaded with corn or bacon. For example, on Dec. 4, 1844 he left for Greensboro with five head of cattle and five loads of corn to sell. Apparently, he slaughtered along the way as he recorded selling "halves" and "quarters." On another occasion he sent 1,595 pounds of bacon consisting of twenty hams and eight shoulders to Charlotte for sale there.[12]

In addition to the movement of foodstuffs into the town or country store and the redistribution of these goods, there was some exchange between individual landholders. The dependence of the larger planters upon the small holders for a portion of their foodstuffs has long been recognized.[13] In general, this has been interpreted as a tie between the cotton planters and the more diversified farmers on the periphery of the cotton belt. However, in addition to this trade, there was some exchange among farmers and planters located adjacent to each other. Often small surpluses of corn, pork, wheat, poultry, eggs, butter, or even fodder were sold, exchanged, or simply borrowed.[14] The terse journal entries of a Virginian illustrate what must have been typical in much of the South.[15]

Oct. 25, 1842   *Let Mr. Trotter have six dozen eggs.*

Aug.   9, 1843   *Lent 36 lbs. of bacon, 7 lbs. of lard and half*
bushel of salt to Leatherwood (another
plantation).

[undated]   *Loaned Mr. A. Thos. Jones 11 lbs. of bacon*
to be returned when Ned returns from
Lynchburg.

Aug. 11, 1843   *Let Mrs. Smith have 7½ lbs. of butter.*

Often foodstuffs were traded for other goods or services. For example, small cotton producers who could not afford to build cotton gins took their crop to nearby plantations for ginning for which they sometimes paid in produce.[16] Where one person or family owned several plantations, it was common to shift foodstuffs from one holding to another.[17] In some cases shortages on one plantation were remedied by shifting manpower from one holding to another.[18] Perhaps the extreme example of this specialization of production was seen in the operation of the Isaac Franklin estates. He had holdings in Tennessee and Louisiana and attempted (though not always successfully) to produce enough corn on the Tennessee plantation to supply the needs of the other farther south.[19]

In addition to the local trade, there was a sizable transfer of goods from one part of the South to another. Perhaps its most significant segment was that which linked the Hill South with the food-deficit areas in the cotton belt. Farmers producing hogs, cattle, and some field crops sought an outlet by moving both live animals and produce into the Deep South. Unfortunately, though, the data on this trade are scanty and fragmentary, and an accurate assessment of its importance to the region's food economy is very difficult. Much of the trade was carried on by farmers and drovers with virtually no central point where records were compiled. Moreover, the ultimate destination of much of the trade is difficult to determine, since some of the routes led into Georgia and Alabama while others supplied the Carolinas. Too, it is possible that a portion of the trade bypassed the southern market by moving into the port cities to be exported (however, in view of the evidence presented in this study, such an export trade must have been small). Finally, a substantial portion of the droving traffic was in work animals rather than animals intended for food and, therefore, of no interest to us here.

The region supplying live animals to the Deep South was primarily central and eastern Tennessee and central Kentucky. Within this area a number of farmers were especially important as livestock producers, and a substantial livestock surplus developed. In Tennessee the most outstanding areas were the valleys of East Tennessee and the Nashville Basin. In Kentucky the lush Bluegrass Basin produced enormous numbers of livestock, and near the Ohio River a number of small valleys as well as that of the Ohio River itself produced surplus animals for sale in the East and South.[20]

The routes used in the droving trade varied considerably, depending upon the source region and the ultimate market area. While the minor routes in the less mountainous parts of central and western Tennessee and Kentucky as well as the area across the Ohio River are not too well known, they probably began in the most intensive cattle producing areas, namely the basins of Kentucky and Tennessee and the Ohio River valley, and then trended southward and eastward. In Kentucky they merged into the Wilderness Trail. Once in the major Appalachian Valleys the routes passed southward into Tennessee (fig. 35). Apparently, the trail leading through Cumberland Gap to the Holston River was used by drovers bound for both the East and South as the Wilderness Road connected easily to the Great Valley and ultimately tidewater Virginia and Maryland. In fact, this is one of the factors that makes quantitative estimates of the droving trade through Cumberland Gap difficult. The stock going through the gap could have gone either south or north, yet it would have been counted as moving through the gap. In Tennessee, Knoxville became the center from which routes radiated to Georgia, the Carolinas, and Alabama. The South Carolina and North Carolina route was via the French Broad River into North Carolina at Asheville and then to eastern North Carolina or through Saluda Gap and along the Saluda River into South Carolina.[21]

The Georgia route branched off at Knoxville and moved down the Tennessee River and entered the state near Chattanooga or to the east of Chattanooga via Unicoi or Woodys Gap.[22] Georgia was also reached from South Carolina simply by crossing the Savannah or Tugaloo Rivers and entering the state from the east.[23]

Alabama was served from two general directions. Drovers who had begun their drives in East Tennessee, or had entered

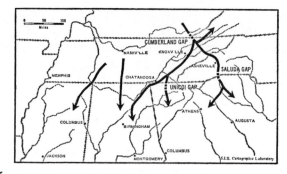

35. DROVING ROUTES INTO THE SOUTH.

Tennessee via the Cumberland Gap, simply moved down the Tennessee River valley into North Alabama. Drovers from farther west in Tennessee and Kentucky tended to converge on Nashville from which they followed the Natchez Trace into western Alabama and possibly Mississippi. In Alabama drovers going south could market their goods along the relatively thickly settled Tennessee River valley or they could move on to the black belt where plantations were most numerous. If this market was insufficient then Mobile could absorb the remainder. Apparently, it was not uncommon for the drover to penetrate rather deeply as there is reference to Florida importing hogs and mules from the interior states via the drover.[24] Being adjacent to a major waterway, Mississippi had easy access to goods moving out of the Old Northwest and was less of a market for foodstuffs moving overland than either Alabama, Georgia, or the Carolinas.

The kinds of livestock driven to southern markets seemed to be limited only by the kinds available in the source regions. While mules, cattle, and hogs were most in demand, there must have been a good market for almost anything, as sheep, goats, and even turkeys and geese were, on occasion, moved along the trails.[25]

Cattle drives to market involved both beef and work cattle. Their quality depended upon where they were bought and the treatment they received in the process of traveling. Most were improved somewhat from the "native" stock of colonial Carolina, yet few were anywhere near purebred. The Durham had been introduced relatively early and was a favorite in the mountains of Tennessee and North Carolina. In Kentucky the cattle would most likely have had some Shorthorn ancestry. Moreover, it is likely that the cattle were, on the average, better than the cattle within the Deep South.

Hogs eclipsed all other stock in both numbers and importance; there were five to eight times as many hogs involved in the trade as all other large animals combined. In addition to whatever need for hogs there might have been in the plantation area, a sizable market also existed in the towns and cities of the area. Columbia, Greenville, Augusta, Savannah, Macon, Montgomery, Mobile, and Tuscaloosa were small by eastern standards, yet their inhabitants had to have meat. But, in addition to the amount consumed by their own inhabitants, these centers served also as "regional markets" to which the drover could turn in order to dispose of unusually large herds.[26]

Sometimes the drives were conducted by the producing farmers themselves, but often it was the experienced professional drover who dominated, making the trip once or twice each year. The professionals either purchased the stock for resale later or received animals on consignment to be paid for after the drive. Occasionally, drovers banded together but usually each drover hired enough assistants, often young boys, to handle the animals he was driving.[27] Reportedly, herds of up to one thousand hogs were driven, but more often the drovers handled only a few hundred head. Cattle, horse, and mule herds were smaller, seldom numbering more than one hundred to two hundred, and frequently herds of a few dozen were seen.[28]

Estimates on the relative importance of these drives in the total southern trade are difficult. Unlike the river trade of New Orleans where detailed records were kept, the routes were so varied and the trade so unorganized that it is almost impossible to get year-by-year figures. Some idea of the size of the overland trade is indicated by the animals driven through Cumberland Gap (table 12). As mentioned previously, these numbers do not necessarily represent the total southern trade accurately, since animals passing through the gap conceivably have gone either north or south depending upon the market. Moreover, those animals destined for the southern market were augmented by stock grown in Tennessee.

A favorite route across the Blue Ridge was the French Broad River valley, and along this stream many of the animals destined

12. Animals driven through Cumberland Gap.[29]

YEAR	SWINE	CATTLE	SHEEP
1835	72,074	2,485	. . .
1838	68,764	4,540	3,250
1842	54,813	2,406	718
1850	43,000	. . .	. . .
1851	21,000	. . .	. . .
1853	53,164	. . .	. . .
1854	11,100	. . .	. . .

for the Carolinas and Georgia passed. Though data on the route are scanty and probably unreliable, it appears that more animals passed through the French Broad River valley than through Cumberland Gap (table 13). This is understandable since the Tennessee Valley was a major livestock producing area, and it lay south of Cumberland Gap.

A number of routes into western Georgia and Alabama also were used during the period, but based on the production/consumption deficiencies calculated earlier it is unlikely that the

13. Animals driven through the French Broad River valley.[30]

YEAR	HOGS	CATTLE
1840	52,255	3,243
1841	54,786	3,049
1842	62,649	3,318
1843	52,642	3,333

numbers of animals moving via these routes were comparable to those that traveled through the French Broad Valley.

General estimates on the total southern trade vary, but it is possible that the annual hog trade may have involved as many as 150,000 head and the cattle trade varied from about 5,000 to 10,000 annually. Charles T. Leavitt placed the hog trade at 120,-000 in 1842, 80,000 in 1850, and 100,000 in 1860.[31] These figures are somewhat higher than the hypothetical needs based on the production/consumption method for 1840 and 1850, but somewhat lower in 1860. According to this writer's estimate, deficits in the inland counties amounted to a total of about 75,000 hogs in 1840, 50,000 in 1850, and 165,000 in 1860 (table 14). In any case, both estimates show the same general trends. If, however, we accept the notion that there was some increase in pork production during the late antebellum years based on a higher slaughter weight per animal, then the deficit postulated for 1860 is much too high. Moreover, if Genovese's assertion that drove animals were heavier than those produced in the Deep South is true, then the number of hogs needed to supply the area's needs is reduced

. *Pork deficiencies in inland areas.*

	1840		1850		1860	
	PORK NEEDED (TONS)	HOG EQUIV. (140 LBS. PER ANIMAL)	PORK NEEDED (TONS)	HOG EQUIV. (140 LBS. PER ANIMAL)	PORK NEEDED (TONS)	HOG EQUIV. (140 LBS. PER ANIMAL)
abama *	...	...	...	...	300	4,300
orgia **	1,400	20,000	1,500	21,400	4,200	60,000
rth Carolina	2,000	28,500	800	11,400	2,600	37,100
uth Carolina ***	1,900	27,100	1,300	18,500	4,500	64,000
tal	5,300	75,600	3,600	51,300	11,600	165,400

Source: *Calculated from U.S. Censuses of 1840, 1850, and 1860.*
)oes not include black belt counties.
Includes several counties containing towns (e.g., Augusta, Macon, Columbus) that im-
rted some meat from the coast.
* Additional pork may have moved through the area to the coast.

even further.[32] Finally, table 14 assumes no intrastate movement of pork, a fact which may be in error since there must have been some trade between hill counties and deficit counties within each state.[33]

In addition to the overland movement of live animals from the Appalachians into the Deep South, there was a notable trade in provisions over the same routes. The Tennessee River acted as an artery for the movement of goods from East Tennessee into Alabama, but the river was relatively unreliable for regular steamboat traffic and both the supply and market tended to be erratic.[34] However, cured pork, flour, fruit, and other foods easily moved the relatively short distance from Tennessee to the Great Bend of Alabama by small boat, though the total quantity was not great.[35] The construction of the Florence bridge in the 1840s gave middle

Tennessee and the northern tier of Alabama counties an outlet for their production of foodstuffs. Toward the end of the antebellum period the penetration of the hill country by railroads was beginning to affect the overland provision trade. After the road into East Tennessee was completed it was used extensively, and by the end of the antebellum period it may have partially replaced droving as a means of moving provisions into Georgia.[36] The eastern droving route into Carolina, however, remained important until well after the war. Not until the railroad was able to penetrate the Blue Ridge barrier did droving suffer a decline, and even then local droving continued on a small scale.

Not all the trade linking the Appalachian hill country originated in Tennessee and Kentucky. Unquestionably, they were major suppliers, yet many farmers in the extreme inland counties of Mississippi, Alabama, Georgia, and the Carolinas had agricultural outputs similar to those of Tennessee and Kentucky. Wheat and corn were fairly important items and, judging from the per capita production in some counties, a sizable surplus was produced. John W. Baker, in discussing the early years in Hart County, Georgia (located about 100 miles upriver from Augusta), lists corn and wheat surplus items shipped down the Savannah River to Augusta.[37] Other parts of northern Georgia and the inland counties of both Carolinas also surely produced some surpluses for shipment into the cotton country.[38] However, northern Alabama is a puzzle. In the Tennessee River valley, cotton became entrenched and much of the valley became partially dependent upon Tennessee for foodstuffs. On the other hand, outside the valley itself (even to the south) a more diversified economy prevailed. It appears that the hill counties bordering Georgia and Tennessee as well as some of the counties situated on the drainage divide between the Tennessee and the Alabama-Tombigbee more closely approached self-sufficiency in foodstuffs than did the Tennessee Valley itself. A number of northern Alabama's counties produced corn quite well and were fair producers of wheat by 1860. For example, a correspondent to the Patent Office gleefully reported "good times" in Jackson County in 1852. He estimated that the county could sell 150,000 bushels of corn easily. A previous report from Jackson reported that the corn crop was responsible for fattening 20,000 swine annually (no doubt this figure included swine from Tennessee being driven South).[39]

Apparently, wheat growing was stimulated greatly during the 1850s. George Powell (writing around 1855) states that wheat growing had been inhibited formerly by lack of milling facilities but that the erection of mills stimulated wheat growing to the point where flour was then being shipped south.[40] This must have been true for a large area since many of the inland counties of the Deep South states showed much higher wheat production ratios in 1860 than in either 1840 or 1850.

Other goods were shipped out of northern Alabama counties toward the south. Jefferson and Blount counties had a trade in apples and peaches that must have been quite extensive. The demand for apples in the plantation counties was substantial and by 1850 "not less than one hundred wagons were sent throughout the state." [41] In addition to the overland routes used, the waterways provided opportunities for rafting goods downriver; even the small tributaries of the Alabama, Warrior, Coosa, and Tombigbee were used.[42]

It appears, then, that the trade from the hill country into the cotton belt was an important one. It provided a market for goods produced in the hill country, helped alleviate possible shortages in the plantation area, and served a number of small cities. Tennessee, Kentucky, northern Georgia and Alabama, and upstate Carolina were important food source areas. Arkansas, northern Louisiana, and northern Mississippi must have been unimportant as food suppliers, as evidence concerning food trade is lacking. Both northern Louisiana and Mississippi were concentrating fairly heavily on cotton production by 1860 and this surely prevented large food surpluses. Furthermore, they both suffered from competition with goods moving down the Mississippi River.

Perhaps, the most notable feature of the Southern intraregional trade was its lack of organization. One searches in vain for evidence of well-established brokers or marketing channels. The usual pattern was for individuals to set out on the trip south from the hill counties trading along the way until their supplies were exhausted. Occasionally, merchants had routes into the hill country along which small quantities of food moved and a few merchants may have had agents, but their numbers were few and the quantities of foodstuffs unimpressive.

Another part of the South's intraregional trade was that which connected the interior and the coast. To be sure, most of the goods moving inland were of extrasouthern origin and will be treated later, but there was a small trade in locally produced items that should be mentioned. Seafood, particularly oysters and fish, were shipped inland from Mobile, Darien, Savannah, Charleston and New Orleans to be consumed in the hotels and restaurants as well as in the home and the quantities were not insignificant. Estimates in Patent Office reports place the oyster trade of Mobile at approximately 25,000 to 50,000 bushels each year.[43]

Evidence of foodstuffs moving into the port cities from the interior is conflicting. As mentioned previously, some students have recognized a substantial movement of livestock into the port cities from the grazing areas and, while there is some evidence of this, its importance is difficult to evaluate.[44] Undoubtedly, the port cities served as markets for foodstuffs produced in the interior, but this trade was small in scale and often competed with goods coming in from outside the region. For example, Mobile attracted foodstuffs from its hinterland and, at the same time, imported western goods from New Orleans. By the late 1850s Mobile was dealing in flour and corn both from upstate Alabama and New Orleans. Receipts of corn from the interior increased during the 1850s (some of it actually may have been produced in Tennessee) and, by 1858, had exceeded that which moved in by sea (see below, fig. 42).[45] However, corn was the only item that offered a serious challenge to that moving coastwise from New Orleans. Other foodstuffs consumed in Mobile came largely from New Orleans. A major reason for this was the lack of large food surpluses in the interior which could move into Mobile. An additional factor, however, may have been that the markets in Mobile were very tightly controlled. Most of the merchants preferred to deal directly with New Orleans and they attempted to keep out competition. Paul Taylor cites an example of a farmer who drove cattle into town only to have the merchants try to buy him out at very low prices.[46] Such practices well might have inhibited the movement of goods into town from the interior.

There appeared to have been a similar trade pattern for other port cities. Both Savannah and Charleston received goods from the interior and, toward the end of the antebellum period, began to export small quantities of foodstuffs.[47] As was the case with the corn moving into Mobile, it is probable that a portion of the trade moving toward the coast was of Tennessee origin, but it is difficult to imagine all the products coming from Tennessee and Kentucky.[48] It is true that the increase in this trade in the 1850s was a result of railroad connections into the Hill South but, in addition to providing an outlet for goods produced in Tennessee and Kentucky, the railroads must have had a stimulating effect on the farming communities along their rights of way and a resulting increase in production. Georgia flour was moving into Charleston via railroad by the 1850s, and it made up a substantial proportion of the flour being exported from that city. The *Charleston Courier* reported that

> previous to 1850 the supplies of flour, wheat, etc., received in the city were exclusively from the ports northward—that is to say, from Richmond, Baltimore, and New York. In the year 1850 we began first to realize the connection by railroad with the granary of the West, and to receive supplies from North Carolina, Georgia, Tennessee, etc.[49]

The chief engineer for the North and South Railway expressed concern over the proposed railroad into northern Alabama encouraging wheat growing to the point where the farmers would cut into the trade from the north. Apparently, Georgians were already noted for their wheat growing.[50] Of course, visions of the area becoming a granary were never realized, but there was a substantial increase in wheat production in northern Georgia during the 1850s and a related movement in wheat toward the coast.

Mississippi waterway trade

The importance of the Mississippi waterway to the western cereal producers and the meat-packing industry is well known to students of the American past. During the first third of the nineteenth century it served as the major outlet for an otherwise isolated agricultural region and helped to make possible the growth and specialization of agriculture and industry in other parts of the country. In the last two or three decades before the Civil War, the Mississippi route was displaced by the northern water routes as the most important outlet for western goods, but the downriver traffic remained important until the war.[51]

The presence of the Mississippi River system and the ready availability of foodstuffs from its headwaters also had profound effects upon the food supply pattern in the South. Not always willing to produce foodstuffs in sufficient quantities to feed their own population, parts of the South depended upon western goods to make up any existing food deficiencies. Obviously, reliance upon extraregional foodstuffs depended upon proximity to such sources and also varied through time.

There are a number of factors which make a detailed assessment of the Mississippi River trade difficult. First, the data on foodstuffs moving downriver into New Orleans are incomplete and probably inaccurate.[52] There was considerable variation in container sizes and types (barrels, tierces, hogsheads, boxes, sacks, etc.) and, at the same time, the methods of compiling data on goods moving in and out of the port must have resulted in underestimates in some cases and duplication in others.[53] Moreover, there is almost no reliable information on the river trade that did not reach New Orleans but trickled off into the town and plantations adjacent to the river upstream from the city. There is little doubt about the existence of such a trade but few clues as to its importance. Much of this trade went into Louisiana, but Mississippi must have attracted a share, too. In addition to the downstream goods absorbed along the river near New Orleans, there was a reexportation of foodstuffs from New Orleans back upriver by New Orleans' factors.

An inventory of items moving onto New Orleans' wharves during the 1840s and 1850s would have revealed a wide assortment of goods. Not only did the city act as an entrepôt for southern-produced cotton and sugar, but through it was funneled much of the commercial output of the entire Mississippi-Ohio-Missouri-Tennessee watershed. It must have been an impressive sight, wharves and warehouses filled with every conceivable item of trade.

> Here is a boat stowed with apples . . . cider, cheese, potatoes, butter, chickens, lard. . . . Flour from Virginia and Ohio . . . cotton from Arkansas and Mississippi, lumber from Tennessee, whiskey from Missouri, tobacco from Kentucky . . . Pork without end, as if Ohio had emptied its lap at the door of New Orleans. Flour by the thousand barrels; rolled out upon the quay.[54]

Foodstuffs were especially important, and hundreds of tons moved through the port. Potatoes, flour, wheat, corn, meal, pork, beef, apples, whiskey, and a host of other items made up the list.

A casual count in the records published in *DeBow's Review* reveals some fifty items arriving in the city from the interior, with twenty-three of these being some type of food.[55] Some of the foodstuffs were exported almost immediately to either foreign ports or to the cities in the eastern United States, while the remainder was used to fill hungry stomachs in the South. A portion (probably much more than we realize) lay there to spoil and rot. The city itself had a tremendous appetite and its markets were huge and well stocked. Even the usually critical Mrs. Trollope described them in 1827 as "handsome and well supplied." [56]

While the variety was impressive, a number of items were outstanding. The most important were the meats and cereals such as corn, wheat, flour, pork, bacon, and beef. Borne on flatboats, keelboats, barges, and steamboats, these foods (as well as some live animals) moved downriver in large quantities throughout the first half of the century. As facilities along the Great Lakes-St. Lawrence-Mohawk routeway improved, an increasing proportion of the western produce was siphoned away from the Crescent City. Its importance relative to the eastern route declined quite sharply, but in absolute figures, the New Orleans' trade maintained itself quite well through the years. This was true of most of the food trade even though there was variation from one item to another. Receipts of pork and beef, for example, suffered a decline in absolute amounts after a peak in the early 1850s. Receipts of wheat flour, on the other hand, showed an overall increase up to the late 1850s. Although it is not within the scope of this study to trace in detail the Mississippi Valley provision trade, it is appropriate to our interests to trace the movement of major foodstuffs into New Orleans and evaluate their importance to the overall supply of food in the South. Moreover, our concern lies with the major southern foods known to have been deficient. Therefore, this section concentrates on the four basic meat-cereal commodities—corn, wheat, pork, and beef.

Of greatest interest and concern to the student of southern agriculture was the downriver movement of pork. We have established previously that in some parts of the South there was a substantial dependence upon nonsouthern pork and in Louisiana, especially on sugar plantations, it supplied the major part of the meat utilized. Movement of pork into the city began in the early part of the century as the packing industry centered in Cincin-

nati began to market surpluses. This trade increased from about
20,000 tons in 1840 to a high of nearly 100,000 tons at mid-century, after which it declined to less than 60,000 tons by 1860
(fig. 36).[57]

The beef trade of New Orleans suffered considerably from
the competition of other routes out of the West. In 1840 New Orleans received a modest 1,000 tons of beef but the trade surged
upward until a peak was reached in the early 1850s. Receipts during the peak period averaged about 6,000 tons, with one year approaching 10,000 tons, after which they declined to about 4,000
or 5,000 tons (fig. 37).

The New Orleans corn trade was much less important to the
food economy of the South than was the trade in pork. A considerable quantity of corn and meal moved into New Orleans each
year, but the immense corn crops produced throughout the remainder of the South as well as the sizable crops grown in northern Louisiana tended to limit the regional demand for corn. New
Orleans and other urban areas did consume fair quantities but,
except in bad crop years, the trade was much less important than
either the wheat or pork trade.

Imports of corn into New Orleans increased from a little
over one million bushels in 1840 to about four million in 1846. A
peak of nearly eight million bushels was reached around 1847
after which the annual trade decreased and leveled off at about
three million bushels during the late 1850s (fig. 38).

The movement of wheat and flour into New Orleans was
quite erratic and the amounts received fluctuated widely from
year to year. And, unlike some other commodities, wheat and
flour imports continued to rise through the two decades. Based on
five-year running averages, imports were around 2.5 million bushels in 1840 but were better than 7 million by the end of the decade (fig. 39).[58] A peak was reached during 1846–47 and a secondary high occurred during the early 1850s but, on the whole,
the trend was upward.

The amount of wheat exported from New Orleans followed
the same general pattern as wheat imports, but the increase during the twenty-year period was not quite as great as the increase
in imports during the same period (fig. 39). This, of course,
meant that an increasing amount of wheat and flour remained
in the city for local or upriver use.

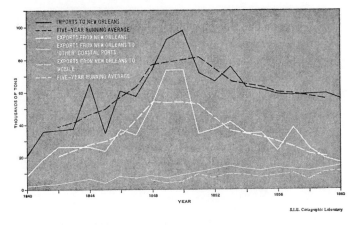

36. PORK TRADE OF NEW ORLEANS.

In addition to the regular river trade connecting New Orleans with the West, was the local trade carried on upstream from
New Orleans. Both itinerant traders and western farmers floated
boats and rafts downriver and peddled their wares among the
small villages and plantations along the rivers.[59] A recent study
by Joe Clark on the western grain trade recognizes the existence
of this local trade and estimates that it was very large, but little
evidence is offered to back up his assertion. It is known that the
larger cities such as Memphis, Vicksburg, Natchez, and Baton
Rouge absorbed some western provisions before they reached
New Orleans, but data on this trade are rare and often difficult to
interpret.[60] For example, exports from Cincinnati give figures for
"other downriver ports" (other than New Orleans) but does not
specify the ports. Furthermore, Cincinnati was not the only center
shipping foodstuffs south so the picture is somewhat hazy. On
the whole, this writer believes the local trade in the major foodstuffs, carried on by farmers and bargemen along the stream
above New Orleans, to have been a relatively minor part of the
total New Orleans trade. For one thing, it is difficult to demonstrate a demand along the river sufficient to account for the
amounts of foodstuffs needed for Clark's estimates. The only item
that was greatly lacking was wheat, and one suspects that the
wheat deficits were not made up fully by imports but that southerners simply consumed considerably less than the national average.

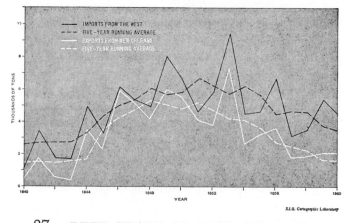

37. BEEF TRADE OF NEW ORLEANS.

It is perhaps best to visualize the interior of Mississippi as being more closely tied to New Orleans than to Cincinnati or St. Louis. That such a situation should exist is puzzling when one considers the proximity of the upstream cities to source areas with the corresponding reduction in transportation expenses. Yet, the advantages of trading with New Orleans merchants apparently offset any attractions the upstream towns offered. More than likely this resulted from the existence of a very active group of factors and merchants in New Orleans. Often handling the accounts of numerous planters in the interior, such businessmen were in a position to offer a wider range of goods and services and thus push out the local merchant who might have operated in places like Vicksburg or Natchez. Too, it appears that the New Orleans merchants were quite aggressive in obtaining their supplies, often traveling deep into the Old Northwest to buy goods.[61]

This is not to say that the local river trade did not exist. Actually, it was quite important at the local level and may have been much more important in trading some perishable commodities (namely, potatoes, apples, cider, butter, cheese, and other fruits and vegetables) than was New Orleans. This trade in items other than meat and cereals probably was limited to the areas adjacent to the major streams, but where available, such items found a welcome market as evidenced by the Natchez newspaper that reported:

Apples and Irish potatoes are good things. We have had good things in Natchez for the last week . . . potatoes, with

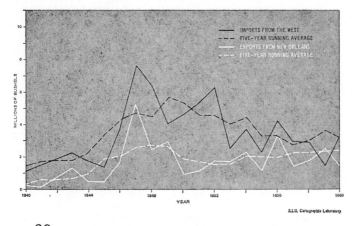

38. CORN TRADE OF NEW ORLEANS.

drawn butter and eggs; and apples raw, and apple dumplings, and apple pies, and baked apples, and roast potatoes,
and potatoes boiled, and hash with potatoes in it . . . and
sundry other fresh articles, for which we are annually in-
debted to the father of rivers, and one of his elder boys.[62]

On the whole, the local trade must have become relatively
less important toward the end of the antebellum period. In the
pre-1830 or -1840 years, it is quite possible that the local river
trade compared quite favorably with that carried on by New Orleans. For one thing, much more of the trade was borne by flatboats in the early years making it easier to do peddling between
the small landings. And second, the trade sphere of New Orleans
appears to have been much less well developed during the early
years. The high cost of keelboating limited the amount of goods
reshipped upriver, thus the local buyer looked to the bargeman
for his produce. This thesis, of course, is difficult to demonstrate
but some hint of it is indicated by the increase in food deficits in
the counties upriver from New Orleans. A portion of this increase
was due to population growth and its effects on upriver demand,
and it is possible that upper Louisiana and Mississippi were becoming more dependent upon western produce, yet it is likely
that the relatively small trade upriver from New Orleans in 1820
or 1830 was heavily supplemented by local river trade but that by
1850 and 1860 the upriver trade from New Orleans represented
a much larger percentage of the total needs of upper Louisiana
and Mississippi.

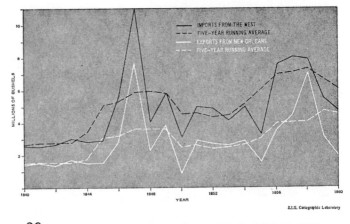

39. WHEAT TRADE OF NEW ORLEANS.

The Gulf and Atlantic port trade

In addition to the movement of goods into the South via the Mississippi River, there was a sizable trade in foodstuffs through the ports of Mobile, Savannah, Charleston, and a number of smaller port cities. This trade, though certainly less significant than that of the Mississippi River, was vital to the economies of the port cities and was of considerable importance in making up food deficits which existed in parts of Alabama, Georgia, and the Carolinas. After about 1840 the greater part of this trade originated in New Orleans and was shown as exports from that city, but a portion of it (especially that entering the Atlantic ports) moved in from northern ports such as Baltimore, Philadelphia, and New York (a good part came from the small ports and wharves of North Carolina and Virginia plantations).[63] The eastern cities were of primary importance in supplying manufactured goods to the South, but surely were secondary to New Orleans in the shipment of foodstuffs.[64]

The most outstanding port receiving foodstuffs was Mobile. Enjoying excellent connections with the cotton producing areas of Central Alabama and portions of Mississippi, Mobile was able to exploit the black belt markets effectively and sell sizable quantities of provisions upriver.

The most important commodity moving up the Alabama-Tombigbee waterways was pork. Fortunately, some data are available on the pork trade of Mobile and, though imprecise, present a fair picture of the city's trade. The importance of early pork is not known, but by the mid-1840s it was approximately five thousand tons annually. The trade increased slowly throughout the next fifteen years to around nine thousand tons by the end of the 1850s. Of the pork exported from New Orleans to United States ports, *other* than the largest northeastern cities (Boston, New York, Philadelphia, and Baltimore), from two-thirds to three-fourths moved into Mobile (figs. 36 and 40).

Unlike the pork trade, the wheat and flour trade of Mobile catered almost exclusively to the white market. A great deal of wheat was grown in northern Alabama and some was grown in the black belt but on the whole, wheat production was insufficient to meet the state's flour needs and imports were necessary to remedy the deficiency. Flour imports into Mobile were equivalent to around 200,000 bushels of wheat in 1846.[65] There was a slight increase throughout the next fifteen years but imports fluctuated between 200,000 and 400,000 bushels. With the exception of the 1858–59 year, imports did not exceed 500,000 bushels (fig. 41).

The source of the wheat and flour that entered Mobile is not absolutely clear. Considering the proximity to New Orleans one would expect the Crescent City to be its major supplier, but there is evidence that wheat came from elsewhere. Data on New Orleans wheat and flour exports are available for the major eastern ports, but Mobile's needs probably were counted under exports to "other coastwise ports." A comparison between Mobile imports and the exports from New Orleans to "other coastwise ports" indicates that New Orleans exports were well able to supply Mobile's needs during the latter part of the antebellum period but that prior to 1849 there must have been alternate sources for the wheat and flour moving into the city. During the years 1847–49, for example, Mobile imported more flour than was exported from New Orleans to "other coastwise ports." The probable source for this flour was the cities of the northeast with perhaps Baltimore being foremost.[66] Baltimore and Virginia flour enjoyed a favorable reputation among a number of planters and sometimes brought premium prices.

There were a host of other goods imported into Mobile with corn, beef, and whiskey being among the most important. Corn imports were fairly low, however, beginning with roughly one

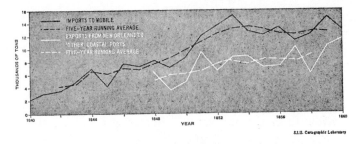

40. PORK TRADE OF MOBILE.

hundred thousand bushels in 1840 and maintaining this annual
rate up to about 1850. After 1850, corn imports climbed steadily
throughout the decade. At the end of the decade, total imports
exceeded half a million bushels (fig. 42).[67]

Though apparently surrounded by thousands of cattle, Mobile's beef needs were not met by local production and beef moved
into the city by ship. The amount of beef imported was relatively
small, however, amounting to only about 115 tons in 1855 and
300 tons in 1859.[68] And, while some of the beef undoubtedly
moved upriver into the interior, it is probable that most remained
in Mobile for urban consumption. This would have been quite
possible since Mobile County's population was approaching 30,-
000 in 1855 and 40,000 by 1860. Actually, this would have
amounted to only about eight pounds per inhabitant in 1855 and
twelve pounds in 1860. Considering the large number of relatively
affluent whites in Mobile and their probable demand for beef, it
is almost sure that the supply of imported beef was augmented by
beef being driven into town from interior Alabama.

The food imports of the eastern South were not confined to
the port of Mobile. Other ports handled goods moving into the
area but in lesser quantities and probably with less regularity. For
these reasons data on goods moving into such ports are scanty.
To further confuse the picture, the larger ports, such as Savannah
and Charleston, showed small exports of certain foodstuffs while
at the same time importing the same articles from New Orleans
or the Northeastern ports.

Charleston was the major port along the South Atlantic
coast. It dominated the Carolina trade and, in addition, had some
influence in parts of Georgia. The Charleston and Hamburg Railway, one of the first railroads built in the nation, linked Augusta,

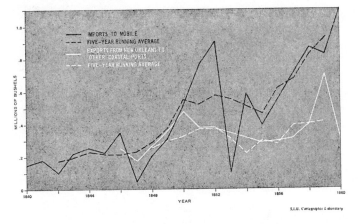

41. WHEAT TRADE OF MOBILE.

Georgia with Charleston. Traffic in foodstuffs and livestock over the road is known from the early 1840s, but these data are primarily for coastward movement and little is known of the movement of goods into the interior.[69] It is likely that the railroad was more important in transporting foodstuffs from the Hill South to the coast than importing food into the interior. Evidence tending to support this view is the increasing amount of produce and livestock that moved *out* of the interior toward the coast. Of course this hardly proves that no foodstuffs moved into the interior from the coast, but it does suggest that the hill country was capable of producing a surplus of provisions, a fact which made large-scale importations from the coast quite unlikely. It is probable that the movement of foodstuffs into Charleston was primarily in response to demands within the city and among rice planters along the coast. The goods moving into the interior from the coast must have been exotics such as salt, sugar, wine, molasses, and coffee.

Importations of food into Savannah and other Georgia ports did not compare with those to Mobile or Charleston; there were scattered imports but the total quantity was quite small.

On the whole, there were a number of sources to which southerners turned for the foodstuffs they did not supply for themselves. Throughout the area both planters and farmers produced small surpluses which they traded or sold to their neighbors. Others produced for a wider market, often traveling substantial distances to sell or trade. In many cases, these food

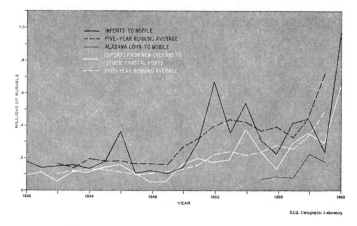

42. CORN TRADE OF MOBILE.

producers were located in the hill states such as Tennessee or Kentucky and made their living almost exclusively by trading with the Deep South. Finally, the trade that has received the most attention was that which connected the northern farmers with the food purchasers in the South. The greater part of this moved down the Mississippi waterway and into the South via the river ports of the area. A portion also went coastwise to a number of Gulf and Atlantic ports, and an additional amount moved south from the ports of the Northeast. The total quantity of foodstuffs that entered this trade was large. Its importance to the overall food producing effort of the South, however, was almost surely not as significant as traditional interpretation would allow. Moreover, there was such great variation between areas within the South that one finds generalization quite difficult. It is with these problems of interpreting the antebellum southern food economy that the next chapter deals.

11 Independence for some

The preceding chapters have demonstrated that the food industry of the South was far from uniform throughout the area. In each of the commodities examined, wide variation existed in both production and consumption with some areas producing well above their mimimum needs and others falling far below. In the last chapter the southern food trade was examined and, where possible, data on the amounts of foodstuffs moving into the area were presented. This leaves us with the task of determining the importance of trade goods in relation to local production and leads us, of course, to the central question of the study, southern self-sufficiency in food.

The pork supply

Of all the major commodities imported into the region, none was so intimately tied to the plantation-slave economy and none evoked such impassioned words from the pens of patriotic southerners pleading for regional independence as pork. We have already established that the South produced an enormous quantity of pork and that in much of the area the production could have supplied the demand easily. The questions that confront us here are, how significant were the pork imports relative to local production and what areas, if any, achieved self-sufficiency?

Looking at the eight-state area as a unit, it is almost certain that potential production was well above its own mimimum needs. There were some 4.3 million people in the area in 1840, 5.5 million in 1850, and about 6.8 million in 1860. Using our figure of 2.2 swine per unit as minimum for subsistence the area *could* have fulfilled its needs in all three census years.

A breakdown into state units, however, gives us a much

more realistic view of potential production relative to consumption. Most of the individual states could have produced their own
pork; some actually could have doubled that amount (table 15).
Only South Carolina and Louisiana consistently fell below their
estimated consumption. Louisiana never came anywhere near
supplying her own needs, apparently preferring to depend upon
meat moving downriver from the Mississippi-Ohio Basin.

Determination of self-sufficiency, however, cannot simply be

15. Potential pork production and consumption by states, in thousands of tons.

1840

	POTENTIAL PRODUCTION	ESTIMATED CONSUMPTION	SURPLUS OR DEFICIENCY
Alabama	50	34	+16
Arkansas	14	6	+8
Georgia	51	39	+12
Louisiana	11	21	−10
Mississippi	35	22	+13
North Carolina	58	43	+15
South Carolina	31	32	−1
Tennessee	102	47	+55

1850

	POTENTIAL PRODUCTION	ESTIMATED CONSUMPTION	SURPLUS OR DEFICIENCY
Alabama	67	45	+22
Arkansas	29	12	+17
Georgia	76	52	+24
Louisiana	21	31	−10
Mississippi	55	35	+20
North Carolina	63	51	+12
South Carolina	37	39	−2
Tennessee	109	58	+51

1860

	POTENTIAL PRODUCTION	ESTIMATED CONSUMPTION	SURPLUS OR DEFICIENCY
Alabama	61	56	+5
Arkansas	41	25	+16
Georgia	71	61	+10
Louisiana	22	43	−21
Mississippi	54	48	+6
North Carolina	66	58	+8
South Carolina	34	41	−7
Tennessee	82	64	+18

Source: *U.S. Censuses of 1840, 1850, and 1860.*

a matter of evaluating state units. While most states had a potential production higher than their needs, there is no assurance that surplus counties within each state supplied those that were deficient. Such a hypothesis would necessitate a lively intrastate trade in either live animals or pork. As discussed in the preceding chapter, there is good evidence of a local trade in foodstuffs, but it is difficult to demonstrate an intrastate trade sufficient to supply the major shortages such as those in coastal Louisiana, Alabama and South Carolina. Moreover, the location of these deficit areas strongly suggests a dependence upon extraregional pork.

Louisiana was the major southern market for extraregional pork. From the very early years of the century until well after the Civil War, it received huge quantities of meat from upriver. Receipts at New Orleans averaged around 20,000 tons in 1840, but this figure increased rapidly thereafter to a peak of almost 1,000,-000 tons at mid-century. After that increasing quantities were shipped from the upper Mississippi Valley directly east, and New Orleans' receipts decreased to around 50,000 tons by the end of the decade. Obviously, this meat was not destined exclusively for plantation use. The urban population of New Orleans was a major consumer, and a substantial proportion was exported to foreign ports or moved coastwise to other American cities. Some, of course, was reshipped upriver to plantations in upstate Louisiana or Mississippi.

The quantity of pork exported from New Orleans showed the same temporal pattern as that imported from upriver.[1] Annual exports fluctuated markedly depending upon receipts from upriver, while the amount remaining in the city showed much less year-to-year variation indicating a fairly steady local market. This does not mean that the local demand remained static. In fact, the proportion retained for consumption in the city and its trade area increased markedly over the two decades. In the early 1840s less than half the pork moving into the city was retained for local consumption, but by 1860 this proportion had increased to almost two thirds (fig. 36). Moreover, the total quantity that remained in the city increased during the two decades. This almost doubled from about 12,000 tons in 1840 to nearly 24,000 tons in 1850 and it reached about 36,000 tons by the end of the decade. There were annual fluctuations, but the five-year running averages show an unmistakable increase.

There were four major users of pork in New Orleans: 1]

the urban population of the city itself;   2] planters and other inhabitants of Louisiana outside New Orleans in which case pork moved into the city and then was sold to consumers located upriver or on streams and bayous in lower Louisiana;   3] ships and steamboats plying the port of New Orleans whose crews needed provisions; and   4] plantations and towns along the Mississippi River and its tributaries within the state of Mississippi. Based on production/consumption ratios the deficit of Louisiana has been estimated at a little less than 10,000 tons in 1840 and 1850, and about 21,000 tons by 1860. However, these figures are based on data for the entire state including a number of high-production counties in northern Louisiana whose surplus hogs probably did not enter the commercial trade. Considering only the southern portion of the state and counties bordering the Mississippi River, the pork deficit was somewhat higher, approximately 12,000 tons in 1840 and almost 30,000 tons by 1860.

A substantial, though unknown, quantity of meat moved upriver from New Orleans into Mississippi. Mississippi had a high production potential in 1840, but it decreased steadily during the next two decades. Moreover, the number of deficit counties along the river increased. Based on the need within these deficit counties Mississippi's needs were around 1,000 tons in 1840, 2,000 in 1850, and possibly 4,000 in 1860.

The pork needed for provisioning ships is unknown but certainly it was not insignificant.[2] From 1851 to 1856 the number of vessels calling at New Orleans varied from about 1,950 to about 2,350 (not including steamboats).[3] If each of these vessels took only one ton of pork (they probably took several tons), ships' provisions alone would have amounted to around 2,000 tons, or nearly 10 percent of the amount that remained in the city around 1850. If the steamboat trade is added the figure easily could be doubled.

The uses outlined above appear to account for the greater part of the pork in New Orleans. We must note, however, that additional pork may have moved into New Orleans, but was unreported. Too, some pork must have trickled into the area upriver from New Orleans, but we can only guess as to the scale of such a trade.[4] In any case there seems little doubt that Louisiana planters preferred to buy rather than raise their pork and that Louisiana depended heavily upon pork from upriver.[5]

In addition to the trade of the lower Mississippi Valley, pork also moved through New Orleans to other parts of the South. Except for the years immediately preceding the Civil War, most of New Orleans' pork exports went either to foreign ports or to the large seaboard cities of the Northeast, but some were shipped coastwise from New Orleans to points other than the large eastern ports (New York, Boston, Philadelphia, and Baltimore). A substantial proportion of this moved into Mobile.

Mobile's imports from the late 1840s to the late 1850s varied from 5,000 to 10,000 tons and represented from two-thirds to three-fourths of the New Orleans shipments to "other coastwise ports" (figs. 36 and 40). Once the pork reached Mobile its destination seems fairly clear. There were no significant pork exports from Mobile during the late antebellum period, thus the entire amount must have been consumed either within the city or in interior Alabama. Perhaps we should consider the demand for pork for ships provisions, but it probably was considerably less than that of New Orleans. Considering the probable demand within Mobile based on its population, consumption amounted to roughly one third of its imports in both 1850 and in 1860, therefore the remaining two-thirds must have moved upriver into the plantation area. Such a trade is known to have existed, and is suggested by the deficit counties appearing on figures 12, 13, and 14.

A portion of the pork that moved upriver from Mobile may have gone into eastern Mississippi, but the great bulk of it remained in Alabama to be utilized by black belt planters and the interior towns such as Selma and Montgomery.

In production/consumption ratios South Carolina was second lowest among the eight southern states (table 15). About one-third of its counties had ratios lower than 2.2 in 1840, and by 1860 the number had increased to more than two-thirds (figs. 12 and 14). The combined needs of these counties averaged about 8,000 tons during the two decades, but the major shortage lay in the rice area, since the coastal counties of Beaufort, Colleton, Horry, Charleston, and Georgetown had a greater combined deficit than that of all the remaining counties.

Scattered data on pork shipped from New Orleans to Charleston substantiate this demand. However, an additional, though unknown, quantity probably entered Charleston from

16. Pork shipped from New Orleans to Charleston.

YEAR	PORK (BARRELS)	BACON (HHDS)	TOTAL MEAT (TONS)
1840	832	289	199
1841	1,681	1,565	794
1842	2,700	2,462	1,255
1843	137	2,906	1,175
1844	2,255	3,986	1,820
1845	1,038	2,533	1,117
1846	2,828	1,962	1,086
1847	1,004	2,875	1,250
1848	2,328	4,218	1,920
1849	. . .	. . .	. . .
1850	4,059	4,246	2,104
1851	1,003	2,872	1,249

Source: DeBow's Review, 2 (1846), 421–22; 6 (1848), 437–38; DeBow, Industrial Resources, 2: 144; and J. Macgregor, Commercial Statistics of America (London: Whittaker and Company, 1847), p. 315.

eastern ports. Only 199 tons were imported from New Orleans, in 1840, but this increased rapidly to 1,255 in 1842 and remained between 1,000 and 2,000 tons for the next nine years (table 16). Since the estimated deficit in the coastal counties was about 6,000 tons, it is clear that the New Orleans supply was augmented from other sources.

Data on livestock moving to the coast over the South Carolina railroad suggest a coastward movement of hogs from the Hill South to the coast. Unfortunately, the available data lists "livestock" rather than specific kinds of animals, leaving the number of hogs unknown (table 17).

17. Livestock moving over the South Carolina railroad.

YEAR	ANIMALS	YEAR	ANIMALS
1848	4,230	1856	11,769
1849	3,285	1857	9,214
1850	5,859	1858	12,001
1851	4,179	1859	14,049
1852	4,894	1860	12,213
1853	8,029	1861	12,257
1854	12,056	1862	8,475
1855	12,021		

Source: U.S. Treasury Department, Report on the Inland Commerce of the United States (1886), p. 266.

A rough indication of the number of hogs involved in this trade comes from an entry in the Patent Office for 1849 in which detailed figures on the trade are given. It lists 1,584 cattle, 3,353 hogs, 328 sheep, and 977 horses with hogs making up about half the total.[6] Admittedly, this is slim evidence upon which to base an interpretation of the railroad trade, but if we assume roughly one-half the livestock to have been hogs, then a substantial quantity of pork was supplied by this route.

The coastwise pork trade was by no means confined to Mobile and Charleston. Other ports received meat but in lesser quantities and probably with less regularity. For these reasons data on meat moving into such ports are scanty. Savannah received small quantities, but the sparsely populated hinterlands of the Georgia ports may have limited the need. Like coastal South Carolina, the important markets were the towns and rice plantations along the coast. There was, of course, some trade between Georgia ports and the interior planting country but, compared to Mobile, Georgia ports were never very important entrepôts for the pork trade. There were several reasons for this difference. First, the distance from Savannah or Darien to the cotton planting area of Georgia was farther and more difficult of access than was the case with Mobile and its hinterland. Second, Alabama rivers focused on one port, Mobile, while those of Georgia flowed into the sea at different points making concentration of the river trade into one port impractical. Moreover, the heads of navigation on Alabama rivers extended well into the planting areas while in Georgia the fall zone effectively blocked large scale upriver transportation to much of the Piedmont cotton area. Finally, the agricultural communities tributary to the Georgia ports were more diversified than those of central Alabama. The Georgia counties most consistently showing pork deficits were in the eastern Piedmont and were supplied overland from Tennessee, but those of southern Georgia had very high ratios.

Since a major theme in this work is southern self-sufficiency, it seems worthwhile at this point to offer estimates on the relative importance of imported pork to the total southern consumption. Obviously, we cannot reconstruct the entire picture, but using the available materials and a bit of "educated" imagination it is tempting to attempt a graphic summary of the entire southern pork supply. The basic data are from the production ratios outlined earlier, but additional information on "flow" was taken from the existing statistics of the Mississippi River trade and port receipts. The results are shown on figures *43* and *44* for the years 1850 and 1860. The total supply for each state is indicated by the size of the circle, the amount imported into the state is shown by the shaded area, while the *width* of the lines indicate the quantity of goods along the trade routes. Where specific data are unavailable, flow lines are based on estimated deficiencies calculated from data on production and consumption in the deficit areas. Dashed lines indicate a probable, but undocumented, movement of pork. Quite likely the data on pork imports are a little low, since a quantity moved into the area but went unreported. This is almost certainly true of the Atlantic coast ports. Even so, this writer is very reluctant to increase the estimates markedly, since it would necessitate an upward revision of pork consumption estimates or a reduction in the output per animal and, based on the evidence examined, neither proposition is feasible.

From the pie graphs and flow lines it is clear that Louisiana and South Carolina were the major buyers of meat. However, significant amounts were needed in other states. Alabama, for example, imported pork equivalent to almost one fifth of her estimated needs in 1860. On the other hand, Tennessee, Arkansas, and Kentucky (not included in this study or shown on map) all were self-sufficient in meat.

That the South depended to some degree upon extraregional sources of pork is unquestionable; the importance of this dependence, however, is less impressive than traditional interpretation would have it. The amount of incoming pork was substantial, yet compared to the total southern production, it remained relatively small. As mentioned previously it is possible that the data outlined on figures *43* and *44* do not represent the complete pork trade. Nevertheless, even if we double the figures postulated on these maps for states such as North Carolina, Georgia, and Mississippi, imports in relation to local production were small. Both Tennessee and Kentucky certainly produced well above their needs, and both supplied pork to the Deep South; thus imported pork often was "southern produced."

The beef supply

Although beef certainly was subordinate to pork as a meat for southern stomachs, enough of it entered the Mississippi and

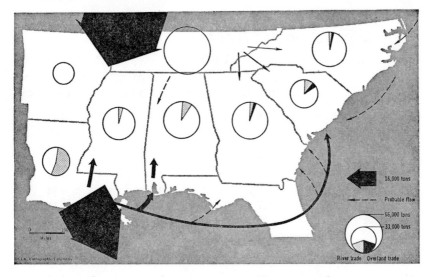

43. SOUTHERN PORK TRADE, 1850.

overland trade to stimulate our curiosity and invite investigation.
The beef and pork trades were similar in the routes they traversed
and the markets they sought, but differed widely in scale. While
pork made up a major segment of the interregional trade, beef
was a minor item. There were two major reasons for this difference. Southerners simply were not major beef eaters, and the
relatively large number of southern cattle obviated the need for
imports.

    The potential southern beef supply was enormous, far in ex-
cess of the demand. At the state level, potential production was
well ahead of consumption even though we are almost certain
that actual production did not reach potential production (table
18).

    Despite this large surfeit of animals throughout the South,
both beef and live animals moved into the area. The most significant amounts moved down the Mississippi into New Orleans and
the surrounding area. From the preceding chapter we noted that
the beef trade of New Orleans increased from about 1,000 to over
4,000 tons during the two decades, with a peak of around 9,000
tons in the early 1850s. Of the beef that moved into New Orleans
from upriver a portion was exported, but a substantial proportion
remained within the city for local use. This amount fluctuated
from 800 to around 1,200 tons during the 1840–50 decade, after

18. *Potential beef production and consumption by states, in thousands of tons.*

1840

	POTENTIAL PRODUCTION	ESTIMATED CONSUMPTION	SURPLUS OR DEFICIENCY
Alabama	20	7	+13
Arkansas	6	1	+5
Georgia	27	8	+19
Louisiana	11	4	+7
Mississippi	19	4	+15
North Carolina	19	9	+10
South Carolina	17	6	+11
Tennessee	25	9	+16

1850

Alabama	22	9	+13
Arkansas	9	2	+7
Georgia	33	10	+23
Louisiana	17	6	+11
Mississippi	22	7	+15
North Carolina	21	10	+11
South Carolina	23	8	+15
Tennessee	23	12	+11

1860

Alabama	23	11	+12
Arkansas	17	5	+12
Georgia	30	12	+18
Louisiana	16	9	+7
Mississippi	22	10	+12
North Carolina	29	12	+17
South Carolina	15	8	+7
Tennessee	23	13	+10

Source: *U.S. Censuses of 1840, 1850, and 1860.*

which it increased steadily until, by the late 1850s, a little over 2,000 tons remained within the city each year. During some years it exceeded this amount but the five-year running average indicate a relatively steady, but increasing quantity.

Determining the ultimate use of this beef presents a somewhat different kind of problem than was the case with pork. The

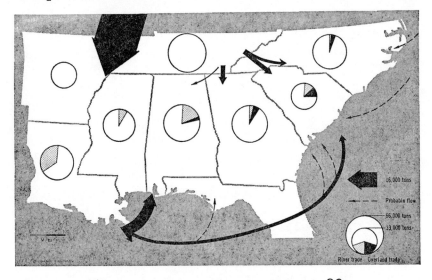

44. SOUTHERN PORK TRADE, 1860.

huge Louisiana market for pork certainly was directly related to
the virtual absence of hogs in southern Louisiana. This was not
true of the cattle industry; in fact, the Louisiana and Mississippi
herders could have supplied the New Orleans market quite easily
had their cattle been depended upon exclusively. However, it appears that herder-owned cattle suffered in comparison to the readily available (and presumably better quality) beef out of the West.[7]
   While the quantity of beef left for use in New Orleans increased during the last decade of the antebellum period, it remained relatively small compared to potential beef production in
Louisiana and lower Mississippi. Moreover, when one considers
the needs of New Orleans' consumers and the demand for beef as
provisions for ships and steamboats, little of the river-borne beef
was left for resale to Louisiana planters or for shipment upriver
into Mississippi. Approximately 1,200 tons were left in New Orleans annually during the 1840s, and during the 1850s this increased to around 2,000 tons. Even so, with a population of some
175,000 in Orleans Parish this would have amounted to only 23
pounds per capita in 1860. Not only could the city have consumed
all the meat that moved downriver, it probably required additional
beef from the Louisiana herds. Of course, there was some local
barge trade along the river above the city, but compared to New

Orleans, upstate Louisiana and Mississippi probably constituted minor markets.

As mentioned in an earlier chapter, small quantities of beef moved from New Orleans to Mobile. Traditionally, this has been interpreted as a response to shortages in the plantation area, but the total quantities were small and the Mobile market probably absorbed virtually all of it. The overland route also supplied some drove beef to the Deep South but the quantity was markedly less than the pork (hogs) that moved over the same routes. (See tables 12 and 13.) Moreover, we should note that a portion of the drove cattle was intended for work stock rather than beef.[8]

The most striking difference between the beef and pork trade is that the beef trade was a trifling one and, compared with southern production, extremely small. There were a number of reasons for this great difference between the two meat industries. Perhaps the most important was the modest demand for beef. Nowhere was it considered the primary meat, and in much of the area was seldom seen on the table. Even where cattle were relatively numerous, beef consumption probably did not exceed the intake of pork. Considering this extremely low consumption of beef by those *involved* in cattle raising, we should not expect the commercial demand for beef to have been outstanding, consequently the beef trade was a minor one.

The corn supply

The corn trade was much less important to the food economy of the South than was the trade in pork. In fact, as we raise the question of southern self-sufficiency, the case of corn is perhaps clearer than for any other major commodity. Despite the impressive Mississippi River trade, the consumption of extrasouthern corn in relation to total southern production was the insignificant. As has been mentioned earlier, corn was grown by all and seldom brought a price high enough to justify its moving long distances. If, for example, it sold at one dollar per bushel (a price it fetched only when scarce) the per pound price would total only about two cents. In contrast bacon commonly sold for ten cents and sometimes more per pound. Obviously, corn could only be transported over short distances without the price becoming exorbitant. The total southern corn crop was huge and, in most cases, sufficient to supply local needs.

The corn and corn meal left in New Orleans varied between one and five million bushels but compared to the production of the eight-state area at the same time, the trade amounted to less than 1 percent in most years. The early 1850s might have been exceptions, but even then imports probably did not exceed 2 or 3 percent. Furthermore, a breakdown by states reveals that none of the eight states was deficient in corn during the three census years (table 19). Of course it does not necessarily follow that *no* externally produced corn was used. Table 19 is based on state units and, undoubtedly, some areas *within* the individual states were deficient. This was especially true where large urban places strained local supplies or where corn production was extremely low. Lower Louisiana was the obvious example of this, and it was the best and most concentrated market for nonsouthern corn.

Imports of corn into New Orleans increased from a little over one million bushels in 1840 to about three million in the late 1850s with peaks of nearly eight million bushels in 1847 and six million in 1852. After that the trade remained between two and four million bushels. Annual exports followed imports closely during most years with the amount remaining in the city varying from one to two million bushels. The only exception was during the early 1850s when the amount retained in the city tripled.

As was the case with beef, we find that the needs of the Crescent City accounted for most of the corn that remained in the city. Louisiana certainly did not have the trouble growing corn that it encountered in pork production, but if we use the rates of consumption postulated in the chapter on grain production and apply them to southern Louisiana there was little corn to spare. Moreover, much of the Louisiana corn produced on small landholdings in the northern part of the state probably did not move off the farms to alleviate shortages in the sugar area. Thus, while the total production for the state might have been adequate, the supply and demand were unbalanced and there was little intrastate trade to offset the situation. Finally, there is reason to suspect higher consumption rates among the sugar planters than elsewhere in the South. Virtually no hay was produced in lower Louisiana and the agriculturists had few substitute items such as cottonseed to feed stock. Consequently, the consumption of corn was quite high. Solon Robinson, while traveling through the sugar country, noted the absence of ancillary feed crops and thought the consumption of corn to be enormous. (This is despite

19. *Corn production and consumption by states, in thousands* ⟨ bushels.

	PRODUCTION	HUMAN CONSUMPTION [a]	HORSE AND MULE CONSUMPTION [b]	HOG CONSUMPTION [c]	TOTAL CONSUMPTION	
1840						
Alabama	20,947	5,808	1,074	5,695	12,577	8,
Arkansas	4,847	954	386	1,572	2,912	1,
Georgia	20,905	6,820	1,182	5,831	13,833	7,
Louisiana	5,953	3,683	749	1,293	5,725	
Mississippi	13,161	3,747	819	4,005	8,571	4,
North Carolina	23,894	7,519	1,250	6,598	15,367	8,
South Carolina	14,723	5,622	974	3,514	10,110	4,
Tennessee	44,986	8,090	2,561	11,706	22,357	22,
1850						
Alabama	28,754	7,721	1,409	7,618	16,748	12,
Arkansas	8,894	2,070	538	3,347	5,955	2,
Georgia	30,080	9,029	1,565	8,674	19,268	10,
Louisiana	10,266	5,455	1,008	2,389	8,852	1,
Mississippi	22,447	6,057	1,275	6,331	13,663	8,
North Carolina	27,941	8,755	1,853	7,251	17,859	10,
South Carolina	16,271	6,790	1,010	4,262	12,062	4,
Tennessee	52,276	9,979	2,595	12,419	24,993	27,
1860						
Alabama	33,226	9,708	1,791	6,993	18,492	14,
Arkansas	17,824	4,336	1,482	4,687	10,505	7,
Georgia	30,776	10,625	1,739	8,144	20,508	10,
Louisiana	16,854	7,450	1,278	2,538	11,266	5,
Mississippi	29,058	8,263	1,712	6,131	16,106	12,
North Carolina	30,079	10,053	1,515	7,532	19,100	10,
South Carolina	15,066	7,160	1,032	3,863	12,055	3,
Tennessee	52,089	11,176	3,129	9,389	23,694	28,

Source: *U.S. Censuses of 1840, 1850, and 18*⟨

[a] Calculated at the rate of 13 bushels per consuming unit.
[b] Calculated at the rate of 7.5 bushels per animal.
[c] Calculated at the rate of 4 bushels per animal.

the fact that Robinson was from the Midwest where large quantities of corn commonly were fed to animals).[9] In addition to that
used within the state, a substantial quantity was used in provisioning boats and ships. Considering these potential markets, it
is almost certain that corn moving into New Orleans was consumed either in the city or in the lower part of the state. Some undoubtedly moved upriver into Mississippi and more trickled in via
the bargeman but the quantity must have been small. The use of
western corn probably was limited to a few large holdings near
the waterways and the urban places such as Vicksburg and Natchez. M. W. Philips, while berating Mississippians for depending
so heavily upon the West for food, noted that 5,952 bushels of
corn moved over the Vicksburg Railroad in 1856. To Philips this
was alarming evidence of the "failure" of southerners to provide
their own sustenance, yet viewed in a regional context, such an
amount was insignificant, since it amounted only to about the
average annual needs of a single large plantation or a small
town.[10]

We noted earlier that the amount of corn left in New Orleans
varied from one to about four million bushels annually during the
three years for which we have production records. Although impressive in absolute number, these figures are not large when we
look at the mouths to be fed in and around New Orleans. Except
for the years 1850–52 when unusually large quantities were left
in the city, the total amounted to only a few bushels per capita.
This does not include the amount needed for draft animals, hogs
or ships provisions. Nor does it include the consumption by plantations located outside Orleans Parish, but near enough to purchase directly from within the city. Consequently, we must conclude that the corn that moved into New Orleans wharves was
either exported from the city or consumed within or near it.

We noted previously that a portion of the corn that moved
into New Orleans from upriver was exported from the city. Of
this, part went to foreign ports, another part was shipped to the
Atlantic ports of the Northeast, and a lesser quantity was shipped
coastwise to Gulf and Atlantic ports of the South. Mobile was the
most important of these corn-receiving ports, yet her corn trade
is puzzling. Alabama was a major corn producer and there appeared to be enough to meet the state's needs, yet Mobile imported
corn throughout the 1840–60 period. The apparent source during

the first fifteen years of the period was New Orleans. Exports from New Orleans to "other coastwise ports" were usually well above the amount moving into Mobile. However, toward the end of the antebellum period corn began to move into Mobile from Alabama. Railroads may have been tapping Tennessee's production but, in any event, sizable and increasing quantities moved south into Mobile. After about 1855 this trade increased steadily until by 1858 it exceeded the amount imported from the Crescent City. Small quantities were exported from Mobile each year, but they were never very important.[11]

The amount of corn that moved upriver from Mobile must have been relatively small. Corn production in the interior was quite high and even the black belt planters, who found it difficult to become self-sufficient in pork, were able to grow enough corn for their needs. The real commercial market for corn in Alabama was in Mobile itself. Being located in the coastal area where corn production was low and having a fairly large urban population, Mobile consumed large quantities. Using the formula on corn consumption oulined previously, the human and animal needs of Mobile County were quite substantial, more than enough to account for the corn listed as being imported into the city (table 20). In fact, it appears that the city's corn needs were not fully

20. *Corn supply of Mobile, in thousands of bushels.*

	1840	1850	1860
Imported into Mobile	100	180	600
Estimated corn needs over local production	180	375	570

met by imports, but this discrepancy could be the result of overestimating corn consumption. It is possible that a number of urban dwellers who had to buy *all* their cereals perferred wheat flour to cornmeal and, with a ready supply of flour in Mobile, corn consumption could have been lower than elsewhere in the south. An alternate explanation is that corn moved downriver but was not reported. This would have been quite possible if the trade had been carried on by small flatboat operators who circumvented the established merchants in town by selling to individuals.[12]

Additional quantities moved into other southern ports especially Charleston, and some undoubtedly came from the North-east.[13] Unfortunately, though, we have no data on this trade. This writer feels this trade was a small one since, based on production/consumption ratios, it appears that there was little market for extraregional corn. If we calculate the corn needs of the deficit Georgia and South Carolina counties appearing on figures 24, 25, and 26, the total comes to only about 1.3 million bushels in 1840, 1.9 million bushels in 1850, and 1.5 million in 1860; a scant 3 to 4 percent of the corn produced by the two states in the respective census years. Considering these facts, it is difficult to argue for a *very* important interregional corn trade along the Atlantic coast. Even when we add this to the Mississippi corn trade the total is unimpressive compared to southern production. Furthermore, we must recognize that the major part of this imported corn was consumed within the urban areas or went to provision the relatively few rice and sugar plantations who produced little or no corn themselves.

A few additional remarks are needed before the discussion of corn is ended. The role of the sweet potato has been discussed earlier, and it should be remembered that potatoes often replaced corn in the slave diet. This was especially true near the Gulf and Atlantic coasts where sweet potato production was high, and if we assume a bushel of potatoes to have replaced one bushel of corn then our postulated needs are reduced drastically. Furthermore, cracked rice also was used in lieu of corn along the Georgia-Carolina coast, further lessening the need for corn. Finally, we must not overlook the use of oats as animal feed. Toward the end of the period oats were being sown as a grazing and as a grain crop, with most of it being used as a replacement for corn.[14]

The wheat supply

The movement of wheat and flour into the South was discussed in the preceeding chapter, but we need to take a closer look at the importance of this trade to the total southern supply. The problem is made difficult, though, by our relative ignorance about wheat consumption. Wheat was such an important farm crop in the Old Northwest and such a popular cereal, both there and in the Northeast, that our knowledge about wheat consumption is somewhat biased. For this reason any attempt at assessing southern self-sufficiency in wheat is to a large extent speculative. Clark estimates white consumption at 3.5 bushels annually and slave consumption at 1.5. The figure for whites may have been accurate for the nation but one must question its applicability over a wide area.[15] The numerous references to low wheat consumption in both published and manuscript materials lead this writer to conclude that the annual per capita consumption of wheat by southern whites was two bushels or less.[16] Even so, there was considerable variation from place to place within the South. Near the coasts wheat production was insignificant, and people either bought wheat from the port merchants or did without. Toward the mountains, wheat culture was more common, and thus wheat was much more commonly used. Slave consumption throughout the area was insignificant.

Estimating southern wheat consumption at two bushels per consuming unit and comparing this to wheat production, we find that Tennessee and the Carolinas produced enough to supply their own needs in all three census years. On the other hand, the Deep South states of Alabama, Mississippi, and Louisiana failed to produce enough to supply their own needs in all three census years. The remaining states fell somewhere in between (table 21).

More states showed a wheat production higher than their postulated needs in 1840 and 1860 than in 1850. The 1849 crop was a bad one in much of the South and it is reflected in these figures. On the other hand 1860 was an exceptionally good year, and many counties in the Hill South produced wheat quite well. We noted previously that upstate Georgia was rapidly becoming known for its wheat growing, and it appears that Tennessee and the Carolinas also were part of this developing "southern wheat belt." [17]

Just as we noted in the section dealing with pork self-sufficiency, the surplus production of a commodity in one part of a state did not necessarily mean that it relieved shortages elsewhere. In fact, existing evidence on the intraregional trade indicates that pork was much more likely to have been a trade item than wheat. For example, the droving trade connecting Tennessee and Kentucky with the Deep South is well known but a similar trade in grain was highly unlikely until, of course, the railroads were built and functioning well.

21. *Wheat production and consumption by states, in thousands of bushels.*

	POTENTIAL PRODUCTION	ESTIMATED CONSUMPTION	SURPLUS OR DEFICIENCY
		1840	
Alabama	828	894	−66
Arkansas	106	147	−41
Georgia	1,802	1,049	+753
Louisiana	1	567	−566
Mississippi	197	576	−379
North Carolina	1,961	1,157	+804
South Carolina	968	865	+103
Tennessee	4,570	1,245	+3,325
		1850	
Alabama	294	1,188	−894
Arkansas	200	318	−118
Georgia	1,089	1,389	−300
Louisiana	1	839	−838
Mississippi	138	932	−794
North Carolina	2,130	1,347	+783
South Carolina	1,066	1,045	+21
Tennessee	1,619	1,535	+84
		1860	
Alabama	1,218	1,493	−275
Arkansas	958	667	+291
Georgia	2,545	1,635	+910
Louisiana	32	1,146	−1,114
Mississippi	588	1,271	−683
North Carolina	4,744	1,547	+3,197
South Carolina	1,286	1,101	+185
Tennessee	5,459	1,719	+3,740

Source: *U.S. Censuses of 1840, 1850, and 1860.*

The most notable trade route bringing wheat into the South was that of the Mississippi River. Of the three states whose production was consistently below their estimated consumption, two (Louisiana and Mississippi) were adjacent to the Mississippi waterway where western grain was readily available. The quantities involved were discussed in the preceeding chapter, but here we must address ourselves to its importance.

The ultimate use for which the wheat and flour that moved down the Mississippi River was intended is as difficult to determine as was the case with the other commodities, yet a major difference was that virtually no wheat was produced in Louisiana, and Mississippi produced well below its postulated needs. Moreover, most of Mississippi's wheat was produced in the northeastern counties and with no significant intrastate trade in wheat the average figure of nearly one bushel per capita for Mississippi is quite misleading, since much of the state was virtually without homegrown wheat.

The amount of wheat left in New Orleans varied from about 1 to 4 million bushels during the two decades, with the peak years being 1846–57. During most other years it fluctuated between 1 and 2 million bushels. Using the data on consumption postulated in a previous section, Louisiana had a potential deficiency of about 600,000 bushels in 1840, 800,000 bushels in 1850, and better than 1 million in 1860. Mississippi's needs were about 400,000 in 1840, 800,000 in 1850, and about 700,000 in 1860. Together, they came close to accounting for the downriver trade. Moreover, we must consider the distinct possibility that urban dwellers consumed more wheat than rural southerners, especially if it were readily available at a reasonable price. Of course, to the New Orleans' trade we must add the "unknown" quantity that entered the South through the ports upriver from New Orleans, but this possibility has been discussed earlier.

The New Orleans-Mobile coastwise trade also carried a portion of the wheat exported from New Orleans, and both Mobile and its hinterland were short of wheat. In our postulates on wheat needs, Alabama was one of the states that consistently showed a deficit. Furthermore, our dot maps of wheat production indicate that the central and southern parts of Alabama were the areas of lowest production. Consequently, these areas attracted wheat to Mobile.

The distribution of the wheat and flour imported into Mobile was similar to that of other goods that moved into the port. A portion was retained for use in the urban area, and the remainder moved upriver into the cotton belt. Based on our estimates of probable consumption, table 22 gives a rough approximation of the ultimate destination of the wheat and flour trade of Mobile. While it is not possible to state conclusively, Alabama appears to

22. Wheat supply of Mobile, in thousands of bushels

	1850	1860
Needed for use in Mobile	45	65
Moved upriver	305	335
Imported into Mobile	350	400

have had some success toward the end of the antebellum period in its attempts to become independent from external grain sources. As discussed earlier, the lack of "flouring" mills was blamed for the lack of wheat growing in Pickens County prior to the 1830s. But, one writer felt that after 1840 "the planters began to calculate on a crop of wheat." [18] There was some increase in the amount of wheat and flour moving into Mobile after 1850, but there was also a concurrent increase in wheat production within the state. Most of this increase occurred in the northern part of the state which still left much of the black belt deficient, yet Mobile imports compared to state production declined from better than 100 percent in 1850 to about a third in 1860. There was even a hint of an intraregional trade to supply Mobile, since Alabama wheat and flour began to appear in Mobile by the late 1850s.[19]

The preceding sections have dealt with a number of characteristics of the southern food system. We have looked at the production and consumption of some of the major southern foods. We also have viewed southern food habits and the trade in foodstuffs. Out of this we can draw a number of tentative conclusions concerning food supply in the area during the 1840–60 period.

The first question that comes to mind is whether the South was self-sufficient or not in foodstuffs. However, raising this question brings others to mind that must be settled first. What do we mean by "the South," and what specific commodities are we discussing?

Obviously, the smaller the area discussed the more accurately one can assess its level of sufficiency. Conversely, if we are referring to the entire South, including those states that became part of the Confederacy, then specific statements must give way to vague generalizations with so many qualifications that they become meaningless. In fact, one of the most important products of this study may be its recognition of the variable character of the food supply—and, indeed, the rural economy—of the South. From Cape Fear to New Orleans and from Knoxville to Mobile a number of agricultural "regions" existed, each with its own system of food supply. Recognition of this fact may be difficult, but this areal variation is striking and it must be grasped before we understand the character of the southern rural economy. If we consider only the "basic four" commodities, counties within the area (even in the "Deep South" states) ranged from those producing huge surpluses to others who depended upon imported food almost exclusively. Using the 1850 census only, we see that in corn production per consuming unit, the variation was from a low of 0.4 bushels per unit in Orleans Parish, Louisiana to a high of over 100 bushels per unit in several counties of Tennessee. The variation in wheat production was even greater. A number of coastal counties reported no wheat at all, but inland production increased markedly. Many counties in Tennessee and North Carolina reported 15 to 20 bushels per consuming unit. Hog numbers also showed wide variation. Orlean Parish, Louisiana was lowest with less than 200 animals while several counties in Arkansas and Tennessee boasted of nearly 10 hogs per consuming unit.

Underlying this areal variation was the relation between food deficits and either large urban populations or commercial crop production. Almost without exception, the areas in which commercial crops were important also were low in one or more of the basic commodities. Rice, cotton, and sugarcane all competed very strongly with subsistence cropping activities. Moreover, they necessitated large labor forces which were difficult to feed easily. Finally, and possibly most importantly, these crops provided a cash income sufficient to pay for commercial foodstuffs.

Perhaps the most neglected aspect of the southern economy is the role of urban places as consumers of goods. Admittedly, urban development in the South was retarded, but a number of urban places existed, and their inhabitants had to be fed. The huge Mississippi River trade is usually taken as prima facie evidence of failure in the southern subsistence economy, yet a major part of the western pork and virtually all the western beef and corn used in the South went to urban tables. The total population of the twenty-five largest cities approached one-half million in 1860; those bordering the Mississippi had almost one-quarter million inhabitants. Their consumption alone would have amounted to about 35,000 tons of pork, well over half that moving down-river at that time. When we add to this the huge amounts of pork, corn, and wheat needed in the small sugar- and rice-planting communities, then the picture of widespread foodstuff deficiency appears to crumble. There is no question about western food moving into the South, but this reflects more the lack of a commercial southern meat-packing industry than a weak subsistence economy. It also points up the weakness of intrasouthern trading organization and transport facilities.

Finally, there is one other factor we should reiterate, the availability of imported foodstuffs. The location of the deficit regions adjacent to the major transport routes or along the coasts was no accident, but a reflection of the economic advantage of being able to purchase food without exorbitant transportation costs. Moreover, this writer has the strong impression that the reliance upon extraregional food was a deliberate decision and, once made, was followed fairly regularly. To be sure, there were planters who tried making all their corn or pork but "ran out" and had to purchase for a few months, but they must have been in the minority. The lack of outstanding annual fluctuations in the amount of foods that remained in New Orleans reflects a steady demand either from urban markets or from planters who relied on the trade year after year. Where abrupt changes in the local demand occurred, a disastrous crop year was to blame.

It is obvious that a description of the South as having been either "self-sufficient" or "dependent upon the West for food" would be unrealistic. From North Carolina to Louisiana, a number of agricultural "regions" existed with each solving its problem of food supply as its situation, resources, and predilections permitted. In this respect the South differed little from other large sections of the country. But there is no justification for seeing the antebellum South as an area of such concentration on staple export agricultural production that it had to import most, or even much, of its food. As a region it was, despite the exceptions noted, largely feeding itself.

NOTES / INDEX

The journals and periodicals used in the notes will be cited by the following abbreviations:

AAAG	*Annals of the Association of American Geographers*
AH	*Agricultural History*
AHQ	*Alabama Historical Quarterly*
AR	*Alabama Review*
BHM	*Bulletin of the History of Medicine*
GHQ	*Georgia Historical Quarterly*
GHSC	*Collections of the Georgia Historical Society*
GR	*Geographical Review*
HQ	*The Historical Quarterly* (Filson Club)
IJHP	*Iowa Journal of History and Politics*
JBUC	*Journal of Business of the University of Chicago*
JMA	*Journal of the Medical Association of Georgia*
JMH	*Journal of Mississippi History*
JNH	*Journal of Negro History*
JPE	*Journal of Political Economy*
JSH	*Journal of Southern History*
LHQ	*Louisiana Historical Quarterly*
MVHR	*Mississippi Valley Historical Review*
NCHR	*North Carolina Historical Review*
PMHS	*Publications of the Mississippi Historical Society*
PMVHA	*Proceedings of the Mississippi Valley Historical Association*
PSHS	*Publications of the Southern Historical Society*
RKSHS	*Register of the Kentucky State Historical Society*
SAQ	*South Atlantic Quarterly*
TAHS	*Transactions of the Alabama Historical Society*
WMHM	*William and Mary College Quarterly Historical Magazine*

Notes

1 Self-sufficiency

[1] Frances Trollope, *Domestic Manners of the Americans* (New York: Dodd, Mead Company, 1901), 1: 88, 2: 129.

[2] Adolph B. Benson, ed., *Peter Kalm's Travels in North America* (New York: Wilson-Erickson Inc., 1937), 1: 285–86.

[3] For a summary of the controversy on the importance of the southern food trade to the national economy, see Ralph L. Andreano, *New Views of American Economic Development* (Cambridge, Mass.: Schenkman Publishing Company, 1965), pp. 187–224. See also National Bureau of Economic Research, *Trends in the American Economy in the Nineteenth Century*, Studies in Income and Wealth, Vol. 24 (Princeton, N.J.: Princeton University Press, 1960), pp. 73–140.

[4] Douglass C. North, *The Economic Growth of the United States, 1790–1860* (Englewood Cliffs, N.J.: Prentice-Hall, 1961), pp. 101–21.

[5] The standard work on northern agriculture during the eighteenth and early nineteenth centuries is Percy W. Bidwell and John I. Falconer, *History of Agriculture in the Northern United States, 1620–1860* (New York: Peter Smith, 1941). See also, Albert L. Olson, *Agricultural Economy and Population in Eighteenth Century Connecticut* (New Haven: Yale University Press, 1935), For contemporary views see Jared Eliot, *Essays Upon Field Husbandry in New England* . . . (London: J. Bew, 1775); *American Husbandry* (London: J. Bew, 1775).

[6] Any grouping of colonies into "regions" has its limitations, but one traditional grouping has been used so often that it should suffice for our purposes: The southern colonies consist of Georgia, South and North Carolina, Virginia, and Maryland; the middle colonies consist of Delaware, New Jersey, Pennsylvania, and New York: the remaining colonies (excluding those that later came to comprise Canada) made up New England.

[7] For treatments of agriculture in the mid-Atlantic area see Bidwell and Falconer; Stevenson W. Fletcher, *Pennsylvania Agriculture and Country Life, 1640–1840* (Harrisburg: Pennsylvania Historical and Museum Commission, 1950); James T. Lemon, "A Rural Geography of Southeastern Pennsylvania in the Eighteenth Century . . ." Diss. University of Wisconsin 1964. Contemporary accounts are Benson, *Peter Kalm's Travels in North America* and *American Husbandry*.

[8] James T. Lemon, "The Agricultural Practices of National Groups in Eighteenth-Century Southeastern Pennsylvania," *GR*, 56 (October 1966), 467–96.

[9] Leonard Brinkman, "The Historical Geography of Improved Cattle in the United States to 1870," Diss. University of Wisconsin 1964.

[10] For a discussion of southern agriculture, see Lewis C. Gray, *History of Agriculture in the Southern United States to 1860* (Gloucester, Mass.: Peter Smith, 1941), 1: 14–436.

[11] The use of slave labor was not confined to the southern colonies or states until well into the nineteenth century. However, slaves were more numerous and made up a much larger proportion of the total labor force in the southern area than elsewhere. Indentured labor was common in both southern and middle colonies during the eighteenth century, but toward the end of the colonial period it tended to be replaced by slaves in the southern colonies and by free labor elsewhere.

[12] Custom House Papers, Fort of Roanoke, Vol. 1 (1682–1760), pp. 11–18 quoted in Harry R. Merrens, *Colonial North Carolina in the Eighteenth Century* (Chapel Hill: University of North Carolina Press, 1964), pp. 111–19.

[13] The distinction between the farm and the plantation was (and is) quite nebulous. Contemporary writers as well as present-day students of agriculture have had a tendency to treat both as if they represented two quite different phenomena. This might well be true as each represents an opposite end of a continuum, yet when one looks at individual units, the problem of classification becomes more difficult. Apparently, most agricultural units were medium in size and could be considered either small plantations or large farms and, for the purposes of this discussion, there is no great need for precise definitions. For the moment, it should be sufficient to define the plantation as a relatively large landholding utilizing large amounts of labor other than that of the managerial family and concentrating upon the production of a cash crop for export, especially rice, cotton, sugar, indigo, or tobacco.

[14] Merrens, 209–20; Gary S. Dunbar, "Colonial Carolina Cowpens," *AH*, 35 (July 1961), 125–30.

[15] For discussions of the origins, characteristics and effects of the American land survey system see William D. Pattison, *Beginnings of the American Rectangular Land Survey System 1784–1800* (Chicago: University of Chicago Press, 1957) and Roy M. Robbins, *Our Landed Heritage: The Public Domain, 1776–1936* (Princeton: Princeton University Press, 1942).

[16] For discussions of pioneer food, hunting, fishing, and farm food production see Thomas D. Clark, *Frontier America: The Story of the Westward Movement* (New York: Charles Scribner's Sons, 1959), pp. 202–19; John A. Caruso, *The Great Lakes Frontier* (Indianapolis: The Bobbs-Merrill Company, Inc., 1961), pp. 320–23; Beverley W.

Bond, Jr., *The Civilization of the Old Northwest* (New York: The Macmillan Company, 1934), pp. 316–50; Roscoe C. Buley, *The Old Northwest Pioneer Period, 1815–1840* (Indianapolis: Indiana Historical Society, 1950), 1: 138–239.

[17] Rodney C. Loehr, "Self-Sufficiency on the Farm," *AH*, 26 (April 1952), 37–45.

[18] Paul C. Henlein, *Cattle Kingdom in the Ohio Valley, 1783–1860* (Lexington: University of Kentucky Press, 1959); Elizabeth L. Parr, "Kentucky's Overland Trade with the Ante-Bellum South," *HQ*, 2 (January 1929), 71–81; Thomas D. Clark, "Livestock Trade Between Kentucky and the South, 1840–1860," *RKSHS*, 27 (September 1929), 569–81.

[19] Charles T. Leavitt, "Transportation and the Livestock Industry of the Middle West to 1860," *AH*, 8 (January 1934), 20–33.

[20] The most recent work on the subject is Joe G. Clark, *Grain Trade of the Old Northwest* (Urbana: University of Illinois Press, 1966).

[21] During these early years before the War of 1812 some of the cotton (the amount is not really known) was produced by the Indians themselves. The bulk of the early production, though, was surely by the whites and their colored bondsmen. Charles S. Davis, *The Cotton Kingdom in Alabama* (Montgomery: Alabama State Department of Archives and History, 1939), p. 12.

[22] J. D. Anthony, "Cherokee County, Alabama, Reminiscences of Its Early Settlement," *AHQ*, 8 (Fall 1946) 331; John S. Bassett, *The Southern Plantation Overseer as Revealed in His Letters* (Northampton, Mass.: Smith College, 1925), pp. 44–45; Martin B. Coyner, "John Harwell Cocke of Bromo: Agriculture and Slavery in the Ante-Bellum South," Diss. University of Virginia, 1961, pp. 408–9; George Powell, "A Description of History of Blount County," *TAHS* (1855), pp. 40–42; Bayrd Still, "The Westward Migration of a Planter Pioneer in 1796," *WMHM*, 21 (October 1941) 320.

[23] In the case of the tobacco region of the Chesapeake Bay, however, the urban functions were performed by cities across the Atlantic. Thus, Virginia developed no "tobacco" port comparable to Charleston, Mobile, or New Orleans.

2   The problems of subsistence

[1] Figure 4 shows the proportion of landholdings over 500 acres in size in 1860. Although this does not indicate precisely where plantations were located, presumably there was a relation between landholding size and the existence of numerous large holdings. Figure 5 shows the average number of slaves per slaveholder, by county. Here, too, there should be a positive relation between large slaveholdings and large landholdings.

[2] The wisdom of concentrating on cash-crop production and

buying provisions was challenged frequently and vociferously by writers of the day. For examples see: *Southern Cultivator*, 3 (1845): 40, 11 (1853): 199–200; *American Cotton Planter*, 3 (1855): 106–7; *Soil of the South*, 4 (1854): 67–68; *The American Cotton Planter and Soil of the South*, 2 (1858): 96.

[3] M. B. Hammond, *The Cotton Industry* (New York: The Mac-Millan Company, 1897), p. 96.

[4] For a discussion of this problem, see: *Southern Cultivator*, 2 (1844): 177–78; *DeBow's Review*, 18 (1855): 339 ff, 21 (1856): 617–20; W. Stanley Hoole, "Advice to an Overseer: Extracts from the 1840–42 Plantation Journal of John Horry Dent," *AR*, 1 (January 1948), 56–62; Frederick L. Olmsted, *A Journey in the Back Country* (New York: Mason Brothers, 1863), p. 59; Franklin L. Riley, "Diary of a Mississippi Planter, January 1, 1840 to April, 1863," *PMHS*, 10 (1909): 311–12. For a recent appraisal of the general abilities of the overseer see William K. Scarborough, "The Plantation Overseer: A Re-evaluation," *AH*, 38 (January 1964), 13–20.

[5] There is a lively and amusing account of this attitude in *Southern Cultivator*, 2 (1844), 177–78. It contains a dialogue between a hypothetical "Col. Cottonbags" and a prospective overseer.

[6] Frank Tannenbaum, *Slave and Citizen: The Negro in America* (New York: Vintage Books, 1963) pp. 65 ff.

[7] U.S. Dept. of Agriculture, *Climate and Man*, Yearbook of Agriculture (Washington: U.S. Government Printing Office, 1941), pp. 756–59, 824–27, 940–43. This work is particularly useful since it contains not only climatic data but also a series of maps of the individual states.

[8] Stephen S. Visher, "Torrential Rains as a Serious Handicap in the South," *GR*, 21 (October 1941), 644–52.

[9] Robert D. Ward, *The Climates of the United States* (Boston: Ginn and Company, 1925), p. 479; Robert B. Lamb, *The Mule in Southern Agriculture*, University of California Publications in Geography (Berkeley and Los Angeles: University of California Press, 1963), p. 21.

[10] John F. H. Claiborne, "Trip Through the Piney Woods," *PMHS*, 9 (1906), 523.

[11] Charles Lyell, *Travels in North America in the Years 1841–42* (New York: Wiley and Putnam, 1845), 1: 127; John H. Moore, "South Mississippi in 1852: Some Selections from the Journal of Benjamin L. C. Wailes," *JMH*, 18 (January 1956), 20.

[12] George W. Featherstonhaugh, *Excursions Through the Slave States* (London: John Murray, 1844), 1: 185–86; *Southern Cultivator*, 17 (1859) 173.

[13] Basil Hall, *Travels in North America* (Edinburgh: Cadel and Company, 1829), 3: 251.

[14] The southern pine is a relatively fire-resistant plant capable of surviving groundfires hot enough to destroy most deciduous trees. Moreover, the longleaf pine seeds have difficulty germinating in the

mulch which develops on nonfired forest floors. The periodic burnings removed this carpet providing bare ground upon which the seeds could germinate. For discussions of the use of fire in southern pine forests see H. H. Chapman, "Is the Longleaf Type a Climax," *Ecology*, 13 (October 1932), 328–34; Kenneth H. Garren, "Effects of Fire on Vegetation of the Southern United States," *Botanical Review*, 9 (November 1943), 617–54; Earl J. Hodgkins, "Effects of Fire on Undergrowth Vegetation in Upland Southern Pine Forests," *Ecology*, 39 (January 1958), 36–46. All have extensive bibliographies on the subject. For an excellent discussion of fire from a historical-geographical perspective see Harry R. Merrins, Colonial North Carolina in the Eighteenth Century (Chapel-Hill: University of North Carolina Press, 1964), pp. 186–93.

[15] Though canes are common throughout the southeast today, many are recent introductions from abroad. The two cane species native to the area (*Arundinaria macrosperma* and *A. tecta*) are much smaller than those commonly used for "fishing poles." Such canes were found in dense patches during the early period and were depended upon heavily for livestock forage during winter. The long, or "switch cane," occurred along stream courses but the smaller cane (*A. tecta*) occurred widely through much of the pine forests.

[16] George G. Smith, Jr., *The History of Methodism in Georgia and Florida from 1785 to 1865* (Macon: Jno. W. Burke and Company, 1877), p. 43.

[17] Erhard Rostlund, "The Myth of a Natural Prairie Belt in Alabama: An Interpretation of Historical Records," *AAAG* 47 (December 1957), 392–411, for a discussion of the black belt as well as other "openings" in the southeast.

[18] *DeBow's Review*, 7 (1849), 40–41; R. C. Beckett, "Antebellum Times in Monroe County," *PHMS*, 11 (1910), 88. George E. Brewer, "History of Coosa County," *Alabama Historical Quarterly*, (Spring 1942), 36; A. J. Brown, *History of Newton County, Mississippi from 1834 to 1894* (Jackson: Clarion-Ledger Company, 1894), pp. 40–42.

[19] This, of course, is not meant to imply that there was no relation between soil fertility and food. In fact, this was one of the subjects that stimulated field work in the field of nutrition. Early in the present century nutritionists began detailed studies of rural diet. For a pioneer study done in the South see Dorothy Dickins, *A Study of Food Habits of People in two Contrasting Areas of Mississippi*, Mississippi Agricultural Experiment Station, Bull. No. 245, 1927.

3 "All kinds of good rations"

[1] Edgar W. Martin, *The Standard of Living in 1860* (Chicago: University of Chicago Press, 1942), pp. 57–64; Wilbur O. Atwater and Charles D. Woods, *Dietary Studies with Reference to the Food of the Negro in Alabama in 1895 and 1896*, U.S. Dept. of Agriculture,

Office of Experiment Stations Bull. No. 38 (Washington: U.S. Government Printing Office, 1897); Richard O. Cummings, *The American and His Food: A History of Food Habits in the United States,* rev. ed. (Chicago: University of Chicago Press, 1941); Dorothy Dickins, *A Study of Food Habits of People in Two Contrasting Areas of Mississippi,* Mississippi Agricultural Experiment Station Bull. No. 245, 1928.

² [Thomas Hamilton], *Men and Manners in America,* 2d ed. (London: T. Cadell, 1834), 2: 255, 258, 262.

³ Ibid.; Harriet Martineau, *Retrospect of Western Travel* (London: Saunders and Otley, 1838), 1: 212. See chapter 4 for detail on this particular food source.

⁴ J. D. Anthony, "Cherokee County Alabama, Reminiscences of Its Early Settlement," *AHQ,* 8 (Fall 1946), 331; Martin B. Coyner "John Hartwell Cocke of Bromo: Agriculture and Slavery in the Ante-Bellum South," Diss. University of Virginia 1961, pp. 408–9; George Powell, "A Description, and History of Blount County," *TAHS* (1855), 40–42; and Bayrd Still "The Westward Migration of a Planter Pioneer in 1796," *WMHM,* 21 (October 1941), 320.

⁵ Harriet Martineau, *Society in America* (2d ed. London: Saunders and Otley, 1837), 2: 203.

⁶ C. D. Arfwedson, *The United States and Canada, in 1832, 1833, and 1834.* (London: Richard Bentley, 1834), 2: 415.

⁷ Ibid. p. 11.

⁸ William H. Willis, "A Southern Sulky Ride in 1837, from North Carolina to Alabama," *PSHS,* 7 (January 1903), 12.

⁹ James R. Creecy, *Scenes in the South* (Washington: Thomas McGill, 1860), pp. 84, 106.

¹⁰ John S. Bassett, *The Southern Plantation Overseer as Revealed in His Letters* (Northampton, Mass: Smith College, 1925), p. 74.

¹¹ Francis M. Trollope, *Domestic Manners of the Americans* (London: Whittaker, Treacher and Company, 1832), p. 238.

¹² *Southern Cultivator,* 13 (1855), 23.

¹³ Ibid.

¹⁴ U.S. Patent Office, *Report of the Commissioner of Patents for the Year 1848,* No. 59, 30th Cong., 2d Sess., p. 724. Hereafter listed as *Patent Office Report.*

¹⁵ Frederick L. Olmsted, *A Journey in the Back Country* (New York: Mason Brothers, 1863), 161.

¹⁶ Emily Burke, *Reminiscences of Georgia* (Oberlin, Ohio: James M. Fitch, 1850), p. 233.

¹⁷ For detail on the current ideas see John C. Gunn, *Gunn's Domestic Medicine or Poor Man's Friend* . . . (Philadelphia: G. V. Raymond, 1840), 182.

¹⁸ John S. Wilson, "Health Department," *Godey's Lady's Book,* 60 February 1860), p. 178.

¹⁹ For descriptions of the curing processes used see *Cotton*

Planter and Soil, 3 (1859), 306; *Southern Cultivator*, 1 (1843), 172, 175, 195, 208; 7 (1849), 114; Burke, *Reminiscences*, p. 223; and Weymouth T. Jordan, *Herbs, Hoecakes and Husbandry: The Daybook of a Planter of the Old South* (Tallahassee: The Florida State University Press, 1960), pp. 45, 47-48, 52-54.

[20] Burke, *Reminiscences*, p. 222.

[21] *Southern Cultivator*, 1 (1843), 174 and 17 (1859), 339.

[22] Letter from Sarah Williams to Samuel Hicks of New Hartford, New York, December 10, 1833. In Sarah Hicks Williams Papers, Southern Historical Manuscript Collection, University of North Carolina, Chapel Hill, North Carolina. Hereafter all documents in this collection cited as *SHMC*, Chapel Hill, North Carolina.

[23] George G. Smith, Jr. *The History of Methodism in Georgia and Florida from 1785 to 1865* (Macon, Georgia: J. W. Burke and Co., 1877), p. 306.

[24] George E. Brewer, *AHQ*, 4 (Spring 1942), 127; Ulrich B. Phillips, *Life and Labor in the Old South* (Boston: Little, Brown and Company, 1929), p. 92.

[25] T. Lynn Smith and Lauren C. Post, "The Country Butchery: A Co-operative Institution," *Rural Sociology*, 2 (September 1937), 335-37.

[26] Ervin E. William, Journal for 1846, Nov. 17, 1846 in *SHMC*, Chapel Hill, North Carolina.

[27] *Patent Office Report*, 1850, p. 287; William P. Dale, "A Connecticut Yankee in Ante-Bellum Alabama," *AR*, 6 (January 1953), 63.

[28] *Soil of the South*, 2 (1852), 294.

[29] Louise Gladney, "History of Pleasant Hill Plantation, 1811-1867," Thesis Louisiana State University 1932, pp. 45-46; William J. Dickey, Diaries, 1858-1859, Manuscript Collection, University of Georgia, Athens, Georgia; Edward M. Steel, "A Pioneer Farmer in the Choctaw Purchase," *JMH*, 16 (October 1954), 235.

[30] Susan Dabney Smedes, *A Southern Planter: Social Life in the Old South* (New York: James Pott and Company, 1900), p. 81; *De Bow's Review*, 30 (1861), 645.

[31] Adam Hodgson, *Letters from North America* (London: Hurst, Robinson and Company, 1824), 1: 21, 31, and Martineau, *Society in America*, 1, 306.

[32] Olmsted, *Back Country*, p. 127.

[33] Sub Rosa [Paul Ravesies], *Scenes and Settlers of Alabama* ([Mobile]: n.p. [1885]), p. 9.

[34] L. C. Gray, *History of Agriculture in the Southern United States to 1860* (New York: Peter Smith, 1941), 2: 832. One questions why Gray chose the word "widespread" since he quotes but two references himself.

[35] J. S. Buckingham, *The Slave States of America* (London: Fisher, Son and Co., 1842), 1: 404; Herbert A. Kellar, *Solon Robinson: Pioneer and Agriculturalist*, Indiana Historical Collections, Vols.

21 and 22 (Indianapolis: Indiana Historical Bureau, 1936), 22, 161; Benjamin M. Norman, *New Orleans and Environs* (New Orleans: By the author, 1845), 56; Tyrone Power, *Impressions of America* (London: Richard Bently, 1836), 2: 250; Frances A. Kemble, *Journal of a Residence on a Georgia Plantation in 1838–1839*, ed. John A. Scott (New York: Alfred A. Knopf, 1961), p. 184.

[36] Martineau, *Society in America*, 2: 4.

[37] *Patent Office Report*, 1848, p. 516; Buckingham, *Slave States*, 1: 404; Kellar, *Solon Robinson*, 22: 161; Norman, *New Orleans*, p. 56; Power, *Impressions*, 2: 250; Smedes, *Southern Planter*, p. 82; Francis and Theresa Pulasky, *White, Red, Black: Sketches of American Society* (New York: Redfield, 1853), 2: 97.

[38] Kellar, 22: 161.

[39] *Patent Office Report*, 1849, p. 161.

[40] *Patent Office Report*, 1850, p. 365.

[41] Gladney, "Pleasant Hill," p. 46 and Wendell H. Stephenson, "A Quarter-Century of a Mississippi Plantation," *MVHR*, 23 (December 1936), 367.

[42] Kemble, *Residence*, p. 184.

[43] Smedes, *Southern Planter*, p. 82, Elizabeth W. A. Pringle, *Chronicles of Chicora Wood* (Boston: Christopher Publishing House, 1940), p. 89; Kolloch Plantation Books Vol. 5, *SHMC*, Chapel Hill, North Carolina.

[44] Martineau, *Society in America*, 1, 306; [Charles A. Clinton], *A Winter From Home* (New York: John F. Trow, 1852), p. 38; Margaret H. Hall, *The Aristocratic Journey* (New York: G. P. Putnam's Sons, 1931), pp. 209–21.

[45] Olmsted, *Back Country*, p. 140.

[46] Hamilton, *Men and Manners*, 2: 255–58; Martineau, *Retrospect of Western Travel*, 1: 212; Fredrika Bremer, *The Homes of the New World: Impressions of America*, trans., Mary Howitt (New York: Harper and Brothers, 1853), 1: 280, 288; William F. Gray, *From Virginia to Texas, 1835* (Houston: Gray, Dillaye and Company, 1909), pp. 40, 51; Frederick L. Olmsted, *The Cotton Kingdom* (New York: Mason Brothers, 1861), 2: 86; Frederick L. Olmsted, *Journey in the Seaboard Slave States* (New York: Mason Brothers, 1859), p. 565; and Wills, *PSHS*, 6 (November 1902), 473, 481.

[47] Sub Rosa, *Scenes*, p. 10; Martineau, *Retrospect of Western Travel*, 1: 212; Hamilton, *Men and Manners*, 2: 255, 258, 262.

[48] Philip H. Gosse, *Letters from Alabama* (London: Morgan and Chase, 1859), p. 128.

[49] Solomon Northup, *Twelve Years a Slave* (New York: Miller, Orton and Mulligan, 1855), p. 201.

[50] *DeBow's Review*, 15 (1853), 70.

[51] Olmsted, *Back Country*, pp. 198, 200, 240; Olmsted, *Cotton Kingdom*, 2: 86; Olmsted, *Seaboard Slave States*, p. 564.

[52] Charles Lyell, *A Second Visit to the United States of North America* (New York: Harper and Brothers, 1849), 1: 144.

[53] Martineau, *Society in America*, 1: 306.

[54] Gosse, *Letters*, pp. 46–47.

[55] *DeBow's Review*, 15 (1853), 70; David W. Mitchell, *Ten Years in the United States* (London: Smith, Elder and Company, 1862), p. 23; A. De Puy Van Buren, *Jottings of a Year's Sojourn in the South* (Battle Creek, Michigan: By the author, 1859), p. 46.

[56] Gosse, *Letters*, p. 46; Olmsted, *Back Country*, p. 242; Lyell, *Second Visit*, 2: 34; and William E. Dodd, *The Cotton Kingdom*, Vol. 27, *Chronicles of America*, ed. Allen Johnson, (New Haven: Yale University Press, 1921), p. 91.

[57] Olmsted, *Seaboard Slave States*, p. 478; Charles Lanman, *Adventures in the Wilds of the United States and British American Provinces* (Philadelphia: John W. Moore, 1856), 2: 137.

[58] Hall, *Aristocratic Journey*, 245; Hamilton, *Men and Manners*, 2: 241; Olmsted, *Back Country*, pp. 161–62.

[59] Lyell, *Second Visit*, 1: 144.

[60] Olmsted, *Seaboard Slave States*, p. 478.

[61] Bremer, *Homes of the New World*, 1: 280.

[62] Olmsted, *Seaboard Slave States*, 454–55.

[63] The process of canning in tins and bottles was in its infancy during the antebellum period, but other methods of keeping fruits preserved by sugar were well-developed. Thus, while the true canning of vegetables and meats was essentially a postwar phenomenon there was an abundance of preserves, jellies, and jams. See Martin, *Living in 1860*, pp. 27–33; Cummings, *The American and His Food*, 85; and Myrtie L. Candler, "Reminiscences of Life in Georgia During the 1850's and 1860's," *GHQ*, 30 (June 1949), 118.

[64] Olmsted, *Back Country*, p. 162; *Cotton Kingdom*, 2: 86; Claiborne, *PMHS*, 9 (1906), 522; Herbert Weaver, *Mississippi Farmers, 1850–1860* (Nashville: The Vanderbilt University Press, 1945), p. 50; Bennie C. Mellown, *Memoirs of a Pre Civil War Community* (Birmingham: The Birmingham Printing Company, 1950), p. 18.

[65] Arfwedson, *U.S. and Canada*, 2: 11 and Rosser H. Taylor, *Ante-Bellum South Carolina: A Social and Cultural History*, The James Sprunt Studies in History and Political Science, 25, No. 2 (Chapel Hill: University of North Carolina Press, 1942), p. 169.

[66] Lyell, *Second Visit*, 2: 158; Martineau, *Retrospect of Western Travel*, 1: 221; Martineau, *Society in America*, 1: 307; Olmsted, *Seaboard Slave States*, p. 625; Timothy Flint, *Recollections of the Last Ten Years* (Boston: Cummings, Hilliard, and Company, 1826), p. 365; James Stuart, *Three Years in North America* (New York: J. and J. Harper, 1833), 2: 123.

[67] U.S. Treasury Dept. *A Report of the Commerce and Navigation of the United States for 1856*, 34th Cong. 3d Sess., 13: 459–63.

[68] Gosse, *Letters*, p. 47; Van Buren, *Jottings*, p. 46; Lyell, *Second Visit*, 2: 158; Mitchell, *Ten Years*, p. 23; and Martineau, *Retrospect of Western Travel*, 1: 212.

[69] Lewis E. Atherton, *The Southern Country Store, 1800–1860*

(Baton Rouge: Louisiana State University Press, 1949), pp. 78–80; Wellington Vandiver, "Pioneer Talladega, Its Minutes and Memories,": *AHQ*, 16 (Spring 1954), 131; and Ernest C. Hynds Jr., "Ante-Bellum Athens and Clarke County," Diss. University of Georgia, 1961, p. 258.

[70] Buckingham, *Slave States of America*, 1: 246, 251, 287.

[71] Hynds, p. 259; John Hardy, *Selma: Her Institutions and Her Men* (fascimile reprint of the original published in 1879 by the Times Book and Job Office, Selma: Bert Neville and Clarence DeBray, 1957) p. 117. For detail on the ice trade during the prerefrigeration period see Richard O. Cummings, *The American Ice Harvests: A Historical Study in Technology, 1800–1918* (Berkeley and Los Angeles: University of California Press, 1949).

[72] Vandiver, *AHQ*, 16 (Spring 1954), 130–31.

[73] "Modern Ice Cream, and the Philosophy of Its Manufacture," *Godey's Lady's Book*, 60 (May 1860), 460–61; Martineau, *Society in America*, 1: 307; Martineau, *Retrospect of Western Travel*, 1: 221; Lyell, *Second Visit*, 2: 158.

[74] John B. Grimball, Diaries, Oct. 18, 1832, SHMC. Chapel Hill, North Carolina.

[75] Ibid., Oct. 16, 1832.

[76] Ibid., July 7, 1832.

[77] Van Buren, *Jottings*, p. 46.

[78] Mitchell, *Ten Years*, pp. 23, 37.

[79] For discussions of slave food see Charles S. Davis, *Cotton Kingdom in Alabama* (Montgomery: Alabama State Department of Archives and History, 1939); James B. Sellers, *Slavery in Alabama* (University, Ala.: University of Alabama Press, 1950); Ralph B. Flanders, *Plantation Slavery in Georgia* (Chapel Hill: University of North Carolina Press, 1933); Joe G. Taylor, *Negro Slavery in Louisiana* (Baton Rouge: Louisiana Historical Association, 1963); Rosser H. Taylor, *Slaveholding in North Carolina;* "Feeding Slaves," *JNH*, 9 (January 1924), 139–43; Charles S. Sydnor, *Slavery in Mississippi* (New York: Appleton-Century Company, 1933; Ulrich B. Phillips, *American Negro Slavery* (New York: D. Appleton and Company, 1918); and Kenneth M. Stampp, *The Peculiar Institution: Slavery in the Ante-Bellum South* (New York: Alfred A. Knopf, 1956). For contemporary views on the subject see *Southern Cultivator*, 8 (1850), 162–64; *Southern Agriculturist*, NS 6 (1846), 224–27; *DeBow's Review*, 3 (1847), 419–20; 7 (1849), 380–83; 14 (1853), 177–78; 25 (1858), 571–72.

[80] Charles S. Sydnor, *A Gentleman of the Old Natchez Region: Benjamin L. C. Wailes* (Durham: Duke University Press, 1938), 98.

[81] Ulrich B. Phillips, ed., *Plantation and Frontier Documents: 1649–1863*, Vols. 1 and 2, *Documentary History of American Industrial Society* (Cleveland: The Arthur H. Clark Company, 1909), 1: 332.

[82] See *DeBow's Review,* 7 (1849), 380–82; *Cotton Planter and Soil,* 2 (1858), 113; *Southern Cultivator,* 12 (1854), 205; James D. B. DeBow, *The Industrial Resources, Statistics, Etc., of the United States,* 3 vols. in one (New York: D. Appleton and Company, 1854), 2: 331.

[83] One doctor actually recommended fat meat for slaves because he thought it to be an excellent "heat generating" substance. This is despite the fact that he considered fat meat and grease detrimental to southern whites. *Cotton Planter and Soil,* 4 (1860), 126 and *DeBow's Review,* 19 (1855), 359.

[84] Davis, *Cotton Kingdom in Alabama,* p. 82.

[85] *DeBow's Review,* 19 (1855), 358–59.

[86] *Soil of the South,* 3 (1853), 753; *Southern Cultivator,* 1 (1843), 172, 175; 7 (1849), 114; *Cotton Planter and Soil,* 3 (1859), 306.

[87] *DeBow's Review,* 12 (1852), 69–70.

[88] Ibid.

[89] *DeBow's Review,* 24 (1858), 325.

[90] Gladney, "Pleasant Hill," p. 25.

[91] Kellar, *Solon Robinson,* 22: 149.

[92] *Southern Cultivator,* VIII (1850), 4 and *Southern Agriculturist,* NS 5 (1845), 314.

[93] Weymouth T. Jordan, *Hugh Davis and his Alabama Plantation* (University, Ala.: University of Alabama Press, 1948), p. 84; Ralph B. Flanders, "Two Plantations and a County of Ante-Bellum Georgia," *GHQ,* 12 (March 1928), 11; Francis Butler Leigh, *Ten Years on a Georgia Plantation Since the War* (London: Richard Bentley and Son, 1883), 233; Taylor, *Ante-Bellum South Carolina,* 54; William H. Holcombe, "Sketches of Plantation Life," *The Knickerbocker Magazine,* 57 (June 1861), 621.

[94] Phillips, *Documents,* 1: 129.

[95] Kellar, *Solon Robinson,* 22: 367; Smedes, *Southern Planter,* pp. 82–84; Pringle, *Chicora Wood,* p. 89; Davis, *Cotton Kingdom in Alabama,* p. 56.

[96] DeBow, *Industrial Resources,* 2: 425; David Doar, *Rice and Rice Planting in the South Carolina Low Country* The Charleston Museum Contributions, No. 8 (Charleston: The Charleston Museum, 1936), p. 32.

[97] Olmsted, *Seaboard Slave States,* 439; Kellar, *Solon Robinson,* 22: 367; *DeBow's Review* 24 (1859), 325; Fredrika Bremer, *America of the Fifties; Letters of Fredrika Bremer,* ed. Adolph B. Benson (New York: The American-Scandinavian Foundation, 1924), p. 111; V. Alton Moody, "Slavery on Louisiana Sugar Plantations," *LHQ,* 7 (April 1924), 255; and M. B. Hammond, *The Cotton Industry* (New York: The Macmillan Company, 1897), p. 91.

[98] Evidence bearing this out appears in journal entries. For example, Ben Sparkman records paying for hogs at four and five cents

per pound from names such as "Sam," "Toby," "Prince," and "Lindy," suggesting he was buying pork from his own slaves. Ben Sparkman, Plantation Record 1853–59, Dec. 22, 1853, Jan. 24, 1854 and Sparkman Family Papers, Vol. 7, 1858, SHMC, Chapel Hill, North Carolina.

[99] Jordan, *Hugh Davis and His Alabama Plantation*, pp. 128–29; Sydnor, *A Gentleman of the Old Natchez Region*, p. 101; DeBow, *Industrial Resources*, 2: 331; *DeBow's Review*, 14 (1853), 177; *Southern Cultivator*, 7 (1850), 162; and *Southern Agriculturist*, NS 6 (1846), 225.

[100] *Southern Cultivator*, 2 (1844), 204; James Ewell, *The Planter's and Mariner's Medical Companion* (Washington: P. Mauro, 1807), p. 197.

[101] *Southern Agriculturist*, 6 (1846), 225 and Jordan, *Hugh Davis and His Alabama Plantation*, pp. 123, 129.

[102] Gosse, *Letters*, pp. 194, 253.

[103] *DeBow's Review*, 13 (1852), 193; Sydnor, *Slavery in Mississippi*, p. 35; John Q. Anderson, "Dr. James Green Carson, Ante-Bellum Planter of Mississippi and Louisiana," *JMH*, 18 (October 1956), 246; John Berkley Grimball, Diary, Dec. 25, 1832; William E. Sparkman, Plantation Record, March 1844–Jan. 1846; Letter from Sarah Williams of North Carolina to her parents in New Hartford, New York, Dec. 10, 1853 in Sarah Hicks Williams Papers. In a letter to his overseer, R. J. Arnold instructed him to "give a little molasses occasionally to the children once a day." R. J. Arnold to A. M. Sanford, May 19, 1840, Arnold-Scriven Papers. The last four items are in SHMC, Chapel Hill, North Carolina.

[104] Olmsted, *Cotton Kingdom*, 2: 180 and Kellar, *Solon Robinson*, 22: 381.

[105] *DeBow's Review*, 14 (1853), 177; Sellers, *Slavery in Alabama*, p. 89; Phillips, *American Negro Slavery*, 266; John B. Cade, "Out of the Mouths of Ex-Slaves," *JNH*, 20 (January 1935), 299–301; John F. H. Claiborne, *Life and Correspondence of John A. Quitman* (New York: Harper and Brothers, 1860), 1: 80.

[106] Cade, *JNH*, 20 (January 1935), 300.

[107] Ibid., 299–301; Flanders, *GHQ*, 12 (March 1928), 7; Pulszky and Pulszky, *Sketches*, 2: 105; DeBow, *Industrial Resources*, 331; *DeBow's Review*, 24 (1860), 359; Guion G. Johnson, *A Social History of the Sea Islands* (Chapel Hill: University of North Carolina Press, 1930), p. 136.

[108] *Southern Agriculturist*, NS 6 (1846), 225; *Southern Cultivator*, 8 (1850), 162; Cade, *JNH*, 20 (January 1935), 299–301; Sellers, *Slavery in America*, pp. 95–97; *DeBow's Review*, 7 (1849), 382; 14 (1853), 177; 25 (1858), 571; 22 (1857), 39, 376; *Cotton Planter and Soil*, 2 (1858), 293.

[109] Letter from R. J. Arnold to A. M. Sanford, May 19, 1840, Arnold-Scriven Papers, SHMC, Chapel Hill, North Carolina.

[110] Dickins, *Food Habits in Mississippi*, p. 33; Dorothy Dickins,

A Nutrition Investigation of Negro Tenants in the Yazoo Mississippi Delta, Mississippi Agricultural Experiment Station Bull., No. 254 (1928), 37.

[111] Cummings, *American and His Food,* p. 74.

[112] *Cotton Planter and Soil,* 4 (1860), 126–27; Wilson, *Godey's Lady's Book,* 60 (February 1860), 178; Gunn, *Domestic Medicine,* p. 182.

[113] *Cotton Planter and Soil,* 2 (1858), 293; 4 (1860), 126–27; Ewell, *Medical Companion,* pp. 65, 197; William D. Postell, *The Health of Slaves on Southern Plantations* (Baton Rouge: Louisiana State University Press, 1951), pp. 32–34.

[114] For details on the general health of slaves and medical care in the South see Postell; Felice Swados, "Negro Health on the Ante-Bellum Plantation," *BHM,* 10 (1941), 460–72; Richard H. Shyrock, "Medical Practice in the Old South," *SAQ,* 29 (April 1930), 160–78; Weymouth T. Jordan, "Plantation Medicine in the Old South," *AR,* 3 (April 1950), 83–107; Victor H. Bassett, "Plantation Medicine," *Journal of the Medical Association of Georgia,* 29 (March 1940), 112–22.

[115] For a discussion of the relative nutritional values of southern foods see Atwater and Woods, *Dietary Studies,* pp. 12–15: These data on food values are somewhat out of date, but they may be more representative of the values of some nineteenth-century southern foods than present day tests.

[116] Lloyd B. Jensen, *Man's Foods: Nutrition and Environments in Food Gathering Times and Food Producing Times* (Champaign, Ill.: The Garrard Press, 1953), p. 189.

[117] Mark Graubard, *Man's Food, Its Rhyme or Reason* (New York: The Macmillan Company, 1943), p. 120. The appearance of vitamin A seems related to the amount of yellow pigment present in vegetables. Carrots are rich in vitamin A but were not widely consumed in the area. Some varieties of sweet potatoes (generally the yellow tubers) were helpful since they contained sizable amounts. See Barnett Sure, *The Vitamins in Health and Disease* (Baltimore: The Williams and Wilkins Company, 1933), pp. 28 ff. and Henry C. Sherman, *Chemistry of Food and Nutrition* (New York: The Macmillan Company, 1952), pp. 482–84 for discussions of this relationship.

[118] Postell, *Health of Slaves,* p. 85.

[119] Ibid.; Graubard, p. 120; Sherman, p. 416; Sure, pp. 128 ff; Josue' de Castro, *The Geography of Hunger* (Boston: Little, Brown, and Company, 1952), pp. 127 ff. See also E. J. Underwood, *Trace Elements in Human and Animal Nutrition* (New York: Academic Press, Inc., 1956).

[120] Atwater and Woods, *Dietary Studies,* pp. 64–69.

[121] Dickins, *Nutrition of Negro Tenants in Mississippi,* 15–17, 26.

[122] Susan B. Mathews, *Food Habits of Georgia Rural People,* Georgia Experiment Station Bull. No. 159, 27. For additional evi-

dence see H. D. Frissell and Isabel Bevier, *Dietary Studies of Negroes in Eastern Virginia*, U.S. Department of Agriculture, Office of Experiment Stations, Bull. No. 71 (1897–98).

[123] Cummings, *The American and His Food*, p. 258.

[124] As share cropping and tenancy become entrenched throughout the cotton belt, the plantation store came to be a landmark. In the store were stored goods sold or "furnished" to the tenants of which "side meat" was one of the more important items. Many people today can recall seeing the "meat box" in the corner of these stores filled with large pieces (perhaps fifteen by thirty inches in size and four inches thick) of white salt meat. Many, too, can remember seeing warehouses in Memphis, Nashville, Atlanta, Montgomery, or Jackson filled with stacks of such white slabs. It is this writer's opinion that extreme dependence upon these white slabs of side meat by tenants in the South during the early twentieth century has influenced students of southern history to assume that southern pork during the antebellum period was similar. Of course, there was a great deal of fat meat consumed before the war, but it appears unlikely that it reached the proportions prevalent by the turn of the century.

[125] Swados, *BHM*, 10 (1941), 471 and Emily S. Maclachlan, "The Diet Pattern of the South: A Study in Regional Sociology," Thesis University of North Carolina 1932, p. 22.

4   The forests, streams, and the sea

[1] Prime examples in twentieth-century America are the opossum and the armadillo. Both have increased their range greatly in the past century. The opossum, traditionally a "southern" animal, can be found over most of the nation, from the garbage cans of New York City to the coniferous forests of central Wisconsin. The armadillo is no longer identified with the West, having invaded a number of other areas. In parts of Florida it is numerous enough to be regarded as a pest.

[2] For some of the works dealing with habitat conditions in relation to forest management see George W. Allen, "The Management of Georgia Deer," *JWM*, 12 (October 1948), 428–32; Coleman Newman and Edward Griffin, "Deer and Turkey Habitats and Populations of Florida," Florida Fish and Game Commission, Technical Bull. No. 1 (1950); Herbert L. Stoddard and Edward V. Komarek, "The Carrying Capacity of Southeastern Quail Lands," Cooperative Quail Study Association Misc. Pub. No. 1 (Tallahassee, Fla.: Tall Timber Research Station, 1961), 477–84; Herbert L. Stoddard, "Relation of Burning to Timber and Wildlife," *Proceedings of the North America Wildlife Conference* (Washington, 1936).

[3] William Elliot, *Carolina Sports by Land and Water* (New York: Derby and Jackson, 1859), p. 271.

[4] This leaves us with a philosophical problem. The statement

rests on the notion of a nature-culture dichotomy in which case all human activity is considered separate from nature's activity. However, considering the place of the American Indian in the "natural" habitat, then one might argue that there was nothing "*un* natural" about him. For our purposes we will assume simply that he was a significant modifier of the habitat.

⁵ Gladys B. Avant, "History of Washington County, Alabama to 1860," Thesis University of Alabama 1929, p. 45; Warren I. Smith, "Structure of Landholdings and Slaveownership in Ante-Bellum Montgomery County, Alabama," Diss. University of Alabama, 1952, pp. 92–95.

⁶ Frank L. Owsley, *Plain Folk of the Old South* (Baton Rouge: Louisiana State University Press, 1949), p. 36.

⁷ Based on U.S. Censuses of 1850, 1860, and 1880. Does not include Florida.

⁸ Bernard Romans, *A Concise Natural History of East and West Florida*, ed. L. Richardson (New Orleans: Pelican, 1961), pp. 58, 64; Benjamin Hawkins, "Letters of Benjamin Hawkins, 1796–1806," *GHSC*, 11 (1916), 87.

⁹ George E. Brewer, "History of Coosa County", *AHQ*, 4 (Spring 1942), 36, 103. See also [Charles A. Clinton], *A Winter From Home* (New York: John F. Trow, 1852), pp. 38–39; James R. Creecy, *Scenes in the South* (Washington: Thomas McGill, 1860), pp. 84, 90–91; Philip H. Gosse, *Letters From Alabama* (London: Morgan and Chase, 1859), pp. 267–68; Charles Lanman, *Adventures in the Wilds of the United States and British American Provinces* (Philadelphia: John W. Moore, 1856), pp. 100, 129, 190, 193–94.

¹⁰ Harriet Martineau, *Retrospect of Western Travel* (London: Saunders and Otley, 1838), 1: 212; [Thomas Hamilton], *Men and Manners in America*, 2d ed. (London: T. Cadell, 1834), 2: 255, 258, 262.

¹¹ Frances A. Kemble, *Journal of a Residence on a Georgia Rice Plantation in 1838–1839*, John A. Scott, ed. (New York: Alfred A. Knopf, 1961), p. 58.

¹² Tyrone Power, *Impressions of America* (London: Richard Bently, 1836), 2: 224.

¹³ Henry B. Whipple, *Bishop Whipple's Southern Diary, 1843–44*, ed. Lester B. Shipee (Minneapolis: University of Minnesota Press, 1937), p. 103.

¹⁴ John F. H. Claiborne, "Trip Through the Piney Woods" *PMHS*, 9 (1906), 522.

¹⁵ *DeBow's Review*, 6 (1848), 429.

¹⁶ *Southern Cabinet . . .* , 1 (1840), 125. Not only was this a bit of perceptive reporting, it proved to be an accurate prophetic statement. The Carolina lowlands were one of the last strongholds of the whitetail after they were decimated elsewhere in the South, and they harbor a huge herd today.

[17] Frederick L. Olmsted, *Journey in the Seaboard Slave States,* (New York: Mason Brothers, 1859), p. 411.

[18] Lanman, *Adventures,* 2: 193–94.

[19] Brewer, *AHQ,* 4 (Spring 1942), 103. For descriptions of deer hunting in Alabama see Gosse, *Letters,* pp. 267–68.

[20] Olmsted, *Seaboard Slave States,* p. 630.

[21] Joe G. Taylor, *Negro Slavery in Louisiana* (Baton Rouge: Louisiana Historical Association, 1963), p. 126.

[22] John B. Cade, "Out of the Mouths of Ex-Slaves," *JNH,* 20 (January 1935), 302.

[23] Henry W. Harrington, Jr., "Excerpts from the Private Journal of Henry William Harrington," in Harrington Papers, *SHMC,* Chapel Hill, North Carolina.

[24] For a detailed description of deer hunting in Louisiana see *DeBow's Review,* 5 (1848), 220–29. The same methods were common to much of the South. See also Claiborne, *PMHS,* 9 (1906), 522–32; James R. Maxwell, *Autobiography* (New York: Greenberg, 1926), p. 102; William H. Sparks, *The Memories of Fifty Years* (Macon: J. W. Burke and Co., 1870), p. 332; Lanman, *Adventures,* 2: 193–94; and Gosse, *Letters,* pp. 267–68.

[25] Ernest T. Seton, *Lives of Game Animals . . .* (Garden City, New York: Doubleday, Page and Company, 1929), 3: 246.

[26] Burton L. Dahlberg and Ralph C. Guettinger, *The White-Tailed Deer in Wisconsin,* Wisconsin Conservation Department Technical Wildlife Bull. No. 14 (Madison: Game Management Division of Wisconsin Conservation Department, 1956), 14–15.

[27] The cottontail was not the only species in the area, but it was the most widespread and the most numerous.

[28] Sparks, *Memories,* p. 331.

[29] Gosse, *Letters,* p. 44.

[30] *Southern Cabinet . . . ,* 1 (1840), p. 125; Frederick L. Olmsted, *A Journey in the Back Country* (New York: Mason Brothers, 1863), p. 27.

[31] Maxwell, *Autobiography,* p. 13.

[32] Everard G. Baker, Diaries, Vol. 1, October 30, 1849, *SHMC,* Chapel Hill, North Carolina.

[33] Charles Lyell, *A Second Visit to the United States of North America* (New York: Harper and Brothers, 1849), 2: 17; William H. Russell, *My Diary North and South* (New York: Harper and Brothers, 1863), p. 88.

[34] [Clinton], *Winter from Home,* p. 38; Lanman, *Adventures,* 2: 193–94.

[35] [Clinton], p. 39; Lanman, 2: 140; Frederick L. Olmsted, *The Cotton Kingdom* (New York: Mason Brothers, 1861), 1: 196; Gosse, *Letters,* pp. 57–58; Brewer, *AHQ,* 4 (Spring 1942), 101.

[36] Gosse, 100–101.

[37] Lanman, 2: 129, 140.

[38] Kemble, *Residence*, p. 58.

[39] David Golightly Harris, Farm Journals, 1857–1858, *SHMC*, Chapel Hill, North Carolina.

[40] Elliot, *Carolina Sports*, p. 270.

[41] Brewer, *AHQ*, 4 (Spring 1942), 101. One conservationist assumes they were plentiful over most of Alabama until about 1880. Robert J. Wheeler, Jr., *The Wild Turkey in Alabama* (Montgomery: Alabama Department of Conservation, 1948).

[42] [Clinton], *Winter from Home*, p. 5; Timothy Flint, *Recollections of the Last Ten Years* (Boston: Cummings, Hilliard, and Company, 1826), p. 365; Whipple, *Southern Diary*, p. 103.

[43] Flint, p. 365.

[44] Francis M. Trollope, *Domestic Manners of the Americans* (London: Whittaker, Treacher, and Company, 1832), p. 239.

[45] John Nevitt, Journal, February 6, 1830, *SHMC*, Chapel Hill, North Carolina.

[46] For an account of the life of one such "market hunter" see John E. Cay, Jr., *Ward Allen: Savannah River Market Hunter* (Savannah: By the author, 1958).

[47] J. D. Anthony, "Cherokee County, Alabama, Reminiscences of Its Early Settlement," *AHQ*, 8 (Fall 1946), 351; John P. Arthur, *Western North Carolina* (Raleigh: Edwards and Broughton Printing Company, 1914), pp. 524–25; Edwin J. Scott, *Random Recollections of a Long Life* (Columbia: Charles A. Calvo, Jr., 1884), pp. 96–97; John R. Swanton, *The Indians of the Southeastern United States*, Bureau of American Ethnology, Bull. No. 137 (Washington: U.S. Government Printing Office, 1946), 310–28.

[48] This was probably true of coastal Carolina, but one suspects they were more common in the deciduous forests nearer the Appalachians. Elliot's book is biased strongly toward the coastal areas. Elliot, *Carolina Sports*, p. 273.

[49] Emily Burke, *Reminiscences of Georgia* (Oberlin, Ohio: James M. Fitch, 1850), p. 140.

[50] Russell, *My Diary North and South*, p. 77.

[51] Earl C. May, *The Canning Clan* (New York: The Macmillan Company, 1937), p. 11; Edward S. Judge, "American Canning Interests," *One Hundred Years of American Commerce*, ed. Chauncy M. Depew (New York: D. O. Haynes and Company, 1895), p. 397.

[52] *DeBow's Review*, 24 (1858), 259–60 and 30 (1861), 112–14.

[53] John C. Butler, *Historical Record of Macon and Central Georgia*, Reprint of 1879 ed. (Macon: J. W. Burke Company, 1958), p. 162; Russell, *My Diary North and South*, p. 88.

[54] Olmsted, *Cotton Kingdom*, 2: 119.

[55] Rosser H. Taylor, *Ante-Bellum South Carolina: A Social and Cultural History*, The James Sprunt Studies in History and Political Science, 25, No. 2 (Chapel Hill: University of North Carolina Press, 1942), p. 169; [Clinton], *Winter from Home*, p. 15.

⁵⁶ Diary of W. Thacker quoted in Taylor, *Ante-Bellum South Carolina,* p. 15.

⁵⁷ Burke, *Reminiscences,* p. 139. The drum commonly taken along the Georgia-Carolina coast is *Pogonia cromis,* and is probably the fish mentioned frequently during the antebellum period. It is possible, though, that the "four or five hundred" pounders described by Miss Burke were groupers, since drum seldom attain a weight in excess of one hundred pounds. It is possible, too, that her report was based not upon fact but upon local information in which case one can forgive the inaccuracy.

⁵⁸ Ulrich B. Phillips, *Plantation and Frontier Documents: 1649–1863,* Vols. 1 and 2 of *Documentary History of American Industrial Society* (Cleveland, Ohio: The Arthur H. Clark Company, 1909), 1: 203 ff.; Guion G. Johnson, *A Social History of the Sea Islands* (Chapel Hill: University of North Carolina Press, 1930), p. 142.

⁵⁹ For descriptions of some of the fish as well as fishing methods see Fredrika Bremer, *America of the Fifties: Letters of Fredrika Bremer,* ed. Adolph B. Benson (New York: The American-Scandinavian Foundation, 1924), p. 296; Phillips, *Documents,* 1: 203 ff.; Burke, *Reminiscences,* pp. 139–40; Johnson, p. 142.

⁶⁰ Weymouth T. Jordan, *Hugh Davis and His Alabama Plantation* (University: University of Alabama Press, 1948), p. 126. For other examples see Taylor, *Slavery in Louisiana,* p. 108; Sub Rosa [Paul Ravesies], *Scenes and Settlers of Alabama* ([Mobile]: n. p. [1885]), p. 9.

⁶¹ John Q. Anderson, "Dr. James Green Carson, Ante-Bellum Planter of Mississippi and Louisiana," *JMH,* 18 (October 1956), 261.

⁶² See Sub Rosa, p. 9 for a description of the baskets, method of using them and the Negroes' system of fishing.

⁶³ J. S. Buckingham, *The Slave States of America* (London: Fisher, Son, and Company, 1842), 1: 262.

⁶⁴ Herbert Weaver, *Mississippi Farmers, 1850–1860* (Nashville: Vanderbilt University Press, 1945), p. 51; Taylor, *Slavery in Louisiana,* p. 108.

⁶⁵ Martineau, *Retrospect,* 1: 217.

⁶⁶ Richard J. Arnold, Plantation Journal for Cherry Hill and White Hall Plantations, January and February, 1847, Arnold Scriven Papers, *SHMC,* Chapel Hill, North Carolina.

⁶⁷ Bryan Grimes, Grimes Family Papers. In a series of journals and account books covering the period from the late 1830s up to the war, Grimes recorded weekly catches of shad and herring, fish rations issued slaves, and commercial sales of fish. He estimated that fishing brought him eight hundred dollars in 1840. For other examples, see William D. Valentine, Diaries, April 12, 1839 and Edward Wood, Greenfield Fishery Records, 1844–60. All of the above are in *SHMC,* Chapel Hill, North Carolina.

⁶⁸ Charles R. Stevenson, "Fisheries in the Ante-Bellum South," in *Economic History, 1607–1865,* ed. James C. Ballagh, Vol. 5 in *The*

South in the Building of the Nation (Richmond: Southern Historical Publishing Society, 1909), p. 267.

[69] Buckingham, *Slave States*, 1: 157; Butler, *Central Georgia*, p. 162.

[70] Buckingham, 1: 273; *American Cotton Planter*, 4 (1856), 314.

[71] David Golightly Harris, Farm Journals, SHMC, Chapel Hill, North Carolina.

[72] Flint, *Reflections*, p. 356. The trout referred to so often in early literature was probably bass. In much of the South today the bass commonly is referred to as trout, though in the mountains only a hundred miles or so away the true trout is found.

[73] William Proctor Gould, Diary, June 16, 1852 in State Department of Archives and History, Montgomery, Alabama.

[74] Russell, *My Diary North and South*, 71; Whipple, *Southern Diary*, p. 29; Taylor, *Negro Slavery in Louisiana*, p. 108; Weaver, *Mississippi Farmer*, pp. 50–51; Anderson, *JMH*, 18 (October 1956), 261; Solomon Northup, *Twelve Years a Slave* (New York: Miller, Orton and Mulligan, 1855), pp. 202–3; A. de Puy Van Buren, *Jottings of a Year's Sojourn in the South* (Battle Creek, Mich.: By the author, 1859), p. 166; Jordan, *Hugh Davis and His Alabama Plantation*, p. 126.

[75] Maxwell, *Autobiography*, p. 16.

[76] John M. Mackie, *From Cape Cod to Dixie and the Tropics* (New York: G. P. Putnam, 1864), p. 185; Charles Mackay, *Life and Liberty in America* (London: Smith, Elder and Company, 1859), 1: 324; Edward J. Thomas, *Memoirs of a Southerner* (Savannah: By the author, 1923), p. 10; Gosse, *Letters*, p. 96; and Lanman, *Adventures*, 2: 137.

[77] Mackie, p. 185. See also Amelia M. Murray, *Letters from the United States, Cuba and Canada* (New York: G. P. Putnam and Company, 1857), p. 202 and Butler, *Historical Record*, p. 162.

[78] Lyell, *Second Visit*, 2: 158; John Berkley Grimball, Diary, June 13, 1832, SHMC, Chapel Hill, North Carolina.

[79] Anne Royall, *Letters from Alabama* (Washington: By the author, 1830), p. 163.

[80] Virginia P. Brown and Jane P. Nabers, "Mary Gordan Duffee's 'Sketches of Alabama,'" *AR*, 9 (April 1956), 285; Buckingham, *Slave States*, 1: 542–43.

[81] Jonathan D. Sauer, "A Geography of Pokeweed," *Annals of the Missouri Botannical Garden*, 39 (May 1952), 113–25.

5   Pork: the South's first choice

[1] Everard Green Baker, Diaries, Vol. I, Aug. 17, 1849, SHMC, Chapel Hill, North Carolina.

[2] For a few examples, see *Southern Cultivator*, 1 (1843), 115–16, 172, 174; 11 (1853), 2–3; 14 (1856), 209–10; *Soil of the*

South, 6 (1856), 67–68; *Cotton Planter and Soil,* 1 (1857), 5, 239; 3 (1859), 305–6; *Farmer and Planter,* 12 (1861), 238.

[3] L. C. Gray, *History of Agriculture in the Southern United States to 1860* (New York: Peter Smith, 1941), 1: 138–51, 200–212, 2: 831–57; James W. Thompson, *A History of Livestock Raising in the United States, 1607–1860,* U.S. Dept. of Agriculture, Agricultural History Series No. 5 (Washington: U.S. Government Printing Office, 1942); Eugene D. Genovese, "Livestock in the Slave Economy of the Old South—A Revised View," *AH,* 36 (July 1962), 143–49.

[4] Philip H. Gosse, *Letters From Alabama* (London: Morgan and Chase, 1859), p. 63.

[5] *Southern Cultivator,* 11 (1853), 2.

[6] For examples see *Southern Cultivator,* 11 (1853), 2–3; 13 (1855), 19; 14 (1856), 209–10; *Cotton Planter and Soil,* 1 (1857), 239; 2 (1858), 60–61. For a discussion of swine improvement in one state, consult John H. Moore, *Agriculture in Ante-Bellum Mississippi* (New York: Bookman Associates, 1958), pp. 95–101. For a more general critique of southern attempts at livestock improvement see Eugene D. Genovese, *The Political Economy of Slavery: Studies in the Economy and Society of the Slave South* (New York: Random House, 1965), pp. 106–23.

[7] *Cotton Planter and Soil,* 3 (1859), 70–71; *Southern Cultivator,* 11 (1853), 2–3; 13 (1855), 19; 14 (1856), 209–10; *Soil of the South,* 6 (1856), 39–40.

[8] Genovese, *AH,* 36 (July 1962), 147.

[9] Moore, *Agriculture in Ante-Bellum Mississippi,* p. 64.

[10] For a description of spaying see *Southern Cultivator,* 2 (1844), 74.

[11] Letter from John M. Chapron of Philadelphia to James H. Haughton of Huntsville, Alabama. October 21 (1840), John M. Chapron Lettercopy Book, *SHMC,* Chapel Hill, North Carolina.

[12] James Stuart, *Three Years in North America* (New York: J. and J. Harper, 1833), 2: 63.

[13] Gosse, *Letters,* p. 271; Herbert A. Kellar, *Solon Robinson: Pioneer and Agriculturalist,* Indiana Historical Collections, Vols. 21 and 22 (Indianapolis: Indiana Historical Bureau, 1936), 22: 137.

[14] Anne K. Walker, *Backtracking in Barbour County* (Richmond: The Dietz Press, 1941), p. 106.

[15] Letter from Howell Adams to William Smith, November 29, 1847 in William R. Smith Papers, *SHMC,* Chapel Hill, North Carolina.

[16] *Southern Cultivator,* 17 (1859), 359; *Patent Office Reports,* 1848, p. 502; 1850, p. 322; Ulrich B. Phillips and James D. Glunt, eds., *Florida Plantation Records from the Papers of George Noble Jones* (St. Louis: Missouri Historical Society, 1927), p. 114; Emily Burke, *Reminiscences of Georgia* (Oberlin, Ohio; James M. Fitch, 1850), p. 126.

[17] *Cotton Planter and Soil,* 1 (1857), 30–31, 239; 2 (1858),

60–61; *Soil of the South,* 5 (1855), 7–8; *Southern Cultivator,* 14 (1856), 365.

[18] References to such systems are legion; see *Southern Cultivator,* 7 (1849), 113; 11 (1853), 2–3, 111; 13 (1855), 305; *Farmer and Planter,* 12 (1861), 235; *Cotton Planter and Soil,* 2 (1858), 60–61; *Soil of the South,* 6 (1856), 39–40; *Patent Office Report,* 1852, p. 66.

[19] *Cotton Planter and Soil,* 2 (1858), 60–61; *Southern Cultivator,* 4 (1846), 107; and *Patent Office Report,* 1848, p. 502.

[20] Stephen A. Norfleet, Farm Records, Vol. 3 (1856–57), SHMC, Chapel Hill, North Carolina.

[21] Rudolf A. Clemen, *The American Livestock and Meat Industry* (New York: The Ronald Press Company, 1923), p. 93.

[22] See *Southern Agriculturist,* 2 (1842), 528; *Southern Cultivator,* 11 (1853), 199; 17 (1859), 253; *Patent Office Reports,* 1850, p. 322; 1851, p. 331; Louise Gladney, "History of Pleasant Hill Plantation, 1811–1867," Thesis Louisiana State University 1932, p. 44.

[23] In similar computations Genovese arrived at about the same figure. He did note, however, that some of the animals may have been bought from drovers thus, presumably, increasing the average. In view of the lack of detailed knowledge of the number and quality of the incoming animals this may be a questionable assumption. Tennessee and Kentucky animals probably were heavier than Deep South hogs before they began the drive, but surely they lost weight during the journey. Furthermore, this writer has found many references to "drove pork" where the agriculturist specifically stated the weight of his own animals separate from the records of the purchased hogs. Where such cases occurred, they were omitted from the calculations on average weights.

[24] Though two litters per year are not necessarily the rule, such frequency is common among penned domestic hogs with the sow being bred back as soon as her litter is weaned. Woods-grazed hogs, however, probably reverted to one litter per year. The number of litters, then, depended upon how the sows were kept.

[25] References for table 4. Example No. 1, *Soil of the South,* 6 (1856), 138; 2, 3, and 4 Gladney, "Pleasant Hill," pp. 41–42; 5, *Southern Cultivator,* 11 (1853), 199; 6, *Soil of the South,* 6 (1856), 207; 7, *American Cotton Planter and Soil,* 2 (1858), 96; 8, 9, 10, 11, and 12, Lucia B. S. Monroe, ed., "Avondale and Deerbrook Plantation Documents," *GHQ,* 17 (June 1933), 154; 13, Letter to Farish Carter from his son, J. F. Carter, January 23, 1851; 14, Farish Carter Papers; Stock Inventory Book, Cameron Papers, Vol. 113; 15, Everard G. Baker, Diaries, Vol. 1 (1849). Last items are part of *SHMC,* Chapel Hill, North Carolina.

[26] The most detailed stock inventory the writer has found is that of the Pettigrew holdings in North Carolina. From 1852 to 1860 detailed records were kept on the number of boars, sows, pigs, and feeders. Sow/pig ratios were, on occasion, lower than 1:3 but usually

stayed well above. Pettigrew Family Books, Vol. 37, *SHMC*, Chapel Hill, North Carolina.

[27] The higher figure may be the more realistic one, but since no allowance was made for boars, sow replacement or meat spoilage this writer favors a more conservative estimate. In order to allow for such factors, this study assumes an increase of 50 percent. This figure also assumes that only one litter was farrowed per year, a fact which may not have been true on the better managed landholdings.

[28] *Southern Cultivator*, 8 (1850), 162; 4 (1846), 27; 18 (1860), 183; *DeBow's Review*, 11 (1851), 370; 7 (1849), 380, 382; *Patent Office Report*, 1851, p. 325; 1852, p. 86; Gosse, *Letters*, p. 253; Gray, *History of Southern Agriculture*, 1: 563; Ulrich B. Phillips, *American Negro Slavery* (New York: D. Appleton and Company, 1918), p. 279; Joe G. Taylor, *Negro Slavery in Louisiana* (Baton Rouge: Louisiana Historical Association, 1963), pp. 106–8; Solomon Northup, *Twelve Years a Slave* (New York: Miller, Orton and Mulligan, 1855), p. 169; Ralph B. Flanders, *Plantation Slavery in Georgia* (Chapel Hill: University of North Carolina Press, 1933), p. 105; Charles S. Sydnor, *Slavery in Mississippi* (New York: D. Appleton-Century Company, 1933), p. 32; Rosser H. Taylor, "Feeding Slaves," *JNH*, 9 (January 1924), 139; Robert Russell, *North America: Its Agriculture and Climate* (Edinburgh: Adam and Charles Black, 1857), pp. 180, 266; Timothy H. Ball, *A Glance into the Great South-East, or Clark County, Alabama* (Grove Hill, Ala.: By the author, 1882), p. 615.

[29] *DeBow's Review*, 14 (1853), 177; 24 (1858), 325; Keller, *Solon Robinson*, 22: 381; Guion G. Johnson, *A Social History of the Sea Islands* (Chapel Hill: University of North Carolina Press, 1930), pp. 85–87; Weymouth T. Jordan, *Hugh Davis and His Alabama Plantation* (University: University of Alabama Press, 1948), p. 88.

[30] Bryan Grimes Plantation Book, Grimes Family Papers, Boxes 1 and 2, and Greenfield Fishery Records, 1844–60. Both are in *SHMC*, Chapel Hill, North Carolina.

[31] Keller, 22: 187; V. Alton Moody, "Slavery on Louisiana Sugar Plantations," *LHQ*, 7 (April 1924), 266; Edwin A. Davis, "Bennet H. Barrow, Ante-Bellum Planter of the Felicianas," *JSH*, 5, (November 1939), 441; Moody cites one planter who issued seven pounds per hand.

[32] Many planters working large groups often allocated work to slaves on an individual or "task" basis. Each was required to perform certain daily tasks. The tasks varied depending upon the age and health of each slave. A healthy adult male was rated as a "full hand" while women, children and the aged were rated "half hands" or "quarter hands," depending upon their abilities.

[33] Rupert B. Vance, *Human Factors in Cotton Culture* (Chapel Hill: University of North Carolina Press, 1929), p. 246.

[34] These calculations are based on an annual yield of 50 percent on swine numbers enumerated in the census and an average weight

yield of 140 pounds per animal. Consumption is estimated at 150 pounds per consuming unit. Converting these data into pork production and measuring it against pork consumption, it appears that approximately 2.20 animals were needed to provide enough pork for one human consuming unit. Since children consumed less than adults and the adult/child ratio varied somewhat within the area, both white and slave populations have been adjusted to represent "adult consuming units" using the formula:

$$\text{adult population} + \frac{\text{population under 15 years}}{2} = z$$

z, then, represents a consuming unit comparable to a single adult.

[35] By varying the estimates on hog production (either weights or numbers) or pork consumption, one can change the number of counties showing pork deficits; but the basic areal pattern is altered surprisingly little.

[36] *DeBow's Review*, 6 (1848), 296; 12 (1852), 67; 16 (1854), 540; *Southern Agriculturist*, NS 4 (1844), 472; Elizabeth L. Parr, "Kentucky's Overland Trade with the Ante-Bellum South," *HQ*, 2 (January 1928), 71–81; Thomas D. Clark, "Livestock Trade between Kentucky and the South, 1840–60," *RKSHS*, 27 (September 1929), 569–81; Charles T. Leavitt, "Transportation and the Livestock Industry of the Middle West to 1860," *AH*, 8 January 1934), 20–33; Wilma Dykeman, *The French Broad* (New York: Rinehart and Company, Inc., 1955), pp. 137–50; James R. Maxwell, *Autobiography* (New York: Greenberg, 1926), p. 25; E. Merton Coulter, *Auraria: The Story of a Georgia Gold-Mining Town* (Athens, Ga.: University of Georgia Press, 1956), p. 21; James Hall, *Notes on the Western States* (Philadelphia: Harrison Hall, 1838), p. 275; Mary Verhoeff, *The Kentucky Mountains: Transportation and Commerce, 1750–1911*, Filson Club Publication No. 26 (Louisville: John P. Morton and Company, 1911), p. 127.

[37] Eugene Genovese, in his scathing (but probably well-deserved) critique of southern hogs gives no recognition of improvement during the antebellum period, and Robert Fogel, in discussing interregional trade, accepts Genovese's views uncritically. This writer feels compelled to take issue with both since their views are contradicted by the evidence. In examining manuscript records of farms and plantations throughout the Deep South, there is no question but that hog weights increased in the decades immediately preceding the war. While the average carcass weight of southern hogs has been estimated at approximately 140 pounds, a breakdown of examples taken from manuscript records into time periods reveals an increase in hog weights through the years. A total of 3,494 samples dated prior to 1845 averaged only 133 pounds, while samples totaling 7,718 animals slaughtered from 1845 to 1861 averaged 153 pounds. Therefore, both Genovese and Fogel may have erred in their assumption of static conditions in the Ante-Bellum South. Genovese, *AH*, 36 (July 1962),

147–48; R. L. Andreano, *New Views of American Economic Development* (Cambridge, Mass.: Schenkman Publishing Company, 1965), p. 206.

6 Beefsteaks and buttermilk

[1] For a discussion of the problem see L. C. Gray, *History of Agriculture in the Southern United States to 1860* (New York: Peter Smith, 1941), 1: 138–51, 200–213, 2: 831–57; James W. Thompson, *A History of Livestock Raising in the United States, 1607–1860*, U.S. Department of Agriculture, Agriculture History Series No. 5 (Washington: Government Printing Office, 1942); Frank L. Owsley, *Plain Folk of the Old South* (Baton Rouge; Louisiana State University Press, 1949); Eugene D. Genovese, "Livestock in the Slave Economy of the Old South—A Revised View," *AH*, 34 (July 1962), 143–49.

[2] Gray, *History of Agriculture*, 1: 138–51; Gary S. Dunbar, "Colonial Carolina Cowpens," *AH*, 35 (July 1961), 125–30; Harry R. Merrens, *Colonial North Carolina in the Eighteenth Century* (Chapel Hill: University of North Carolina Press, 1964), pp. 134–41; Thompson, pp. 77–78; Archer B. Hulbert, *Paths of Inland Commerce* (New Haven: Yale University Press, 1920), pp. 22–23.

[3] Charles Arnade, "Cattle Raising in Spanish Florida, 1513–1763," *AH*, 35 (July 1961), 118–19; Lauren C. Post, *Cajun Sketches From the Prairies of Southwest Louisiana* (Baton Rouge: Louisiana State University Press, 1962); Lauren C. Post, "Cattle Branding in Southwest Louisiana," *The McNeese Review*, 10 (Winter 1958), 101–17.

[4] Elizabeth L. Parr, "Kentucky's Overland Trade with the Ante-Bellum South," *HQ*, 2 (January 1928), 71–81; Thomas D. Clark, "Livestock Trade between Kentucky and the South, 1840–60," *RKSHS*, 27 (September 1929), 569–81.

[5] Thompson, *Livestock*, p. 105; Philip H. Gosse, *Letters From Alabama* (London: Morgan and Chase, 1859), p. 271; Laura S. Walker, *History of Ware County Georgia* (Macon: J. W. Burke Company, 1934), p. 100.

[6] Adolph B. Benson, ed. and trans., *Peter Kalms Travels in North America* (New York: Wilson-Erickson, Inc., 1937), 1: 110.

[7] Timothy Flint, *Recollections of the Last Ten Years* (Boston: Cummings, Hilliard, and Company, 1826), pp. 317–19, 328–29; [Robert Baird], *View of the Valley of the Mississippi . . .* , 2d ed. (Philadelphia: H. S. Tanner, 1834), pp. 276, 304; John F. H. Claiborne, "Trip Through the Piney Woods," *PMHS*, 9 (1906), 514 ff; and Basil Hall, *Travels in North America* (Edinburgh: Cadell and Company, 1829), 3: 270–71.

[8] Adam Hodgson, *Letters From North America* (London: Hurst, Robinson and Company, 1824), 1: 148; Benjamin M. Norman, *New Orleans and Environs* (New Orleans: By the author, 1845), 38–40;

Emily Burke, *Reminiscences of Georgia* (Oberlin, Ohio: James M. Fitch, 1850), 127; Baird, p. 304; and Claiborne, *PMHS*, 9 (1960), 516.

[9] In many respects, the development of "woods ranching" in the Gulf South closely paralleled the "cowpens" of the Carolinas and, as such, was merely an extension of the eastern system. Frank L. Owsley has recognized the existence of such a system during the nineteenth century and argues strongly that the grazier must be reckoned as an important element in the economy of the frontier areas and as a minor figure even after the plantation economy was well established. See Owsley, *Plain Folk*, pp. 24–36 and Herbert Weaver, *Mississippi Farmers, 1850–1860* (Nashville: Vanderbilt University Press, 1945). His contentions are not universally accepted, and there is little evidence to support an important commercial cattle industry, yet the existence of such huge herds deserves further discussion. For a critique of Owsley's thesis and a discussion of southern cattle see Genovese, *AH*, 36 (July 1962), 143–49.

[10] Timothy Flint, *Recollections*, p. 317.

[11] Claiborne, *PMHS*, 9 (1906), 521–22.

[12] John H. Goff, *Cow Punching in Old Georgia* Emory University Studies in Business and Economics, No. 5 (Atlanta: Emory University, 1950), p. 22.

[13] See, for example, George G. Smith, Jr., *The History of Methodism In Georgia and Florida from 1785 to 1865* (Macon: Jno. W. Burke and Company, 1877), pp. 34–35; William P. Fleming, *Crisp County Georgia: Historical Sketches* (Cordele, Ga.: Ham Printing Co., 1932), p. 24; John B. Pate, *History of Turner County* (Amboy, Ga.: By the author, 1933), pp. 41–42; Simon P. Richardson, *Lights and Shadows of Itinerant Life: An Autobiography* (Nashville and Dallas: Methodist Episcopal Church, 1901), p. 26.

[14] Smith, p. 305. Hammock is a variation of hummock. In the South the term has come to refer to a plot of relatively rich land often supporting a growth of hardwood trees.

[15] *Patent Office Report*, 1850, p. 260.

[16] William H. Sparks, *The Memories of Fifty Years* (Philadelphia: Clayton, Remsen and Haffelfinger, 1870), p. 331.

[17] Claiborne, *PMHS*, 9 (1906), 521–22; John H. Moore, "South Mississippi in 1852," *JMH*, 18 (January 1956), 20, 22, 30; Weaver, *Mississippi Farmers*, p. 58; Gladys B. Avant, "History of Washington County, Alabama to 1860," Thesis, University of Alabama 1929, p. 22. Traugott Bromme, "Mississippi: A Geographic-Statistic-Topographic Sketch . . ." (trans., Charles F. Heartman) *JMH*, IV (April, 1942), 103; Cyril E. Cain, *Four Centuries on the Pascagoula* (n.p.: By the author, 1953), pp. 127–31.

[18] Sparks, 332 and Fleming, *County Georgia*, p. 119.

[19] Claiborne, *PMHS*, 9 (1906), 522.

[20] Flint, *Recollections*, p. 319.

[21] Claiborne, *PMHS*, 9 (1906), 522; Sparks, *Fifty Years*, pp. 331–32; J. S. Buckingham *The Slave States of America* (London: Fisher, Son, and Company, 1842), 1: 308; George E. Brewer, "History of Coosa County," *AHQ*, 4 (Spring 1942), 36, 119; Fleming, p. 119.

[22] Owsley, *Plain Folk*, pp. 24–34.

[23] Goff, *Cow Punching*, p. 18; Claiborne, *PMHS*, 9 (1906), 516.

[24] Claiborne, *PMHS*, 9 (1906), 521; Goff, p. 19; Pate, *Turner Country*, p. 42; Burke, *Reminiscences*, p. 127; and Cain, *Pascagoula*, p. 128.

[25] Goff, p. 19; Pate, pp. 41–42.

[26] Goff, p. 19.

[27] Cattle numbers were reported in the published census records after 1840 for county-size units, and such data are used in this study. For more detailed data, one also can use Schedule 4 of the census manuscripts which reports cattle by landholder. Several students have used these records to advantage. A good example is John H. Moore, *Agriculture in Ante-Bellum Mississippi* (New York: Bookman Associates, 1958). However, even such detailed records as the census manuscripts may not provide us with a precise view since there is some question about their accuracy. No doubt many of the entries are simply estimates, and many of the herders may have gone unreported.

[28] Burke, p. 127.

[29] Hodgson, *Letters*, 1: 148; Bromme, *JMH*, 4 (April 1942), 103; Claiborne, *PMHS*, 9 (1906), 516.

[30] Norman, p. 40; Flint, *Recollections*, p. 329; Baird, *View of the Valley*, p. 276; Edward King, *The Great South* (Hartford: American Publishing Co., 1875), 85.

[31] Values of these cattle must have been low. Estimates for cattle prices in Alabama and Louisiana place then at seven to twelve dollars per head for three- and four-year-old steers. *Patent Office Reports*, 1849, p. 279 and 1850, p. 260.

[32] [Charles A. Clinton], *A Winter From Home* (New York: John F. Trow, 1852), pp. 38–39, 32; Hodgson, *Letters*, 1: 148–49; Harriet Martineau, *Society in America* (2nd ed. London: Saunders and Olley, 1837), 2: 49; Basil Hall, *Travels in North America*, 3: 270–71.

[33] Gosse, *Letters from Alabama*, p. 271; Burke, *Reminiscences*, p. 127; Warren P. Ward, *History of Coffee County, Georgia* (Atlanta: By the author, 1930), pp. 95–96.

[34] Avant, *Washington County*, p. 21; *Patent Office Reports*, 1852, p. 64; 1849, pp. 161, 297; Claiborne, *PMHS*, 9 (1906), 522; Sparks, *Fifty Years*, p. 333; A. J. Brown, *History of Newton County, Mississippi from 1834 to 1894* (Jackson: Clarion-Ledger Co., 1894), p. 55.

[35] Pate, *Turner County*, p. 42.

[36] *DeBow's Review*, 6 (1848), 429; 7 (1849), 446; 9 (1850), 657; *Patent Office Report*, 1855, p. 405; Robert L. Robinson, "Mobile in the 1850s: A Social, Cultural and Economic History," Thesis University of Alabama 1955, p. 65.

[37] *DeBow's Review*, 21 (1856), 399; 25 (1858), 567; 28 (1860), 221.

[38] Owsley, *Plain Folk*, p. 136; Paul W. Taylor, "Mobile: 1818–1859 As Her Newspapers Pictured Her," Thesis University of Alabama 1951, pp. 43–44.

[39] *Patent Office Reports*, 1856, p. 407; and 1855, p. 419; *DeBow's Review*, 22 (1857), 202; U.S. Treasury Department, *Report of the Commerce and Navigation of the United States for 1856*, 34th Congress, 3d sess., 1856, 13: 305–7.

[40] Herbert A. Kellar, *Solon Robinson: Pioneer and Agriculturalist*, Indiana Historical Collections, Vols. 21 and 22 (Indianapolis: Indiana Historical Bureau, 1936), 21: 486–87; Charles S. Sydnor, *A Gentleman of the Old Natchez Region: Benjamin L. C. Wailes* (Durham: Duke University Press, 1938), pp. 82–83.

[41] Ralph B. Flanders, "Planters Problems in Ante-Bellum Georgia," *GHQ*, 14 (March 1930), 20.

[42] James B. Sellers, *Slavery in Alabama* (University: University of Alabama Press, 1950), pp. 23 ff. For other specific examples see Sydnor, pp. 82–83; Louise Gladney, "History of Pleasant Hill Plantation, 1811–1867," Thesis Louisiana State University 1932, p. 41; Willie D. Halsell, "Migration Into and Settlement of Leflore County, 1833–1876," *JMH*, 9 (October 1947), 231; Wendell H. Stephenson, *Isaac Franklin: Slave Trader and Planter of the Old South* (Baton Rouge: Louisiana State University Press, 1938), pp. 102–3, 157–85.

[43] Sydnor, pp. 82–83; Kellar, *Solon Robinson*, 21: 486–87; James C. Bonner, "Profile of a Late Ante-Bellum Community," *AHR*, 49 (July 1944), 675; Edwin A. Davis, ed., *Plantation Life in the Florida Parishes of Louisiana, 1836–1846 as Reflected in the Diary of Bennet Hilliard Barrow* (New York: Columbia University Press, 1943), p. 410.

[44] John H. Moore, *Agriculture in Ante-Bellum Mississippi,* (New York: Bookman Associates, 1958) pp. 64–65.

[45] Oxen usually are not considered food animals though they often were eaten for food after a few years of service. In fact, this is one of the factors that led to their continued use as draft animals long after the horse and mule were proved to be more suitable.

[46] After examining and comparing the census material on butter production and number of cows, the writer has concluded that there were no real "milch" cows in the South. The appellation would be more accurate if it were changed to read "lactating females" or simply "any cows" since that is about all it meant.

[47] For an analysis of this system of cattle improvement see Leonard Brinkman, "The Historical Geography of Improved Cattle in the United States to 1870," Diss. University of Wisconsin 1964. Brinkman has gone to the "herd books" of the various breeds and has mapped the diffusion of improved cattle through time. His work deals mainly with the Northeast and Midwest, primarily because this was

the area of greatest impact. In fact, his work is convincing evidence against any outstanding improvement in southern cattle, yet if his notion of bloodline diffusion through the use of imported bulls is accepted, then we can visualize a similar, though much less important, diffusion occurring in parts of the South.

[48] William Proctor Gould, Diary for 1857, November 9 and December 2, SHMC, Chapel Hill, North Carolina.

[49] Bromme, JMH, 4 (April 1942), 103; Kellar, Solon Robinson, 22: 181; James Stuart, Three Years in North America (New York: J. and J. Harper, 1833), 2: 102; A. de Puy Van Buren, Jottings of a Year's Sojourn in the South (Battle Creek, Mich.: By the author, 1859), p. 85.

[50] J. R. York to William M. Otey, August 20, 1856, Wyche-Otey Papers, SHMC, Chapel Hill, North Carolina.

[51] Patent Office Report, 1850, p. 188.

[52] Patent Office Report, 1851, p. 331.

[53] Kellar, Solon Robinson, 21: 469 and Moore, JMH, 17 (January 1956), 21.

[54] R. J. Arnold to A. M. Sanford, May 19, 1840, Arnold-Scriven Papers, SHMC, Chapel Hill, North Carolina.

[55] Patent Office Report, 1851, p. 325.

[56] John D. Ashmore, Plantation Journal, April 10, 1853, SHMC, Chapel Hill, North Carolina.

[57] See Soil of the South, 5 (1855), 76; Southern Cultivator, 16 (1858), 366–67; DeBow's Review, 26 (1859), 580 for a few examples.

[58] Davis, Plantation Life, 410; W. Stanley Hoole, "Advice to an Overseer," AR, 1 (January 1948), 57–58; Weymouth T. Jordan, Hugh Davis and His Alabama Plantation (University: University of Alabama Press, 1948), p. 30; Brewer, AHQ, 4 (Spring 1942), 218; and Walker, Backtracking, p. 105.

[59] Moore, Agriculture in Ante-Bellum Mississippi, p. 100.

[60] Frederick L. Olmsted, A Journey in the Back Country (New York: Mason Brothers, 1863), pp. 224–25.

[61] Lewis E. Atherton, The Southern Country Store, 1800–1860 (Baton Rouge: Louisiana State University Press, 1949), pp. 49, 96–97; John W. Baker, History of Hart County (Atlanta: By the author, 1933), p. 56; Charles Lanman, Adventures in the Wilds of the United States and British American Provinces (Philadelphia: John W. Moore, 1856), 1: 375.

[62] Patent Office Report, 1851, p. 320.

[63] In addition to the inaccuracies inherent in any system of estimating reproduction rates, weights, or quality, one faces the obvious problem of census inaccuracy. Not only are there many sources of probable error in the census data, but there is the questions about the single census year being typical of the decade it supposedly represents. For this reason, comparisons between censuses are of doubtful validity. On the other hand, one can observe spatial distributions within the area studied for any one census year and be on relatively safe

ground, since biases toward absolute errors, either up or down, can be expected to have affected most of the area rather uniformly. In any study of the period 1840–60, however, one is drawn to the Federal Censuses as being the best quantitative data available. The writer has utilized such data in this study but cautions the reader against too precise an interpretation of the results.

[64] Estwick Evans, *A Pedestrious Tour* . . . (Concord, New Hampshire: Joseph C. Spear, 1819), Vol. 8 of Reuben G. Thwaites, *Early Western Travels* (Cleveland: The Arthur Clark Company, 1904), p. 331.

[65] William G. DeBrahm, "Philosophico-Historico-Hydrogeography of South Carolina, Georgia, and East Florida," in *Documents Connected With the History of South Carolina*, ed., P. C. J. Weston (London: n.p., 1856), p. 200.

[66] Gladney, "Pleasant Hill," p. 45; Lucia B. S. Monroe, "Avondale and Deerbrook Plantation Documents," *GHQ*, 17 (June 1933), 154; Lenoir Family Papers, Vol. 177, December 2, 1850–January 29, 1851; William L. Macay, Account Books, Vols. 5 and 7 in Macay-McNeely Papers; and Robert W. Withers, Books, Vol. I, 1834–35, pp. 11–12. Last three items in *SHMC*, Chapel Hill, North Carolina.

[67] Richard D. Cummings, *The American and His Food: A History of Food Habits in the United States*, rev. ed. (Chicago: University of Chicago Press, 1941), pp. 258–59.

[68] White consumption in the South may have been close to the national average but the large slave population probably depressed the overall average considerably since beef was not issued to slaves regularly.

[69] *Patent Office Report*, 1849, p. 724.

[70] Rupert B. Vance, *Human Factors in Cotton Culture* (Chapel Hill: University of North Carolina Press, 1929), p. 246.

[71] *DeBow's Review*, 24 (1858), 325; Rosser H. Taylor, *Ante-Bellum South Carolina: A Social and Cultural History*, The James Sprunt Studies in History and Political Science, 25, No. 2 (Chapel Hill: University of North Carolina Press, 1942), p. 54; Charles S. Davis, *The Cotton Kingdom in Alabama* (Montgomery: Alabama State Department of Archives and History, 1939), p. 56; Ulrich B. Phillips, *American Negro Slavery* (New York: D. Appleton and Company, 1918), p. 265; Kellar, *Solon Robinson*, 22: 367; David Doar, *Rice and Rice Planting in the South Carolina Low Country*, The Charleston Museum Contributions, No. 8 (Charleston: The Charleston Museum, 1936), p. 32; and Gladney, "Pleasant Hill," p. 45.

[72] The ratios are calculated on the basis of the following: 1] an annual herd increase of 20 percent;   2] a carcass weight of three hundred pounds; and   3] a consumption of thirty pounds of beef per consuming unit. Based on these assumptions a ration of 0.5 animals per consuming unit would have been necessary to produce an adequate supply of meat.

[73] Gray, *History of Agriculture*, 1: 489.

[74] H. H. Biswell, et al., *Native Forage Plants of Cutover Forest Lands in the Coastal Plain of Georgia*, Georgia Coastal Plain Experiment Station Bull. No. 37, 1943, pp. 5–7, 41–43.

[75] Stuart, *Three Years*, 2: 102; *Patent Office Report*, 1852, p. 64; and Van Buren, *Jottings*, p. 52.

[76] Biswell, p. 42.

[77] Calculated from figures given in the census for 1850, p. lxxxii. The animal figure includes all types of cattle.

[78] *Southern Cultivator*, 14 (1856), 43–44, 173.

[79] *Patent Office Report*, 1848, p. 501.

[80] *Southern Cultivator*, 14 (1856), 43.

[81] *Patent Office Report*, 1850, p. 262.

[82] John Berkley Grimball, Diary, January 29 and April 30, 1849; Louis M. DeSaussure, Plantation Record, 1846, p. 8 and 1852, pp. 11–12; William E. Sparkman, Plantation Record, August 1, 2, 3, and 7, 1844; Ben Sparkman, Plantation Record, September 13–18, 1854; and Phanor Prudhomme, Papers, Vol. 11, July 18, 1860; all are in *SHMC*, Chapel Hill, North Carolina.

[83] Cameron Papers, Vol. 122, November 6, 1845 to July 25, 1846. *SHMC*, Chapel Hill, North Carolina.

[84] His weights were based on samples. He found that 10 bundles weighed 36 pounds. Lamar Papers, January 26, 1850, Manuscript Collection, University of Georgia Library, Athens, Georgia and Jackson-Prince Papers, Vol. 17, 1850, *SHMC*, Chapel Hill, North Carolina.

[85] Kolloch Plantation Books, Vol. 5, *SHMC*, Chapel Hill, North Carolina.

[86] Thomas F. Hunt, "The History of Cereal Farming in the South," *Economic History, 1607–1865*, ed. James C. Ballagh, Vol. 5, *The South in the Building of the Nation* (Richmond: The Southern History Pub. Society, 1909), pp. 212–22.

[87] *Southern Cultivator*, XIV (1856), 43; XVIII (1860), 166; *Patent Office Reports*, 1848, p. 508; 1847, p. 389; 1851, p. 324; Louis M. DeSaussure, Plantation Record, 1846, p. 8; 1852, p. 12; *SHMC*, Chapel Hill, North Carolina.

[88] *Southern Cultivator*, 4 (1846), 71, 165; *Patent Office Report*, 1849, pp. 150, 154; Jordan, *Hugh Davis*, p. 30; Benjamin M. Duggar, "Grass and Forage Crop Farming in the South," *Economic History, 1607–1865*, ed. James C. Ballagh, Vol. 5 *The South in the Building of the Nation*, pp. 222–29; and Ben Sparkman, Plantation Record, September 15–18, 1854, *SHMC*, Chapel Hill, North Carolina.

[89] *Patent Office Reports*, 1847, p. 389; 1851, pp. 324–25; Olmsted, *Back Country*, p. 49; *Southern Cultivator*, 18 (1860), 364; and Walker, *Backtracking*, p. 105.

[90] Buckingham, *Slave States*, p. 150.

7 The occasional diversion

[1] Sheep did not adapt to the forest environment along the Eastern Seaboard as well as did swine and cattle. Wild predatory animals took a heavy toll of lambs during the frontier period and, later, dogs came to be almost as pesky. Swine and cattle, on the other hand, were quite able to care for themselves.

[2] Cyril E. Cain, *Four Centuries on the Pascagoula* (n.p.: By the author, 1953), pp. 132–34; Traugott Bromme, "Mississippi: A Geographic-Statistic-Topographic Sketch for Immigrants and Friends of Geography and Ethnology," *JMH*, 4 (April 1942), 103; John B. Pate, *History of Turner County* (Amboy, Ga.: By the author, 1933), p. 29; Daughters of the American Revolution, *History of Pulaski County Georgia* (Atlanta: Walter W. Brown Publishing Company, 1935), p. 53.

[3] *Southern Cultivator*, 6 (1848), 2. Very likely his angry observation on the dog/sheep ratio was accurate. For details on this controversy see Earl W. Hayter, *The Troubled Farmer* (Dekalb: Northern Illinois University Press, 1968), pp. 123–41.

[4] Sheep parasites are spread among animals via the animal feces which are dropped and thence transmitted orally to other animals, though in some cases a third host animal is required. Having a wide grazing area, woods-grazed animals scattered their feces freely thereby reducing the chance of infection. Many "old timers" in the South today who remember the "no-fence" era tend to attribute the near elimination of sheep to the effectiveness of fence laws which confined the animals to fenced lots, where they were wiped out by parasites.

[5] *Southern Cultivator*, 3 (1845), 105; 10 (1852), 70; *Southern Agriculturist*, 5 (1845), 268.

[6] For a discussion of the quality of the native sheep, treatment, and efforts toward improvement see Edward N. Wentworth, *America's Sheep Trails* (Ames, Iowa: Iowa State College Press, 1948), pp. 102–8; John H. Moore, *Agriculture in Ante-Bellum Mississippi* (New York: Bookman Associates, 1958), pp. 63, 106–7; *Southern Cultivator*, 1 (1843), 86; 3 (1845), 105; 10 (1852), 70; 11 (1853), 355–56; and 14 (1856), 80–81.

[7] A column for "value of poultry" was included as early as the 1840 census, but meaningful interpretations of such data are hardly possible.

[8] Sparkman Family Papers, Vol. 5, *SHMC*, Chapel Hill, North Carolina.

[9] Hairston Wilson Papers and Books, *SHMC*, Chapel Hill, North Carolina.

[10] For a description of the barnyard poultry conditions, see Julia

E. Harn, "Old Canoochee Backwards Sketches," *GHQ*, 24 (September 1940), 276.

[11] Charles E. Cauthen, *Family Letters of the Three Wade Hamptions, 1782–1901* (Columbia: University of South Carolina Press, 1953), p. 34.

[12] Guion G. Johnson, *A Social History of the Sea Islands* (Chapel Hill: The University of North Carolina Press, 1930), p. 86.

[13] Ulrich B. Phillips, ed., *Plantation and Frontier Documents: 1649–1863*, Vols. 1 and 2, *Documentary History of American Industrial Society* (Cleveland, Ohio: The Arthur H. Clark Company, 1909), 1: 127; Charles S. Davis, *The Cotton Kingdom in Alabama* (Montgomery: Alabama State Department of Archives and History, 1939), p. 48; Edwin A. Davis, ed. *Plantation Life in the Florida Parishes of Louisiana, 1836–1846 as Reflected in the Diary of Bennet Hilliard Barrow* (New York: Columbia University Press, 1943), p. 410.

[14] Davis, *Cotton Kingdom*, p. 48; Charles S. Sydnor, *A Gentleman of the Old Natchez Region: Benjamin L. C. Wailes* (Durham: Duke University Press, 1938), p. 98.

[15] Frances A. Kemble, *Journal of a Residence on a Georgia Plantation in 1838–1839*, ed. John A. Scott (New York: Alfred A. Knopf, 1961), p. 82; Davis, *Cotton Kingdom*, p. 48; Philip H. Gosse, *Letters from Alabama* (London: Morgan and Chase, 1859), p. 158; Weymouth T. Jordan, *Ante-Bellum Alabama; Town and Country* (Tallahassee: Florida State University Press, 1957), p. 55; George C. Osborn, "Plantation Life in Central Mississippi as Revealed in the Clay Sharky Papers," *JMH*, 3 (October 1941), 280; Franklin L. Riley, "Diary of a Mississippi Planter, January 1, 1840 to April, 1863," *PMHS*, 10 (1909), 370.

[16] Bromme, *JMH*, 4 (April 1942), 103.

[17] Lewis E. Atherton, *The Southern Country Store, 1800–1860* (Baton Rouge: Louisiana State University Press, 1949), 49; Rosser H. Taylor, *Ante-Bellum South Carolina: A Social and Cultural History*, The James Sprunt Studies in History and Political Science, 25, No. 2 (Chapel Hill: University of North Carolina Press, 1942), p. 14; Davis, *Cotton Kingdom*, p. 167.

[18] Adam Hodgson, *Letters from North America* (London: Hurst, Robinson and Company, 1824), 1: 32; Hairston-Wilson Papers and Books, Vol. 6 (1833–40); Kollack Plantation Books, Vol. 5 (1842–43); Henry Clay Warmoth, Papers and Books, Vol. 2 (1856–57). The last three items are in *SHMC*, Chapel Hill, North Carolina. The Warmoth Papers reveal an almost unbelievable record of commercial egg production. During 1856 and 1857 the plantation shipped an average of 2.7 dozen eggs per day. During the spring of 1857 as many as 50 dozen were shipped per week. On June 8 his weekly shipment, placed aboard the *Ceres* (presumably a steamboat), amounted to 73 *dozen eggs*. Most likely, they moved to New Orleans.

[19] Riley, *PHMS*, 10 (1909), 307; Osborn, *JMH*, 3 (October 1941), 280.

²⁰ Ibid.; Gosse, *Letters from Alabama*, p. 158; Edward M. Steel, "A Pioneer Farmer in the Choctaw Purchase," *JMH*, 16 (October 1954) 235; Louise Gladney, "History of Pleasant Hill Plantation, 1811–1867," Thesis Louisiana State University 1932, pp. 41–42.

²¹ Bromme, *JMH*, 4 (April 1942), 103; Hodgson, *Letters from North America*, pp. 21, 32; Gosse, p. 158; Osborn, *JMH*, 3 (October 1941), 280; Margaret H. Hall, *The Aristocratic Journey* (New York: G. P. Putnam's Sons, 1831), p. 208.

²² Gladney, pp. 41–42. See also Sparkman, Family Papers, Vol. 5 (1851); and William W. White, *Diary of Captain William Wallace White, 1857–1910* (Birmingham: Leonard Henderson White, 1956), Nov. 1858, pp. 2, 6, 13.

²³ Bromme, *JMH*, 4 (April 1942), 103; Riley, *PMHS*, 10 (1909), 307; Gosse, *Letters from Alabama*, p. 158; Osborn, *JMH*, 3 (October 1941), 280.

²⁴ James B. Sellers, *Slavery in Alabama* (University: University of Alabama Press, 1950), p. 55 and Kemble, *Journal*, pp. 83–85.

²⁵ Frederick L. Olmsted, *Journey in the Seaboard Slave States* (New York: Mason Brothers, 1859), p. 439.

²⁶ *DeBow's Review*, 10 (1851), 624.

8   Corn pone and light bread

¹ Donald L. Kemmerer, "The Pre-Civil War South's Leading Crop, Corn," *AH*, 23 (October 1949), 236–39.

² Ulrich B. Phillips, *American Negro Slavery* (New York: D. Appleton and Company, 1918), p. 207.

³ Sparkman Family Papers, Vol. 5 (1845–52); Letter from Howell Adams to William Smith; July 18, 1849. William R. Smith Papers; John Berkley Grimball Diary, February 28, 1833; Tristram L. Skinner Plantation Record (1842–60); Nicholas B. Massenburg, Farm Journal (1843); and James Hamilton Couper, Plantation Records (1820–31). Above items are in *SHMC*, Chapel Hill, North Carolina.

⁴ Since acreage data are not given in the manuscripts, it was necessary to estimate acreage from production data. In this case the computations were based on assumed yields of ¼ bale per acre for cotton and twenty bushels per acre for corn.

⁵ Louis M. DeSaussere, Plantation Record, p. 10, *SHMC*, Chapel Hill, North Carolina.

⁶ *Patent Office Reports*, 1848, p. 502. See also John H. Moore, *Agriculture in Ante-Bellum Mississippi* (New York: Bookman Associates, 1958), p. 59.

⁷ Daybooks and other manuscript materials are filled with references to pulling, curing, or even selling corn blades or "fodder." Cameron papers, Vol. 122, No. 6, 1845 through July 25, 1846; Bayside Plantation Records, Vol. I, No. 53; William E. Sparkman Plantation

Record, August 1–7, 1844; Phanor Prudhomme Papers, Vol. 11, July 18, 1860; Louis M. DeSaussere Plantation Records, 1852, p. 11; John Berkley Grimball Diary, January 29 and April 30, 1849; Preceding items in *SHMC*, Chapel Hill, North Carolina. Lamar Papers and Dennis Papers (1863), Georgiana Manuscript Collection, University of Georgia, Athens, Georgia. For further discussion of the importance of fodder see chapter 5.

⁸ Letter from Howell Adams to William Smith, January 16, 1846, William R. Smith Papers; John B. Grimball Diary, July 31, 1832, *SHMC*, Chapel Hill, North Carolina.

⁹ Grimes Family Papers, Box 2 (1832–40); Pettigrew Family Books, Vol. 27 (1948), p. 17; Tristrim L. Skinner Plantation Record (1843–51); *SHMC*, Chapel Hill, North Carolina; Dennis Papers (1858), p. 416. Georgiana Collection, University of Georgia, Athens, Georgia. Both Pettigrew and Skinner also shipped corn and wheat by schooner to Charleston, Baltimore, and New York.

¹⁰ A few of the many available examples are: *Southern Cultivator*, 8 (1850), 162; *DeBow's Review*, 3 (1847), 420; 10 (1851), 623; 24 (1858), 325; Ulrich B. Phillips, *American Negro Slavery* (New York: D. Appleton and Company, 1918), pp. 265–79. A good example was the rations listed by a Mr. Thomas E. Cox who carefully listed allowances for his servants.

	Bacon (lbs.)	Other Meat (pecks)
Lewis	3½	1½
Joe	2½	1
Rose	2	1
Mary	1½	1
Eug [enia]	1½	½
Ellen	3	1
Emily	2	½
Ella	1	½
Robert	1	½

¹¹ *Southern Cultivator*, 18 (1860), 183; 8 (1850), 162; 12 (1854), 205; V. Alton Moody, "Slavery on Louisiana Sugar Plantations," *LHQ*, 7 (April 1924), 266; James B. Sellers, *Slavery in Alabama* (University: University of Alabama Press, 1950), p. 88; Herbert A. Kellar, *Solon Robinson: Pioneer and Agriculturalist*, Indiana Historical Collections, Vols. 21 and 22 (Indianapolis: Indiana Historical Bureau, 1936), 22: 172.

¹² Martin B. Coyner, "John Hartwell Cooke of Bremo: Agriculture and Slavery in the Ante-Bellum South," Diss. University of Virginia 1961, p. 410.

¹³ For details on fattening hogs see chapter 5.

¹⁴ *DeBow's Review*, 6 (1848), 147.

¹⁵ The estimate on corn consumption was made for farm work animals and was certainly low when applied to animals used in towns. The lack of pasture grazing and relatively constant work demanded

by draying necessitated higher grain consumption in which case the corn (or equivalent grain) consumption would have been much higher.

[16] If the production of sweet potatoes is added to the amount of corn produced in a ratio of one bushel of potatoes to one peck of corn, then the total corn-potato production either approaches or exceeds the 1.000 figure in almost all the counties in the coastal area.

[17] Alfred G. Smith, Jr., *Economic Readjustment of an Old Cotton State: South Carolina, 1820–1860* (Columbia: University of South Carolina Press, 1958), p. 74.

[18] *DeBow's Review*, 23 (1857), 505.

[19] *Patent Office Report*, 1850, pp. 231–32.

[20] John W. Baker, *History of Hart County* (Atlanta: By the author, 1933), p. 56; *Patent Office Report*, 1850, p. 400; Pettigrew Family Papers, Vol. 27, p. 17; Tristrim L. Skinner Plantation (1843–51).

[21] Although the absence of documentary evidence does not prove the absence of a particular phenomenon, this writer has been amazed at the lack of references to either the reaper or the thresher in documents relating to the South. A few have been unearthed, but only a pitiful few. This writer knows of no more striking way of illustrating this notion than by asking the reader to scan the pages of comparable issues of the *Wisconsin Farmer and Northwestern Cultivator* and the *Southern Cultivator*.

[22] U.S. Dept. of Agriculture, *Yearbook of Agriculture, 1921* (Washington: U.S. Government Printing Office, 1922), pp. 159–60.

[23] *DeBow's Review*, 22 (1857), 202; 17 (1854), 541–42; XXV (1858), 471; 23 (1857), 503–4; U.S. Treasury Dept., *A Report of the Commerce and Navigation of the United States for 1856*, 34th Cong., 3d Sess., 1856, 13: 305–13.

[24] *Patent Office Report*, 1852, p. 31; John S. Bassett, *The Southern Plantation Overseer as Revealed in His Letters* (Northampton, Mass.: Smith College, 1925), p. 62; and Coyner, "John Hartwell Cooke," p. 410.

[25] David Doar, *Rice and Rice Planting in the South Carolina Low Country*, The Charleston Museum Contributions, No. 8 (Charleston: Charleston Museum, 1936), p. 32; James D. B. DeBow, *The Industrial Resources, Statistics, Etc. of the United States*, 3d ed. (New York: D. Appleton and Company, 1854), p. 425. James H. Couper, a prominent Georgia planter, believed the food value of small rice was slightly higher than corn. He estimated their relative values at a ratio of 8 to 10. Taking shipping and other expenses into account he calculated the following table to indicate whether to consume the small rice or buy corn.

Price of Small Rice (100 lbs.)	Price of Corn (bu.)
$1.50	$ .50
1.75	.61
2.00	.74

Price of Small Rice (100 lbs.)	Price of Corn (bu.)
2.25	.87
2.33	.91
2.50	1.00

James H. Couper, "Notes on Agriculture and Rural Economy" (1824), *SHMC*, Chapel Hill, North Carolina.

[26] John H. Moore, "South Mississippi in 1852: Some Selections from the Journal of Benjamin L. C. Wailes," *JMH*, 18 (January 1956), 21; Sam B. Hilliard, "Birdsong: Sequent Occupance on a Southwestern Georgia Plantation," Thesis University of Georgia 1961, pp. 59–60. Though absent from most scholarly works on the antebellum South, inland rice production may have been important locally. While traveling through the South and talking to "old timers" this writer has met several who told of "rice patches" worked by their fathers and grandfathers. Many, too, can point out "ridges" marking the boundaries of the old fields and remnants of ditches used to flood and drain the fields, both invariably covered with a dense growth of huge trees.

9 Rounding out the fare

[1] Sarah William to Samuel Hicks of New Hartford, N.Y., March 17, 1853, Sarah Hicks William Papers, *SHMC*, Chapel Hill, North Carolina.

[2] Martin B. Coyner, "John Hartwell Cocke of Bremo: Agriculture and Slavery in the Ante-Bellum South," Diss. University of Virginia 1961, pp. 236–37. For another outstanding example see Charles S. Sydnor, *A Gentlemen of the Old Natchez Region: Benjamin L. C. Wailes* (Durham: Duke University Press, 1938), pp. 82–83.

[3] These "fragmented" gardens survived until the twentieth century. This writer remembers very well his father's propensity to plant plots all over the farm; the sweet potato patch, the watermelon and cantaloupe patch, the turnip patch, and the pea patch were yearly "musts" and each was separate from the regular garden. The reasons for this fragmentation were twofold. First, it permitted one to choose a site where soil and drainage conditions were best for the specific crop. Often a small forest clearing or "new-ground" was used for turnips or watermelons. Second, the need for large quantities necessitated substantial acreages which the garden could not spare. Since the barnyard fowls had the run of the premises, the garden usually was fenced "chicken tight." Consequently, its size was limited and there was little room for crops such as watermelons. Of course, in antebellum times the no-fence conditions required fenced fields, but even then the garden required special care since it usually was close enough to the barnyard to suffer from the depredations of poultry.

⁴ Louis M. DeSaussere, Plantation Record (1836), *SHMC*, Chapel Hill, North Carolina. He must have relied very heavily upon potatoes. His writings refer to "slips" much more than either corn or pork.

⁵ John Berkley Grimball Diary, September 15 and 27, 1832 and January 13, 1833. Grimball planted both corn and potatoes but constantly referred to being short or running out of corn. It is doubtful whether he ever expected to be self-sufficient.

⁶ "Banking" is a term used to describe a method of food preservation commonly used in America where frosts were a danger. Since sweet potatoes are susceptible to frosts, southerners piled the tubers on a bed of straw or pine needles and then covered them with another layer of bedding. The entire bank was then covered with sand. The roots were removed as needed with the remaining potatoes carefully recovered to insure frost protection. Occasionally, a crude door was made of boards and stuffed with burlap or some other insulating material allowing easy removal of the potatoes. This method was used for the tubers intended for both food and "seed."

⁷ William J. Dickey, Diary, July 1858, Georgiana Manuscript Collection, University of Georgia, Athens, Georgia; *Southern Cultivator*, 14 (1856), 172; Louis M. DeSaussere, Plantation Record and John Berkley Grimball, Diary, July 28, 1832. Last two items in *SHMC*, Chapel Hill, North Carolina.

⁸ Letter from R. J. Arnold to A. M. Sanford, May 19, 1840, Arnold-Scriven Papers, *SHMC*, Chapel Hill, North Carolina.

⁹ *Patent Office Report*, 1848, p. 501 and *DeBow's Review*, 19 (1855), 592–94.

¹⁰ There may be some confusion between the sweet potato and the yam. The tuber so common in the South is *Ipomea batatas* and is entirely different from the true yam. Some varieties of southern potatoes are called yams, but this name belongs, properly, only to the family *Dioscorea* which is a common root crop in the tropics.

¹¹ *Patent Office Report*, 1848, p. 501; and Amos A. Parker, *Trip to the West and Texas* (Concord, N.H.: White and Fisher, 1835), p. 108.

¹² There were several varieties of peas grown in the southeastern states. Known locally by such names as "crowders," or "blackeyes," they were much more commonly grown than green peas or any of the beans. The species was *Vigna sinensis*. Occasionally, some strains are found which produced extremely long pods (sometimes considered a separate species, *V. sesquipedalis*), but in either case, the cowpea should should not be confused with the "garden," or "green" pea, a distinctly different plant (*Pisum sativum*).

¹³ John H. Moore, *Agriculture in Ante-Bellum Mississippi* (New York: Bookman Associates, 1958), pp. 59–60; Ulrich B. Phillips, ed., *Plantation and Frontier Documents: 1649–1863*, Vols. 1 and 2, *Documentary History of American Industrial Society* (Cleveland, Ohio:

The Arthur H. Clark Company, 1909), 1: 128; R. C. Beckett, "Ante-Bellum Times in Monroe County," *PHMS*, 11 (1910) 88; *Southern Agriculturist*, NS 3 (1843).

¹⁴ *Patent Office Report*, 1848, p. 502.

¹⁵ *Patent Office Report*, 1852, p. 86.

¹⁶ *Patent Office Reports*, 1852, p. 195 and 1853, p. 81.

¹⁷ Benjamin L. C. Wailes, *Report on the Agriculture and Geology of Mississippi*, ([Jackson]: E. Barksdale, 1854), p. 195.

¹⁸ Herbert Weaver, *Mississippi Farmers, 1850–1860* (Nashville: Vanderbilt University Press, 1945), p. 98.

¹⁹ John S. Bassett, *The Southern Plantation Overseer as Revealed in His Letters* (Northampton, Mass.: Smith College, 1925), p. 74; Louise Gladney, "History of Pleasant Hill Plantation, 1811–1867," Thesis Louisiana State University 1932, p. 8.

²⁰ *Patent Office Report*, 1848, pp. 159, 501. Considering the dearth of references to such practices, encountering the following was a surprise: "I must raise them [turnips] or I can't make out with my milk cows." Undoubtedly, Mr. Lumpkin was not a typical southerner. Letter from George Lumpkin to Wilson Lumpkin, July 23, 1854. Barrow Papers, Folder 8 (1854). Georgiana Manuscript Collection, University of Georgia, Athens, Georgia.

²¹ Emily Burke, *Reminiscences of Georgia* (Oberlin, Ohio: James M. Fitch, 1850), p. 129; Edwin A. Davis, "Bennet H. Barrow, Ante-Bellum Planter of the Felicians," *JSH*, 5 (November 1939), 437.

²² For a short discussion of this new interest see Edgar W. Martin, *The Standard of Living in 1860* (Chicago: University of Chicago Press, 1942), p. 28.

²³ Burke, p. 129; Philip H. Gosse, *Letters From Alabama* (London: Morgan and Chase, 1859), p. 194; Frederick L. Olmsted, *Journey in the Seaboard Slave States* (New York: Mason Brothers, 1859), p. 566; Timothy Flint, *Recollections of the Last Ten Years* (Boston: Cummings, Hilliard, and Company, 1826), p. 326; Anne Royall, *Letters From Alabama* (Washington: By the author, 1830), p. 163.

²⁴ Flint, p. 326.

²⁵ For details on individual planters and their plantations, see Weymouth T. Jordan, *Hugh Davis and His Alabama Plantation* (University, Alabama: University of Alabama Press, 1948), pp. 43–44; Sydnor, *A Gentleman of the Old Natchez Region*, pp. 82–83; George C. Osborn, "Plantation Life in Central Mississippi as Revealed in the Clay Sharkey Papers," *JMH*, 3 (October 1941), 280; Albert G. Seal, "John Carmichael Jenkins: Scientific Planter of the Natchez District," *JMH*, 1 (January 1939), 17–23.

²⁶ Gosse, *Letters from Alabama*, p. 194; *DeBow's Review*, 29 (1860), 790–91; *Patent Office Reports*, 1848, p. 503; 1850, p. 196; Claiborne, *PMHS*, 9 (1906), 530.

²⁷ *Southern Cultivator*, 13 (1855), 305; 14 (1856), 91; Gosse, p. 194; Rosser H. Taylor, *Ante-Bellum South Carolina: A Social and*

Cultural History, The James Sprunt Studies in History and Political Science, 25, No. 2 (Chapel Hill: University of North Carolina Press, 1942), p. 169.

[28] Virginia P. Brown and Jane P. Nabers, "Mary Gordon Duffee's 'Sketches of Alabama,'" *AR,* 9 (April 1956), 143; James R. Maxwell, *Autobiography* (New York: Greenberg, 1926), p. 27.

[29] Olmsted, *Seaboard Slave States,* pp. 566, 659; Gosse, *Letters from Alabama,* p. 194; L. C. Gray, *History of Agriculture in the Southern United States to 1860* (New York: Peter Smith, 1941), 1: 489, 2: 824–27.

[30] Herbert A. Kellar, "Solon Robinson: Pioneer and Agriculturalist," Indiana Historical Collections, Vols. 21 and 22 (Indianapolis: Indiana Historical Bureau, 1936), 2: 483.

[31] Andrew M. Soule, "Vegetables, Fruit and Nursery Products, and Truck Farming in the South," *Economic History, 1607–1865,* Vol. 5, *The South in the Building of the Nation* (Richmond: Southern Historical Publication Society, 1909), pp. 236–37.

[32] Olmsted, *Seaboard Slave States,* pp. 422, 682, 693; Frederick L. Olmsted, *The Cotton Kingdom* (New York: Mason Brothers, 1861), 2: 180, 196.

[33] Basil Hall, *Travels in North America* (Edinburgh: Cadell and Company, 1829), 3: 180; Charles Lanman, *Adventures in the Wilds of the United States and British American Provinces* (Philadelphia: John W. Moore, 1856), 2: 185–86; Charles Lyell, *A Second Visit to the United States of North America* (New York: Harper and Brothers, 1849), 1: 327; Francis and Theresa Pulszky, *White, Red, Black: Sketches of American Society* (New York: Redfield, 1853), 2: 104.

[34] Gray, *History of Agriculture,* 1: 564.

[35] Gladney, "Pleasant Hill," pp. 27–28; Fredrika Bremer, *America of the Fifties: Letters of Fredrika Bremer,* ed. Adolph B. Benson (New York: The American-Scandinavian Foundation, 1924), p. 111; Burke, *Reminiscences,* pp. 112, 208; Olmsted, *Seaboard Slave States,* p. 682; A de Puy Van Buren, *Jottings of a Year's Sojourn in the South* (Battle Creek, Mich.: By the author, 1859), p. 208; William H. Holcombe, "Sketches of Plantation Life," *The Knickerbocker Magazine,* 57 (June 1861), 622–24.

[36] Gray, *History of Agriculture,* 1: 564.

[37] Olmsted, *Seaboard Slave States,* p. 422; *DeBow's Review,* 13 (1852), 193.

[38] *Patent Office Report,* 1852, p. 86; Lanman, *Adventures in the Wilds,* 2: 185–86; Ulrich B. Phillips, *American Negro Slavery* (New York: D. Appleton and Company, 1918), p. 265; John F. H. Claiborne, *Life and Correspondence of John A. Quitman* (New York: Harper and Brothers, 1860), 1: 80; Dorothy S. Magoffin, "A Georgia Planter and His Plantations, 1873–1861," *NCHR,* 15 (October 1938), 373.

[39] William D. Postell, *The Health of Slaves on Southern Plantations* (Baton Rouge: Louisiana State University Press, 1951), p. 34.

[40] Fredrika Bremer, *The Homes of the New World: Impressions of America*, trans. Mary Howitt (New York: Harper and Brothers, 1853), 1: 305; Magoffin, *NCHR*, 15 (October 1938), 376.

[41] Gladney, "Pleasant Hill," pp. 27–28; Magoffin, *NCHR*, 15 (October 1938), 376.

[42] Olmsted, *Seaboard Slave States*, p. 565.

[43] Ibid., p. 689; Olmsted, *Cotton Kingdom*, 2: 196; M. B. Hammond, *The Cotton Industry*, Publications of the American Economic Association, NS 1 (New York: The Macmillan Company, 1897), p. 91; *Debow's Review*, 13 (1852), 193; V. Alton Moody, "Slavery on Louisiana Sugar Plantations," *LHQ*, 7 (April 1924), 264

[44] *DeBow's Review*, 13 (1852), 193; Holcombe, *The Knickerbocker Magazine*, 57 (June 1861), 622–24.

[45] Moody, *LHQ*, 7: 256–60.

[46] *DeBow's Review*, 17 (1854), 424.

[47] *Southern Cultivator*, 8 (1850), 163.

[48] Bremer, *America of the Fifties*, p. 111; Charles Mackay, *Life and Liberty in America* (London: Smith, Elder and Company, 1859), 1: 327.

10   Making up the shortage

[1] Lewis E. Atherton, *The Southern Country Store, 1800–1860* (Baton Rouge: Louisiana State University Press, 1949), pp. 47, 50–51, 96–97.

[2] Frederich L. Olmsted, *Journey in the Seaboard Slave States* (New York: Mason Brothers, 1859), p. 414.

[3] This writer has examined a number of accounts of stores that operated in the South during the antebellum period. The Southern Historical Manuscript Collection at the University of North Carolina has an excellent group, and the Georgiana Library at the University of Georgia has amassed an impressive collection. Some of these store accounts are quite large and contain both store accounts (daily sales) and individual credit accounts. Thus, one can follow the total trade of the store as well as the consuming habits of individual families.

[4] See chapter 3 for detail on luxury goods in southern stores.

[5] Lenoir Family Papers, Vol. 177 (1854), SHMC, Chapel Hill, North Carolina.

[6] Crane and Cape's Accounts Books, Vol. 1 (1837), SHMC, Chapel Hill, North Carolina.

[7] Baxter Davidson Papers, Farm Account and Daybook, Vol. 8 (1846–49), SHMC, Chapel Hill, North Carolina.

[8] Lenoir Family Papers (1853–54), SHMC, Chapel Hill, North Carolina.

[9] In addition to the examples quoted above, the writer has examined a number of other accounts which support this observation;

the Dennis Family Papers (1857–58); Carter Papers; Thomas Accounts (1836); and the Job Bowers Store Accounts. The first three are in the Georgiana Manuscript Collection, University of Georgia, Athens, Georgia; the last is in the hands of Mssrs. Joe F. White of Lavonia, Georgia and Charles M. Bowers of Canon, Ga.

[10] Lenoir Family Papers, Vol. 177 (1850–52), *SHMC*, Chapel Hill, North Carolina.

[11] Wyche-Otey Papers (1852–57), *SHMC*, Chapel Hill, North Carolina. His total bill with Devlin amounted to $3,480.98 in 1852 but most was for "cash" rather than food. The Otey and Dorin accounts lend credence to Morton Rothstein's recent comments on the dual nature of the southern economy, "The Antebellum South as a Dual Economy: A Tentative Hypothesis," *AH*, 41 (October 1967), 373–82. He has offered a tantalizing notion which may help resolve the conflicting interpretation of the South as a home for the "planter" and the "yeoman." To his basic hypothesis, this writer must add a comment. Too many students of the antebellum South have virtually ignored the *areal* variation in southern agriculture. Thus, while there might have been a "dual economy" operating, there were also agricultural "regions" each with its own crops, landholding sizes and types, labor system and marketing emphases.

[12] Lenoir Family Papers, Vol. 197 (1844–58) and Vol. 177 (1852), *SHMC*, Chapel Hill, North Carolina.

[13] Lewis C. Gray, *History of Agriculture in the Southern United States to 1860* (New York: Peter Smith, 1941), 1: 451–52; Alfred G. Smith, Jr., *Economic Readjustment of an Old Cotton State: South Carolina, 1820–1860* (Columbia: University of South Carolina Press, 1958), p. 70; Atherton, *Southern Country Store*, pp. 50–51; Robert R. Russell, "The Effects of Slavery Upon Nonslaveholders in the Ante-Bellum South," *AH*, 15 (April 1941), 113.

[14] Edward M. Steel, "A Pioneer Farmer in the Choctaw Purchase," *JMH*, 16 (October 1954), 235; Frederick L. Olmsted, *The Cotton Kingdom* (New York: Mason Brothers, 1861), 2:79; John S. Bassett, *The Southern Plantation Overseer as Revealed in His Letters* (Northhampton, Massachusetts: Smith College, 1925), pp. 59, 107; Mack Swearingen, "Thirty Years of a Mississippi Plantation; Charles Whitmore of 'Montpelier,'" *JSH*, 1 (May 1935), 209.

[15] Hairston-Wilson Papers and Books, Vol. 6 (1842–43), *SHMC*, Chapel Hill, North Carolina.

[16] Louise Gladney, "History of Pleasant Hill Plantation, 1811–1867," Thesis Louisiana State University 1932, p. 5; Weymouth T. Jordan, *Hugh Davis and His Alabama Plantation* (University: University of Alabama Press, 1948), p. 134.

[17] Charles S. Sydnor, *A Gentleman of the Old Natchez Region: Benjamin L. C. Wailes* (Durham: Duke University Press, 1938), p. 97; Ulrich B. Phillips and James D. Glunt, eds., *Florida Plantation Records From the Papers of George Noble Jones* (St. Louis: Missouri

Historical Society, 1927), pp. 121–23, 519–21; James B. Sellers, *Slavery in Alabama* (University: University of Alabama Press, 1950), p. 30.

[18] Ulrich B. Phillips, ed., *Plantation and Frontier Documents: 1649–1863*, Vols. 1 and 2 of *Documentary History of American Industrial Society* (Cleveland, Ohio: The Arthur H. Clark Company, 1909), 1: 181–82.

[19] Wendell H. Stephenson, *Isaac Franklin: Slave Trader and Planter of the Old South* (Baton Rouge: Louisiana State University Press, 1938), p. 98.

[20] For details on the cattle industry of the hill states see Thomas D. Clark, "Livestock Trade between Kentucky and the South, 1840–60," *RKSHS*, 27 (September 1929), 569–81; Elizabeth L. Parr, "Kentucky's Overland Trade with the Ante-Bellum South," *HQ*, 2 (January 1928), 71–81. John P. Arthur, *Western North Carolina* (Raleigh: Edwards and Broughton Printing Company, 1941); Paul C. Henlein, *Cattle Kingdom in the Ohio Valley, 1783–1860* (Lexington: University of Kentucky Press, 1959).

[21] For a discussion of the droving trade along the French Broad River see Wilma Dykeman, *The French Broad, Rivers of America,* (New York: Rinehart and Company, Inc., 1955), pp. 137–50; Edmund C. Burnett, "Hog Raising and Hog Driving in the Region of the French Broad River," *AH*, 20 (April 1946), 86–103.

[22] Eulalie M. Lewis, "Roads and Steamboats in North Georgia," *GHQ*, 27 (September 1959), 91.

[23] Arthur, *Western North Carolina,* pp. 285–87; Parr, *HQ*, 2 (January 1928), 72; Clark, *RKSHS*, 27 (September 1929), 570–74.

[24] *DeBow's Review,* 6 (1848), 296.

[25] Dykeman, *French Broad,* p. 139; E. Merton Coulter, *Auraria: The Story of a Georgia Gold-Mining Town* (Athens: University of Georgia Press, 1956), p. 21.

[26] Parr, *HQ*, 2 (January 1928), 77–79.

[27] Dykeman, p. 141; Clark, *RKSHS*, 27 (September 1929). Since local drives continued until the closing decades of the nineteenth century there are a few persons who can recall seeing them. This writer has talked with a few who, as young boys, hired out as assistants to drovers operating in western North Carolina.

[28] Arthur, *Western North Carolina,* p. 287 and Parr, *HQ*, 2 (January 1928), 73.

[29] Parr, *HQ*, 2 (January 1928), 77; *DeBow's Review,* 12 (1852), 67; 16 (1854), 540; James Hall, *Notes on the Western States* (Philadelphia: Harrison Hall, 1838), p. 275; Mary Verhoeff, *The Kentucky Mountains: Transportation and Commerce, 1750–1911,* Filson Club Publications, No. 26 (Louisville: John P. Morton and Company, 1911), p. 127.

[30] *Southern Agriculturist,* NS 4 (1844), 472.

[31] Charles T. Leavitt, "Transportation and the Livestock Industry of the Middle West to 1860," *AH*, 8 (January 1934), 29.

[32] Eugene D. Genovesee, "Livestock in the Slave Economy of the Old South—A Revised View," *AH*, 36 (July 1962), 148.

[33] *Patent Office Report*, 1850, p. 320 and 1852, p. 74.

[34] Thomas P. Abernathy, "The Origin of the Whig Party in Tennessee," *MVHR*, 12 (March 1926), 512; Thomas J. Campbell, *The Upper Tennessee* (Chattanooga: By the author, 1932), pp. 41–42; Donald Davidson, *The Tennessee, Rivers of America* (New York: Rinehart and Company, Inc., 1946), I: 213.

[35] Mary J. Welsh, "Recollections of Pioneer Life in Mississippi," *PMHS*, 4 (1901), 354.

[36] *Southern Cultivator*, 12 (1854), 159 and 17 (1859), 338.

[37] John W. Baker, *History of Hart County* (Atlanta: By the author, 1933), p. 56.

[38] This study depends very little upon oral history techniques, yet one often is impressed by "oldsters" who reminisce about stories they were told as children. According to Mr. Carey Mills of Sylva, North Carolina (now deceased), there were regular trading trips made out of the Smoky Mountains into the towns of Georgia and the Carolinas. Entire communities often sent caravans of wagons loaded with hams, beef, venison, hides, apples, cider, honey, cornmeal, bearskins, pigeons, beeswax, and tallow to exchange for the "store goods" once or twice a year. The major trip was begun in late fall, after harvest. The small Piedmont towns were visited, but large caravans often sought the larger cities. During the early years of the century, they journeyed as far south as Augusta, Georgia.

[39] *Patent Office Reports*, 1852, p. 74 and 1849, p. 230.

[40] George Powell, "A Description and History of Blount County," *TAHS* (1855), 48–51.

[41] Ibid.; Virginia P. Brown and Jane P. Nabers, "Mary Gordon Duffee's 'Sketches of Alabama,'" *AR*, 9 (April 1956), 142–43; James R. Maxwell, *Autobiography* (New York: Greenberg, 1926), p. 27.

[42] Powell, *TAHS* (1855), 52; Charles S. Davis, *The Cotton Kingdom in Alabama* (Montgomery: Alabama State Department of Archives and History, 1939), p. 165; *Patent Office Report*, 1855, p. 191.

[43] *Patent Office Report*, 1855, p. 405 and 1856, p. 512.

[44] Frank L. Owsley, *Plain Folk of the Old South* (Baton Rouge: Louisiana State University Press, 1949), p. 136; John F. H. Claiborne, "Trip through the Piney Woods," *PMHS*, 9 (1906), 522; Gladys B. Avant, "History of Washington County, Alabama to 1860," Thesis University of Alabama 1929, p. 21; Paul W. Taylor, "Mobile: 1818–1859 As Her Newspapers Pictured Her," Thesis University of Alabama 1951, pp. 43–44.

[45] *DeBow's Review*, 18 (1855), 239; 19 (1855), 459; 25 (1858), 567; 28 (1860), 221–22.

[46] Taylor, "Mobile: 1818–1859," pp. 43–44.

[47] *DeBow's Review*, 17 (1854), 541; 23 (1857), 503; 25 (1858), 471; U.S. Treasury Department, *Report of the Commerce and Naviga-*

tion of the United States for 1856, 34th Cong., 3d Sess., 1856, 13: 305–13.

[48] For data on goods moving over the South Carolina Railway see U.S. Treasury Department, *Report on the Inland Commerce of the United States for 1886*, 49th Cong., 2d Sess., 1886, No. 7, pt. 2, p. 266.

[49] *DeBow's Review*, 25 (1858), 225.

[50] Davis, *Cotton Kingdom*, p. 166.

[51] Isaac Lippincott, "Internal Trade of the United States 1700–1860," *Washington University Studies*, 4 (October 1916), pp. 63–150; Louis B. Schmidt, "Internal Commerce and the Development of the National Economy Before 1860," *JPE*, 47 (December 1939), 798–822; R. B. Way, "The Commerce of the Lower Mississippi in the Period, 1830–1860," *PMVHA*, 10 (1918–21), 57–68; Albert L. Kohlmeier, *The Old Northwest as the Keystone of the Arch of American Federal Union* (Bloomington: The Principia Press, Inc., 1938).

[52] They are, however, infinitely better than those for the overland trade. In the case of the former, we are dealing with inaccuracies, in the latter with an almost total absence.

[53] Since the usual containers (barrels, hogsheads, etc.,) are based upon volume rather than weight, variations in weight were inevitable. For estimates on inaccuracies as well as the problems involved in calculating weights of the various containers, see Charles T. Leavitt, "Some Economic Aspects of the Western Meat-Packing Industry," *JBUC*, 4 (January 1931), 69. The most comprehensive collection of data on the trade can be found in William F. Switzler's *Report on the Internal Commerce of the United States*, 50th Cong., 1st Sess., 1888, No. 6, pt. 2. However, data also are found in the various issues of *DeBow's Review* and *Hunt's Merchant's Magazine* as well as many of the southern agricultural periodicals.

[54] James D. B. DeBow, *The Industrial Resources, Statistics, Etc. of the United States* (New York: D. Appleton and Company, 1854), 2: 137–38.

[55] *DeBow's Review*, 27 (1859), 477–78.

[56] Francis M. Trollope, *Domestic Manners of the Americans* (London: Whittaker, Treacher, and Company, 1832), 1: 8.

[57] Since the data on imports are listed under different categories such as bacon, pork, or hams, it is difficult to sort out the various kinds of meat. The term "pork" is somewhat ambiguous since it is commonly used to designate "swine flesh." On the other hand, it apparently was used during the antebellum period to mean barreled pork as opposed to bacon or smoked pork. In the data on meat moving downriver there was a fairly sharp distinction between bacon and pork. Throughout the decade the proportion of bacon to pork increased. During the early 1840s bacon made up approximately 25 to 30 percent of the total but increased to better than 50 percent by 1859 and 1860. This could have reflected an increased demand in the South where smoked meat was preferred, but it is difficult to be positive

since this same increase was reflected in the meat exported from the city. In order to simplify computations on the meat trade the data represented in figure 36 include all pork rather than barreled pork.

[58] Computing imports of both wheat and flour into wheat equivalents must entail some error. At the same time, wheat imports were given in both barrels and sacks which further complicated the tabulation. The data used for compiling figure 39 were computed as follows: One barrel of wheat, five bushels; one sack of wheat = two bushels; and a barrel of flour is equivalent to five bushels of wheat.

[59] Way, PMVHA, 10 (1918–21), 57–58 and John A. Johnson, "Pre-Steamboat Navigation on the Lower Mississippi River," Diss. Louisiana State University 1963, pp. 185–86.

[60] John G. Clark, Grain Trade of the Old Northwest (Urbana and London: University of Illinois Press, 1966) pp. 47–49. He estimates the trade to have been at least equal to that moving into New Orleans. Clark's claims are simply guesses and poor ones at that. Data on meat and grain moving over the Vicksburg-Jackson Railway suggests a notable West-to-East movement of foodstuffs, but there is no way of knowing whether this represented a direct trade linking Mississippi to the West or the reexport trade of New Orleans, a trade known to have been significant. In fact, one writer estimated that as much as 75 percent of New Orleans' receipts were sent back upstream. Way, PMVHA, 10 (1918–21), 62. For scattered data on the railroad trade see Debow's Review, 11 (1851), 595.

[61] James Stuart, Three Years in North America (New York: J. and J. Harper, 1833), 2: 191; Fred M. Jones, Middlemen in the Domestic Trade of the United States, Illinois Studies in the Social Sciences, 21, No. 3 (Urbana: University of Illinois Press, 1937), p. 27.

[62] Phillips, Documents, 1: 299.

[63] Pettigrew Family Books, SHMC, Chapel Hill, North Carolina.

[64] In his discussion with Professor Fishlow over the importance of the antebellum interregional trade, Fogel argues strongly for an active food trade connecting the eastern seaboard cities and the South. We know that the trade did exist; we also know that foodstuffs were among the items traded; yet, the importance of the food trade has yet to be demonstrated. He bases his argument on estimates of southern production relative to consumption which, in this writer's opinion, are unrealistic.

[65] The data on flour are converted into the equivalent of wheat in bushels at a ratio of $5:1$. There was some wheat imported into Mobile, but the great bulk of the trade was in flour.

[66] Davis, Cotton Kingdom, p. 160.

[67] Conversion from sacks and barrels to bushels presented a problem. The major part of the imports was of shelled corn in sacks of about two bushels. However, the corn moving down the Alabama-Tombigbee was barreled ear corn which probably contained about four bushels.

[68] *DeBow's Review*, 21 (1856), 399 and 28 (1860), 221–22.

[69] U.S. Treasury Department, *Report on Internal Commerce for 1886*, p. 266.

11   Independence for some

[1] The terms "export" and "import" may present some confusion. They usually refer to foreign trade, but in this case "import" is used to designate goods of a nonsouthern origin. Thus, pork from Ohio, Indiana, and Illinois was "imported" into the South.

[2] James Hall, *The West: Commerce and Navigation* (Cincinnati: B. W. Derby and Company, 1848), p. 191.

[3] *DeBow's Review*, 17 (1854), 623 and 23 (1857), 374.

[4] See chapter 10 n. 61 for more detail.

[5] Of all the plantation records this writer has examined no single group of plantations rivals those of Louisiana in their dependence upon commercial meat. Many planters kept no hogs at all, and their records show them purchasing huge quantities of meat during January and February (the hog-killing season). Bayside Plantation Records, Vol. 1 (1849); Phanor Prudhomme, Papers, Vol. 2; R. R. Barrow, Residence Journal (1858); and Henry C. Warmoth, Papers, Vol. 2 (1857). The Warmoth Papers are extremely detailed and are among the best plantation records extant. All are in *SHMC*, Chapel Hill, North Carolina.

[6] *Patent Office Report*, 1848, p. 536. The total number of livestock, however, differs by about 1,000 animals from the data given in the table above.

[7] In fairness to the Louisiana-Mississippi herder it should be noted that a substantial proportion of the animals and beef brought into New Orleans might well have originated in parts of Louisiana and Mississippi. However, the extent to which these local herders were able to enter the market is not known. Lawren C. Post, "Cattle Branding in Southwest Louisiana," *McNeese Review*, 10 (Winter 1958), 101–17.

[8] Even if we assume an annual trade of 3,000 beeves into South Carolina and Georgia, it was lost among the million or so animals listed as "other cattle" in the 1850 and 1860 censuses of the two states.

[9] Herbert A. Kellar, *Solon Robinson: Pioneer and Agriculturist*, Indiana Historical Collections, Vols. 21 and 22 (Indianapolis: Indiana Historical Bureau, 1936), 22: 166.

[10] *Cotton Planter and Soil*, 1 (1857), 135. It must be noted, however, that this writer's conclusions are in direct contrast with those of Joe G. Clark. As mentioned in the previous chapter, Clark estimates the river trade that trickled into southern markets upriver from New

Orleans to have been very important (pp. 47–48). He goes on to discuss the southern need for corn, and estimates the per-capita and per-hog consumption at thirteen bushels each (p. 130). This was fairly accurate for humans but grossly extravagant for swine. His two sources for determining the amount of corn used for fattening hogs are both works dealing with conditions in the Old Northwest and are useless as references on the southern hog-producing system. To make matters worse he assumes *all* hogs to have consumed thirteen bushels annually, an assumption which should bring a smile to the lips of those who have delved into the various southern manuscript collections. If true, it would have brought an even bigger "smile" to those scrawny southern "land pikes," many of whom saw no corn all year save that which they snitched after rooting their way into a cornfield.

[11] *DeBow's Review,* 6 (1848), 429; 7 (1849), 446; and U.S. Treasury Department, *A Report of the Commerce and Navigation of the United States for 1856,* 34th Cong., 3d Sess., 1856, 13: 305–11.

[12] George Powell, "A Description and History of Blount County," *TAHS,* (1855), 52; Paul W. Taylor, "Mobile: 1818–1859, "As Her Newspapers Pictured Her," Thesis University of Alabama 1951, pp. 43–44.

[13] A portion of this undoubtedly was southern produced as we have evidence of corn being exported from the coastal counties of North Carolina to Charleston. Pettigrew Family Books, *SHMC,* Chapel Hill, North Carolina.

[14] In the calculations on corn needs, the corn consumption of humans, horses and mules, and hogs were computed for each county and the total compared to county production. If we add the oat production to the corn production (using the ratio: 2 bushels oats = 1 bushel corn) the total corn supply was augmented. In some counties, oat production was quite small but in others it was enough to account for a 15 to 20 percent rise in available corn.

[15] John G. Clark, *Grain Trade of the Old Northwest* (Urbana: University of Illinois Press, 1966), p. 31.

[16] One cannot help but be impressed by the numerous references to the lack of wheat bread in the South. A traveler journeying from Ohio through Virginia, North and South Carolina, Georgia, Alabama, Tennessee, and Kentucky in 1822–23 had wheat bread as he passed near Charleston, Virginia on the way south and did not taste another bite until he was near Harrodsburg, Kentucky on the return trip the next year. Of course, this was quite early in the century and might not have been representative of the later period, but it does indicate that wheat bread in the South was by no means as common as in the West. Lucius V. Bierce, *Travels in the Southland, 1822–1823,* ed. George W. Knepper (Columbus, Ohio: Ohio State University Press, 1966).

[17] Although wheat production was much higher in the Hill South than in other parts of the area, surplus production was in no way

Index

Absentee ownership: effects on food production, 25

Acorns: for swine feed, 99

Agriculture: regional specialization, 3; semitropical crops, 4; colonial period, 4–5; colonial New England, 5; middle colonies, 6–7; southern colonies, 7–9; in the Old Northwest, 13–15

Agriculture, diversified: common goal of farmers, 2; in colonial New England, 5; middle colonies, 6–7; southern colonies, 8–9

Agricultural plants: temperate-zone, 5; Environmental limits, 28–36 passim

Agricultural regions: United States, 3; in the South, 235

Alcoholic beverages: attitudes toward, 52

Alston plantation: meal described, 54

Amenities: slaves desire for, 27

Andropogon. See Broomsedge

Animal husbandry: in colonies, 5–6, 7, 9

Apples: dried, 51; pudding, 54; dumplings, 55; widely grown, 180–82; local trade in, 199; in Mississippi River trade, 202

Aristida. See Wiregrass

Armadillo: extended range of, 252n1

Augusta, Georgia: market for drovers, 195

Backbone and ribs: as part of slave ration, 58

Bacon: common on frontier, 39; high consumption, 41; overuse, 42; as slave food, 57, 58; peddled in North Carolina, 191

Bananas: on table at Alston plantation, 54

Banking vegetables: description, 275n6; mentioned, 175

Barbecue: special occasion for slaves, 59; mentioned, 44

Barley: seldom grown, 168

Bass: saltwater, 85; freshwater, 86

Beans: cooking methods, 51; as garden crop, 173; in slave provision patches, 182

Bear meat: food in Mississippi, 55

Beef: use in South, 44; techniques of preservation, 44; eaten fresh, 44; as replacement for pork, 44; consumption, 44, 130; cooperative slaughtering, 44–45; cooking methods, 45; apparent prejudice against, 58–59; consumed by slaves, 58–59; as supplementary meat for slaves, 59; carcass weights, 129; annual production, 129–30; deficit regions, 131–34; in Mississippi River trade, 202; consumed in Mobile, 224

Beef trade: local sources, 189; of New Orleans, 204; of Mobile, 210

Birds: use for food, 80–82

Black belt: as a natural grassland, 35

Blackberry: preserved, 51–52; used for food, 89–90

Blackeyes. *See* Cowpeas

Bluegrass Basin: as food supplier, 193

Bluestem: used as grazing, 134; mentioned, 34, 35

Bread pudding: dish at Alston plantation, 54

Broomsedge: used for forage, 34

Buckingham, J. S.: on confectioneries, 53; on freshwater fishing, 86; on persimmons, 90

Buckwheat: not widely grown, 50, 168

Buffalo: used for food, 86

Burke, Emily: comment on high port consumption, 41: on meat curing, 43; comments on oysters, 84; on drum fishing, 85; on cattle, 119

Butter: regional production, 128, 131–32; local trade in, 187, 191; in Mississippi River trade, 206

Butter beans, 173

Buttermilk: for food, 52; used by slaves, 61